MW01155987

MARY IN THE MIDDLE AGES

LUIGI GAMBERO, S.M.

MARY
IN THE MIDDLE AGES

The Blessed Virgin Mary in the Thought of
Medieval Latin Theologians

Translated by Thomas Buffer

IGNATIUS PRESS   SAN FRANCISCO

Title of the Italian original:
Maria nel pensiero dei teologi latini medievali
© 2000 Edizioni San Paolo, Milan

Cover art:
The Virgin Taking Leave of the Apostles
(detail from the *Maesta* altarpiece)
Duccio di Buoninsegna
© Scala / Art Resource, New York

Cover design by Roxanne Mei Lum

Contents

Abbreviations   15

Introduction   17
    READING: *Mary's True Role in the Economy of Salvation*   21

PART ONE

AUTHORS OF THE EARLY MIDDLE AGES
Seventh–Eleventh Centuries

Prologue   25

1 ILDEPHONSUS OF TOLEDO (d. 667)   27
  Invocation of the Virgin   28
  Divine Motherhood   29
  Ever-Virgin   29
  The Blessed Virgin and Human Salvation   30
  Consecration to the Blessed Virgin   31
  READING: *A Prayer Inspired by the Mystery of the Incarnation*   32
  READING: *Consecration to the Virgin Mary*   34

2 THE VENERABLE BEDE (d. 735)   36
  Mary's Greatness   37
  Virgin and Bride   38
  Eve-Mary   38
  Mary and the Church   39
  Witness to Marian Devotion   40
  READING: *As It Was Fulfilled in Mary, May the Word of God
    Also Be Fulfilled in Us*   41
  READING: *Mary's Spirit of Humility and Service*   41

3 AMBROSE AUTPERT (d. 781)   43
  The Feast of the Purification of Mary   44
  Mary Our Mother   45
  The Sword of Simeon   45

The Feast of Mary's Assumption into Heaven   46
Mary, Worthy of Praise   47
Mary's Heavenly Intercession   47
Mary, Type of the Church   48
READING: *Mary, Image of the Church*   48
READING: *Mary's Greatness*   49

4   THE CAROLINGIAN RENAISSANCE   51

5   PAUL THE DEACON (d. ca. 799)   53
Symbol and Reality in Exalting Mary   53
The Humble Virgin   54
Mary's Love for Jesus   55
Mary's Assumption into Heaven   56
The Virgin's Heavenly Mission   57
READING: *The Heavenly Glory of the Mother of God*   57
READING: *Mary's Mercy Extended to Human Creatures*   58

6   ALCUIN (d. ca. 804)   60
Defender of Christological and Marian Dogma   61
Alcuin's Deep Personal Devotion to the Virgin   62
READING: *The Virgin Mother of the Incarnate Word*   64
READING: *An Anonymous Prayer*   65

7   RABANUS MAURUS (d. 856)   66
Mary in Messianic Prophecy   67
The Name of Mary   68
Summary of Rabanus Maurus' Marian Teaching   69
Mary's Glorification and Heavenly Mission   71
READING: *Mary's Humility in the Mystery of the Visitation*   71
READING: *Greatness of the Divine Motherhood*   72

8   PASCHASIUS RADBERTUS (d. 865)   74
Controversy over Mary's Virginity during the
    Birth of Christ   75
Mary's Assumption into Heaven   77
Marian Devotion   78
READING: *The Glory of the Blessed Virgin in Heaven*   80

9 FULBERT OF CHARTRES (d. 1028)   81
   The Woman of the Prophecies   82
   Predestined from the Moment of Her Conception   83
   The Star of the Sea   84
   Mary's Power of Intercession   85
   READING: *The Woman Who Crushes the Serpent's Head*   86
   READING: *Mary's Glory and Intercession in Heaven*   87

10 THE CLUNIAC REFORM AND
   MARIAN DEVOTION (Tenth Century)   88
   Odo of Cluny (d. ca. 943)   88
   Odilo of Cluny (d. 1049)   89
   Mary, Model of the Monk   90
   The Blessed Virgin and Monastic Virtues   91
   READING: *Mary Appears to the Monk Converted by Odo*   93
   READING: *Mary's Poverty*   93
   READING: *Mary, Perfect Mirror of Holiness*   94

11 PETER DAMIAN (d. 1072)   95
   Outstanding Dignity and Perfection of the Mother of God   96
   Eve's Curse and Mary's Blessing   97
   The Mother of God and the Eucharist   98
   Mary and the Church   99
   Devotion to the Mother of the Lord   99
   READING: *The Entire History of Salvation Is Reflected in Mary*   100
   READING: *Mary and John Assumed Bodily into Heaven*   101
   READING: *Praise for the Greatness of the Mother of God*   101

                        PART TWO

            A GOLDEN PERIOD FOR MARIAN DOCTRINE
                       Twelfth Century

   Prologue   105

1 ANSELM OF CANTERBURY (d. 1109)   109
   The Problem of the Immaculate Conception   110
   Marian Theology and Prayer to the Virgin   111
   Mary, Mother of All Believers   114

The Spiritual Inspiration of Anselm's Marian Teaching   114
READING: *It Was Fitting That Christ Should Be Born of a Virgin*   115
READING: *Calling upon Mary for Salvation*   115

2   EADMER OF CANTERBURY (d. 1124)   117
Mary Preserved from Original Sin   118
Mary as Exalted Creature   119
Prayer to Mary   121
READING: *Mary's Role as Our Mother*   122
READING: *Mary's Glory in the Ascension of Christ*   123

3   RUPERT OF DEUTZ (d. 1130)   124
The Problem of the Immaculate Conception   125
The Mystery of the Blessed Virgin, Bride of
   the Eternal Father   125
Mary at the Foot of the Cross   126
Queen of Heaven and Earth   127
READING: *Model of the Church*   128
READING: *The Kiss of God*   129
READING: *Mother of Us All*   130

4   BERNARD OF CLAIRVAUX (d. 1153)   131
Mary in the Mystery of the Incarnation   133
Mary Stands between Christ and Humanity   135
Devotion to Mary   137
Mary and Original Sin   137
Mary's Assumption into Heaven   138
READING: *The Name of Mary*   139
READING: *The Sword of Simeon*   140

5   PETER THE VENERABLE (d. 1156)   142
His Marian Piety   143
Faith and Devotion   144
Mary and the Holy Spirit   145
READING: *In Honor of the Mother of the Lord*   146

6   ARNOLD OF BONNEVAL (d. after 1156)   148
Mary and Redemption   149

Mary in the Glory of God   151
READING: *Mary and the Mystery of the Incarnation*   152
READING: *Mary on Calvary*   153

7   AMADEUS OF LAUSANNE (d. 1159)   155
His Mariological Legacy   155
Mary between the Two Testaments   156
Mary and the Gifts of the Holy Spirit   157
Mary's Role in the Glory of God   160
READING: *Mary in the Glory of God*   160
READING: *Our Helper and Mediatrix*   161

8   AELRED OF RIEVAULX (d. 1167)   162
Mary, the Ideal Creature   163
Assumed into Heaven   164
Mary's Mediation   165
Spiritual Mother   166
Devotion to Our Lady and Queen   167
READING: *Sorrow at the Loss of Jesus*   168
READING: *Mary, the Bride of Christ*   169

9   ISAAC OF STELLA (d. ca. 1169)   170
An Ecclesiological Mariology   171
Mary, the Virgin Earth   171
Mary in the Mystical Body   172
The Motherhood of Mary and the Motherhood
   of the Church   173
Mary in Heavenly Glory   173
READING: *Mary and the Church Are One and the
   Same Mother*   175
READING: *Mary Assumed into Heaven*   175

10   PHILIP OF HARVENG (d. 1183)   177
Mary and Her Son   178
Assumed into the Glory of Heaven   179
Mary and the Church   180
The Virgin's Mediation in Heaven   181
Philip's Mariology   182

READING: *Most Beautiful among All Women*   182
READING: *The Virgin's Love for the Most Wretched*   184

11   ALAIN DE LILLE (d. ca. 1203)   185
His Life and Works   185
The Commentary on the Song of Songs   186
Bride of Christ   187
Mary and the Church   188
The Ultimate Destiny of the Blessed Virgin   189
READING: *The Four Virtues of the Incarnation*   190

PART THREE

THE AGE OF SCHOLASTICISM
Thirteenth Century

Prologue   195

1   ANTHONY OF PADUA (d. 1231)   197
The Evangelical Doctor   197
His Kerygmatic Mariology   198
The Virgin Mother of God   199
Mediatrix of Salvation and Grace   201
A Woman Filled with Gifts and Virtues   202
READING: *The Virgin and the Allegory of the Bee*   203

2   BONAVENTURE (d. 1274)   206
The Seraphic Doctor   206
His Marian Doctrine   207
Mary and the Incarnation   209
Mary's Mediation   210
Mary's Spiritual Motherhood   212
Devotion to Mary   213
READING: *"Standing by the Cross of Jesus"* (Jn 19:25)   213

3   CONRAD OF SAXONY (d. 1279)   216
Mary's Blessed Birth   217
Mary's Spiritual Beauty   218
Queen of Earth and Heaven   218

Mary's Intercession 219
READING: *Mary's Wonderful Beauty* 220
READING: *The Humble Sweetness of the Mother of God* 221
READING: *The Exalted Dignity of the Mother of God* 221

4 ALBERT THE GREAT (d. 1280) 222
A Great Son of St. Dominic 222
His Marian Doctrine 223
Mary's Immaculate Conception and Holiness 225
Mother and Spouse of Christ 226
The Virginity of the Mother of God 227
Mary Assumed into Heaven 228
Mary's Place in the Economy of Salvation 228
Mother of Men 230
Devotion to Mary 231
READING: *Blessed Are You Because You Believed!* 231
READING: *The Virgin's Intervention at Cana* 232

5 THOMAS AQUINAS (d. 1274) 234
Marian Doctor 234
His Marian Doctrine 235
A New Mariological Perspective 236
The Sanctification of the Virgin 237
Mary and Salvation 239
READING: *The Marriage between Mary and Joseph Was
a True Marriage* 240
READING: *The Body of Christ Was Formed from the
Most Pure Blood of Mary* 241
READING: *Mary Is Exempt from the Curses of Sin* 242

6 JOHN DUNS SCOTUS (d. 1308) 243
Outline of His Life and Times 243
Scotus' Marian Doctrine 244
Mary's Motherhood 245
Mary's Virginity 247
The Virgin Is Preserved from Original Sin 248
READING: *The Immaculate Conception and the Mediation
of Christ* 251

PART FOUR

TOWARD NEW EXPRESSIONS
OF MARIAN FAITH AND DEVOTION
Fourteenth and Fifteenth Centuries

Prologue   255

1 RAYMUND LULL (d. 1315)   257
   Lull and the Immaculate Conception   258
   Mary's Divine Motherhood and Her Humility   259
   Fullness of Grace   260
   Trinity and Incarnation   260
   READING: *The Fruit of Mary's Womb*   262

2 UBERTINO OF CASALE (d. after 1325)   264
   An Eventful Life   264
   Mary in the Life of Jesus   265
   Mary in the Mysteries of Jesus' Infancy   265
   Mary in the Paschal Mystery   269
   The *Arbor Vitae*, Witness to a Spirituality   271
   READING: *Jesus Teaches Us to Love His Mother*   272
   READING: *Mary's Mission after the Resurrection of Her Son*   273

3 BRIDGET OF SWEDEN (d. 1373)   275
   Her Life and Writings   275
   A Follower of the Franciscan School   276
   Mary and Redemption   277
   The Six Sorrows of the Mother of God   278
   Mediatrix of Grace   279
   READING: *The Beauty of Mary's Son*   279
   READING: *The Virgin Praises Her Husband, Joseph*   280

4 JEAN GERSON (d. 1429)   281
   A Difficult and Committed Life   281
   Theological Prudence and Abundant Thought   283
   Supporter of the Immaculate Conception   284
   Mary's Role in the Work of Salvation   285
   Mary's Greatness   287

READING: *Mary's Temptations and Other Trials* — 288

READING: *Invocation of the Blessed Virgin* — 288

5 BERNARDINE OF SIENA (d. 1444) — 290

A Son of St. Francis, in Love with Mary — 290

Doctrinal Exaggerations? — 292

Mary, a Matchless Mother — 293

Mary's Holiness — 294

Mary's Assumption into Heaven — 295

Universal Queen and Mediatrix — 295

READING: *Mary, Tabernacle of God* — 297

READING: *Milady Obedience* — 298

READING: *Milady Diligence* — 299

6 ANTONINUS OF FLORENCE (d. 1459) — 300

Mary's Holiness — 301

Mary's Cooperation in Redemption — 302

Mary's Spiritual Motherhood — 303

Mediatrix — 304

READING: *Mary at Cana* — 305

READING: *Mary's Pilgrimage to the Holy Places* — 306

7 DIONYSIUS THE CARTHUSIAN (d. 1471) — 307

An Authoritative Witness to the Marian Tradition

of the Church — 308

The Problem of the Immaculate Conception — 309

Mary's Gratitude for the Gift of Her Divine Motherhood — 309

Mary's Cooperation in Redemption; Mediatrix of Grace — 310

Mary and the Church — 311

READING: *The Virgin's Extraordinary Faith* — 312

READING: *The Virgin's Perfect Hope* — 313

READING: *The Virgin's Outstanding and Ardent Charity* — 313

READING: *Mary and the Gifts of the Holy Spirit* — 314

8 ALANUS DE RUPE (d. 1475) — 315

Teacher and Preacher — 315

His Marian Devotion — 316

His Writings — 316

The Holy Rosary   317

The Confraternity of the Rosary   318

READING: *Private Revelations of Mary regarding Christ's Passion*   320

READING: *The Rosary Is Presented as an Ancient Practice*   320

9   BERNARDINE DE BUSTIS (d. ca. 1515)   321

The Immaculate Conception   322

Mary's Divine Motherhood   323

The Mother of God and Redemption   323

Mary's Glory in Heaven   324

READING: *Mary Received Baptism*   325

READING: *Mary Received the Sacrament of Penance*   326

READING: *Mary Received the Eucharist*   326

Select Bibliography   329

Index   331

Scripture Index   337

Abbreviations

AnHymn	G. M. Dreves, C. Blume, H. M. Bannister, *Analecta Hymnica Medii Aevi*, 55 vols. (Leipzig, 1886–).
AnPraem	*Analecta Praemonstratensis* (Tongerlo [Belgium], 1914–).
CCL	*Corpus Christianorum*, series latina (Turnhout, 1953–).
CCM	*Corpus Christianorum*, continuatio mediaevalis (Turnhout, 1971–).
CivCatt	*Civiltà Cattolica* (Rome, 1850–).
Clar	*Claretianum* (Rome, 1961–).
CollFranc	*Collectanea Franciscana* (Rome, 1931–).
CollOrdCistRef	*Collectanea Ordinis Cistercensium Reformatorum* (Westmalle [Belgium], 1934/1935–).
CongrLourd	*Maria et Ecclesia, Acta Congressus Mariologici-Mariani in civitate Lourdes anno 1958 celebrati* (Rome, 1959).
CongrRom	*De cultu mariano saeculis XII-XV* (Rome, 1980).
CongrZag	*De cultu mariano saeculis VI-XI* (Rome, 1972).
CPL	E. Dekkers and A. Gaar, *Clavis Patrum Latinorum*, Sacris Erudiri, 3 (Steenbrugge, 1961).
CPSal	*Corona Patrum Salesiana* (Turin: SEI, 1934–).
DS	*Dictionnaire de spiritualité ascétique et mystique* (Paris, 1933–).
EphMar	*Ephemerides Mariologicae* (Madrid, 1951–).
EstEcl	*Estudios Eclesiásticos* (Madrid, 1922–).
EstMar	*Estudios Marianos* (Salamanca, 1941–).
EtMar	*Études Mariales*, Bulletin de la Société Française d'Études Mariales (Paris, 1944–).
FrancEducConf	*The Franciscan Educational Conference* (Washington, D.C., 1919).
Greg	*Gregorianum* (Rome, 1920–).
Hesbert	R. G. Hesbert, *Corpus Antiphonalium Officii*, 6 vols. (Rome: Herder, 1963-1979).

Mar	*Marianum* (Rome, 1939–).
Maria	*Maria: Études sur la Sainte Vierge*, ed. H. du Manoir, 8 vols. (Paris, 1949-1971).
MGH	*Monumenta Germaniae Historica* (Hannover-Berlin, 1826–).
MiscFranc	*Miscellanea Francescana* (Rome, 1886–).
MSR	*Mélanges de science religieuse* (Lille, 1944–).
NDM	*Nuovo Dizionario di Mariologia*, ed. S. De Fiores and S. Meo (Cinisello Balsamo: Edizioni Paoline, 1985).
PG	J. P. Migne, ed., *Patrologia Graeca*, 161 vols. (Paris, 1857-1866).
PL	J. P. Migne, ed., *Patrologia Latina*, 221 vols. (Paris, 1841-1864).
RB	*Revue Bénédictine* (Maredsous [Belgium], 1884–).
RBPhH	*Revue Belge de philologie et d'histoire* (Brussels, 1922–).
RSPhTH	*Revue des sciences philosophiques et théologiques* (Paris, 1907–).
RSR	*Recherches de science religieuse* (Paris, 1913–).
RTAM	*Recherches de théologie ancienne et médiévale* (Louvain, 1934–).
SC	*Sources chrétiennes* (Paris: Les Éditions du Cerf, 1941–).
ScriptaMar	*Scripta de Maria* (Saragossa, 1978–).
StMar	*Studia Mariana, cura Commissionis Marialis Franciscanae edita* (Rome, 1948–).
TMPM	*Testi mariani del primo millenio*, ed. G. Gharib, E. Toniolo, L. Gambero, and G. Di Nola, 4 vols. (Rome: Città Nuova, 1988-1991).
TMSM	*Testi mariani del secondo millenio*, vols. 3 and 4, ed. L. Gambero (Rome: Città Nuova, 1996).

Introduction

In an earlier publication, dedicated to the patristic era,[1] we attempted to gather together the essential elements of the most ancient Christian tradition about the Church's teaching on the Mother of the Lord. We drew these elements from the writings of the Church Fathers and other Christian authors who lived in their time. That book was intended as a kind of immersion in the original sources of the Church's tradition. The present volume aims to continue the journey already begun, moving on into the next period of history. This period has been called "medieval"—a rather debatable term that still has negative and pejorative connotations. For our part, we consider this period to be a time full of cultural value, in every sense of the word "cultural". We will go through the writings of Christian authors from this period, gathering together the most weighty and significant moments in the development of Marian doctrine and devotion.

The historical period we are considering embraces a span of time reaching from the end of the patristic age (eighth century) to the end of the fifteenth century. The close of this long series of centuries may be fixed by two historical events critical to both East and West, events so significant as to determine the end of an era.

In the East, with the conquest of Constantinople by the Turks (1453), the fall of the Byzantine Empire gave rise to particular difficulties within the life of the Byzantine Church. Many scholars of Greek origin and education decided to take refuge in the West, while those who stayed behind found the continuation of theological research and study an arduous and difficult undertaking.

In the West, the medieval era appeared to be in irreversible decline as early as the thirteenth century. Nevertheless, today it is customary to prolong the medieval era by two centuries, right up to the close of the

---

[1] Luigi Gambero, *Mary and the Fathers of the Church: The Blessed Virgin Mary in Patristic Thought*, trans. Thomas Buffer (San Francisco: Ignatius Press, 1999).

fifteenth century. In reality, the historical factors that were destined to open the door to the Renaissance were already well under way. The political rivalries of various kings and princes, as well as actual wars, the outbreaks of plagues, the incursions and invasions of the Muslims into European countries, along with a certain stagnation within European culture, such as an obsessive and sterile tendency toward speculation, and other, less important factors, heavily influenced Western learning and culture. On the level of religious learning, properly speaking, one may observe an exaggerated move toward an individualistic approach, which emphasized the desire to pursue the interior life at the expense of a religious commitment to live out the faith in practice. Finally, there occurred the catastrophic events that ensnared whole regions of Christendom, namely, the Protestant Reformation and the English schism. We think, then, that the end of the fifteenth century can be taken as the end of the Middle Ages, during which Marian doctrine and piety were seen as vital components of the Church's life, as much in the East as in the West, and the figure of Mary was considered an indisputable sign of sure faith in the mystery of the incarnate Word.

In the eighth century, the Christian West was still deeply under the influence of the impetus that the Council of Ephesus had given to Marian devotion. Shrines dedicated to the Theotókos sprang up in almost every place. Homiletic literature was notably enriched by Marian sermons, devised according to a more or less fixed plan, in which the salient steps of the story of salvation were traced: the sin of our first parents, the Eve–Mary parallel, the angel's Annunciation to Mary and the Incarnation of the Son of God, the birth of Christ at Bethlehem, the adoration of the Magi. But it was especially the feast of the Dormition and Assumption of Mary into heaven that inspired the most enthusiastic homilies about the Virgin. The Nestorian controversy was ended by the Second Council of Nicaea (787), with the solemn legitimation of the cult of images of Christ, the Virgin, and the saints. Additionally, the triumph of the orthodox faith opened a new epoch of newfound political and religious tranquillity. Consequently, strong pressure was exerted by renewed dogmatic demands, which promoted the exploration of new Marian expressions in art.

Marian liturgy and piety both benefitted from this climate. In the East, there was an increase in the number of liturgical texts, composed for the most part by poets and hymn-writers who were also profound theologians. These texts resonated with the authentically Marian spirit of the people of God.

In the West, by contrast, the Church's life was badly shaken by historical events that radically altered the religious situation of Europe. Over a period of several centuries, successive barbarian invasions led to continuous political, social, and economic transformations, which finally coalesced in the formation of the Holy Roman Empire and the Carolingian renaissance. Also in contrast with the Christian East, where Marian devotion was clearly a popular phenomenon, devotion to Mary in the West was expressed in limited circles, particularly in monastic environments. And in fact, the majority of Western Marian writers during these centuries belonged to the monastic tradition. They saw the Mother of God, not so much as a subject for doctrinal reflection, but as a person, as someone with importance for the lives of the faithful. In particular, the Benedictines considered her a marvelous model of the religious life, because Mary, in her purity and humility, showed them the safe way to the heavenly homeland.

In the eleventh century, the Byzantine Empire was enjoying a golden period under the reign of Basil II. In the Latin world, this was paralleled by an incipient reawakening of civilization and culture in all areas of life, in the various countries of Europe. This phenomenon, however, unfolded in continuity with a past whose treasures and positive values could not be forgotten. The ecclesiastical writers of that age, which today is called the Low Middle Ages, did not give up the task of carrying forward the tradition of the Church Fathers, even if they did not always refer to them with the most rigorous exactitude. Indeed, to us today, the connections they made sometimes appear to be invalidated by their excessive formalism. But even though this way of appealing to the Fathers was not totally correct and is considered critically questionable today, nevertheless it might merit a kind of certificate of authenticity if interpreted as the sincere and enduring expression of the traditional Christian life.[2]

At this important historical turning point, monasticism was able to carry out its role in an acceptable and effective way. The monks provided a connection to and continuity with the positive values of a past that was

---

[2] See H. Barré, *Prières anciennes de l'Occident à la Mère du Sauveur* (Paris 1963), p. 7.

fading away. They revived it within a renewed and dynamic historical context in which the doctrinal tradition and example of the Fathers had clearly begun to regain the privileged place they deserved.

Marian theology and piety, while not giving up their strong bonds with past centuries, reached new objectives. This marked a turning point in the doctrinal and spiritual history of the Latin Middle Ages, demonstrating a vitality and depth that belie the negative judgments made against that era.

By the end of the Middle Ages, Marian feasts were firmly and definitively established in the calendar of the liturgical year. At that time, the feasts of the Purification, the Annunciation, the Assumption, and Birth of Mary were being celebrated everywhere in the West. Other feasts, such as the Conception of Mary and the Sorrows of Mary, still awaited more solid and universal acceptance. Thus, devotion to the Mother of the Lord appeared fully legitimated by its entry into the Church's liturgical worship, and the faithful could turn to her without fear of going beyond the limits demanded by an authentic understanding of the Faith.

In this religious climate, prayers addressed to Mary, publicly or privately, greatly increased in number. These texts, in Latin and the languages of the people, form a rich patrimony of prayer, handed down as a precious inheritance to later generations. Marian hymn-writing also developed to an amazing degree, which favored the flowering of compositions that, in some cases, reached the highest peaks of poetry and lyricism.

Unfortunately, the limits within which our work must be confined do not allow us fully to demonstrate the impressive growth of the Marian religious phenomenon during the Middle Ages. We will present the thought of a rather limited number of authors. Our selection is determined by each author's reputation, the importance of his contribution, and the influence he exercised during his life and in later ages. In any case, we trust that the great figures whose Marian thought we have chosen to present can still act as wise guides for the reader who wishes to pursue the study of Mariology. They were the powerful protagonists of the extraordinary flowering of Marian thought during the Middle Ages; they breathed an atmosphere of intense Christian faith and piety; they placed their own genius at the service of a Lady and Queen who, in her turn, has never ceased to offer her maternal assistance to the people of God, in total humility. Moreover, we are firmly convinced that their human and religious genius are truly unsurpassed and, consequently, capable of influencing our own thinking and our lives.

READING

MARY'S TRUE ROLE IN THE ECONOMY OF SALVATION

But surely when [God] became man, He brought home to us His incommunicable attributes with a distinctiveness, which precludes the possibility of our lowering Him merely by our exalting a creature. He alone has an entrance into our soul, reads our secret thoughts, speaks to our heart, applies to us spiritual pardon and strength. On Him we solely depend. He alone is our inward life; He not only regenerates us, but (to use the words appropriated to a higher mystery) *semper gignit*; He is ever renewing our new birth and our heavenly sonship. In this sense He may be called, as in nature, so in grace, our real Father.

Mary is only our mother by divine appointment, given us from the Cross; her presence is above, not on earth; her office is external, not within us. Her name is not heard in the administration of the Sacraments. Her work is not one of ministration towards us; her power is indirect. It is her prayers that avail, and her prayers are effectual by the *fiat* of Him who is our all in all. Nor need she hear us by any innate power, or any personal gift; but by His manifestation to her of the prayers which we make to her. When Moses was on the Mount, the Almighty told him of the idolatry of the people at the foot of it, in order that he might intercede for them; and thus it is the Divine Presence which is the intermediating Power by which we reach her and she reaches us.

Woe is me, if even by a breath I sully these ineffable truths! but still, without prejudice to them, there is, I say, another range of thought quite distinct from them, incommensurate with them, of which the Blessed Virgin is the centre. If we placed our Lord in that centre, we should only be dragging Him from His throne, and making Him an Arian kind of God; that is, no God at all. He who charges us with making Mary a divinity, is thereby denying the divinity of Jesus. Such a man does not know what divinity is. Our Lord cannot pray for us, as a creature prays, as Mary prays; He cannot inspire those feelings which a creature inspires. To her belongs, as being a creature, a natural claim on our sympathy and familiarity, in that she is nothing else than our fellow. She is our pride,—in the poet's words, "Our tainted nature's solitary boast".

—Ven. John Henry Newman, *Certain Difficulties Felt by Anglicans in Catholic Teaching Considered* (London and New York: Longmans, Green, and Co., 1900–1901), pp. 83-85

PART ONE

Authors of the Early Middle Ages

(Seventh to Eleventh Centuries)

Prologue

In the West, the last years of the patristic age more or less coincide with the beginning of the Middle Ages. During this period, under the lasting influence of Byzantine theology, Marian doctrine continued to have capable and enthusiastic promoters. The teaching of such authors as Ildephonsus of Toledo, Aldhelm of Malmesbury, the Venerable Bede, and Ambrose Autpert emphasizes themes that show clear signs of the charismatic influence of the Fathers of the Church.

Marian piety also continued to be influenced positively by Eastern spirituality. Marian feasts, born within the Byzantine Church, began gradually to spread into Western Christianity. These celebrations underwent a remarkable enrichment in the Latin liturgy, as well as in literature and art, which have obvious connections to the liturgy. And so it is that we see new celebrations, such as the feast of Mary's Conception or the keeping of Saturday as a liturgical memorial of the Mother of the Lord, being added to those already widespread in the West: the Nativity, the Annunciation, the Purification, and the Assumption.

Sacred art became more and more interested in the icon of the Theotókos, especially during the iconoclast crisis in the East. There the Church of Rome openly came to the defense of sacred images, stressing the legitimacy of the cult rendered to them and condemning the persecutory policies of the Byzantine emperors. Many images of Christ, the Virgin, and the saints were sent to the West for safekeeping. At the end of the first phase of iconoclasm, the Second Ecumenical Council of Nicaea, in 787, defined the theological correctness and legitimacy of the cult of icons. In 843, having overcome a new round of persecutions in the first decades of the ninth century, the Eastern Church decided to immortalize the event by proclaiming the solemnity of the Triumph of Orthodoxy. This feast is celebrated every year on the first Sunday of Lent.

As far as literature is concerned, it suffices to consider the extraordinary success and broad circulation in the West of the Latin version of the *Akáthistos* hymn, the unsurpassed masterpiece of Marian poetry and

praise. In Western Christianity, this hymn sparked an amazing prolifera-
tion of songs and other Marian poems that took their inspiration from
it.[1] Nor can one undervalue the fact that the oldest known Marian
prayer, the *Sub tuum praesidium confugimus*, the Greek text of which had
been lost,[2] was, in its Latin translation, one of the invocations most
widely found and treasured within Western Marian piety.

It may be observed that the Eastern Church of those days was still
disposed to recognize the primatial authority of the See of Rome,
while the Latin Church, for her part, readily gave a favorable reception
to initiatives proceeding from the rich spiritual life of the Byzantine
Church.

---

[1] See G. G. Meersseman, *Der Hymnos Akathistos im Abendland*, 2 vols. (Fribourg, 1958–1960).

[2] The Greek text was discovered in a papyrus in the John Rylands Library, Manches-
ter, and published in 1938, after several attempts at reconstructing the text, which had
suffered serious damage. See F. Mercenier, "L'Antienne mariale grecque la plus anci-
enne", *Le Muséon* 52 (1939): 229–33; O. Stegmiller, "Sub tuum praesidium: Bemer-
kungen zur ältesten Überlieferung", *Zeitschrift für katholische Theologie* 74 (1952): 76–82.

I

ILDEPHONSUS OF TOLEDO
(d. 667)

Seventh-century Spanish Christianity, despite the serious trials it had to endure because of the Muslim invasion, also experienced moments of particular strength as well as a reassuring increase in the faith of its members. Viewing the scene against the historical background of the time, it is easy to identify some positive results of great importance. In particular we refer to the victory over the threat of Arianism, which had been brought to Spain earlier by the Vandals. The Visigoths, after their conversion to the orthodox Christian religion, were able to banish Arianism from the kingdom they established in Spain. We may also recall the strong impetus given pastoral and missionary efforts, especially by the regional councils celebrated in Toledo. For a long time, these were held nearly every year. One must also take into account the dynamic and influential theological activity of such outstanding churchmen as the brothers Leander and Isidore of Seville and Ildephonsus of Toledo. Where Marian doctrine is concerned, this last-named author is undoubtedly its most important witness and the teacher who made the richest and most important contribution.

Born in Toledo around 617, Ildephonsus became a Benedictine monk and later abbot of the monastery of Agli, located in the outskirts of his native city. In 657, he was named metropolitan archbishop of Toledo, where he died in 667. His theological reflection developed within the current of the great tradition of the Latin Fathers, especially Jerome, Augustine, and Gregory the Great. Among his writings, a treatise on the virginity of Mary is of special interest: *Libellus de virginitate perpetua sanctae Mariae contra tres infideles*. This treatise had an enormous influence on all subsequent Marian literature in Spain. It won Ildephonsus the title "The Virgin's Chaplain", given him many centuries later by the great

Spanish poet and dramatist Lope de Vega, who wrote a play about Ildephonsus called *The Virgin's Chaplain*.

Of the three infidels against whom Ildephonsus directs his refutations, two were the heretics Jovinian and Helvidius, who lived in the fourth century and had already been the target of St. Jerome's forceful and harsh attacks. The third is identified with an anonymous Jew, whom Ildephonsus views as the personification of the large Jewish colony present in Spain during his day. At that time, the Jews continued to oppose and mock the truths of the Christian faith, aiming most directly at the dogma of the virginity of the Mother of the Lord. Ildephonsus' argument is directed especially against these Jews, whom he engages in an impassioned debate in defense of this Marian dogma.[1]

Invocation of the Virgin

Ildephonsus begins the twelve chapters that make up his treatise with an ardent prayer addressed directly to Mary in which he expresses all his impassioned admiration in the face of the mysteries of the wondrous vocation and the fullness of grace found in this creature, so favored by God. He invokes her intercession to obtain the gift of the Holy Spirit. He considers the Annunciation to be the central moment of her whole divine adventure. The author remains lost in ecstasy as he contemplates this unique creature, who was entrusted with such wonderful divine miracles and "promoted to a new state of glory, hitherto unknown".[2]

---

[1] The *De virginitate perpetua sanctae Mariae* was published in the original Latin in Migne, PL 96, 53–110. Among other editions, we refer the reader to that of J. Campos Ruiz in the series Biblioteca de Autores Cristianos (Madrid, 1971; with Spanish translation). Among the numerous studies on Ildephonsus' Marian doctrine we recall: J. M. Cascante Davila, *Doctrina Mariana de S. Ildefonso de Toledo* (Barcelona, 1958); idem, "La devoción y el culto a María en los escritos de S. Ildefonso de Toledo", in CongrZag 3:223–48; J. M. Canal, "Fuentes del 'De virginitate sanctae Mariae' de San Ildefonso de Toledo", Clar 6 (1966): 115–30; idem, "San Ildefonso de Toledo: Historia y legenda", EphMar 17 (1967): 437–62; H. M. Köster, "Ildefons von Toledo als Theologe der Marienverehrung", in CongrZag 3:197–222; J. Ballesteros Mateos, *El Tratado "De virginitate Sanctae Mariae" de San Ildefonso de Toledo*, Estudio teológico de San Ildefonso (1985); TMPM 3:647–88.

[2] *De virginitate perpetua sanctae Mariae* 1; PL 96, 58AB.

Divine Motherhood

The basic reason for Mary's privileged condition is the gift of the divine motherhood, which makes her unique, a person without equal. Certainly she is part of a human context, but she is also distinct from all human beings because of the exceptional graces with which God adorned her. Our author writes:

> Behold, you are blessed among women, intact one among women in childbirth, mistress among handmaids, queen among sisters. For behold, henceforth all generations will call you blessed; all the powers of heaven recognize you as blessed; all the prophets preach you as blessed; all the nations celebrate you as blessed.[3]

Ildephonsus' almost uncontrollable enthusiasm pushes him to make some rather bold statements, which reach the point of considering Mary to be, from a certain point of view, even greater than her Son. These statements can be understood only as the external manifestations of the impulse of love and devotion that he felt for the Mother of God in the depths of his being. Here is one example:

> In receiving the only God [into your womb], you remain inferior to God the Son. In giving birth to him, who is both God and man, you rank first with regard to your Son as man. For when you receive him, God is merely your guest, but when you conceive him, he dwells within you as both man and God.[4]

Ever-Virgin

In addition to the divine motherhood, virginity also played an important role in determining the glorious destiny of the Mother of the Lord. The bishop of Toledo underscores this, as if to give value to a feminine condition that the Jews tended to disdain, seeing it as identical to sterility:

> While you are filled with great glory because of your Son, you have glory equally great because you remained untouched by any man whatever.[5]

---

[3] Ibid., PL 96, 58D–59A.

[4] Ibid., PL 96, 59A.

[5] Ibid.

Consequently, Ildephonsus puts those who would deny Mary's virginity on their guard with a severe statement: To attack the glory of the Virgin Mary is equivalent to showing a serious lack of respect to her Son. This is how he reproves Jovinian:

> You declare that he honored the Virgin in creating her but covered her in shame when he was born. If anyone is thinking such thoughts, his heart ought to dry up.[6]

Taking possession of Mary's womb in the mystery of the Incarnation, the Lord miraculously preserved its virginal state even after his birth, since he is the Almighty and can arrange such a blessing as he pleases:

> He alone came forth from that gate, and he is its guardian. No one else entered with him, and no one else came forth with him (cf. Ezek 44:2–3). . . . When he entered this house, he did not despoil it of its chastity, and when he came forth from it, he enriched its integrity.[7]

Mary was a virgin in conceiving and bearing the Son of God, and she remained a virgin throughout her earthly existence. For this reason, the glory of her virginity is higher even than the nobility of the angels. This explains why the bishop of Toledo readily made superlative statements about the greatness of this creature, on whom the Creator poured out his most extraordinary gifts of grace. In his treatise, one frequently reads statements such as the following:

> And certainly her virginity remained forever incorrupt, whole, intact, inviolate. . . . This woman is a vessel of sanctification, eternally virgin; she is the Mother of God; she is the shrine of the Holy Spirit; she alone is the unique temple of her Creator.[8]

The Blessed Virgin and Human Salvation

Ildephonsus considers the miracle of virginal motherhood, not only as a privilege strictly connected to Mary personally, but also as an event that God ordained for the salvation of all human beings:

> Because of this Virgin, all men have seen the salvation of God (see Is 52:10; Lk 3:6). All the ends of the earth, thanks to this Virgin, have

---

[6] Ibid., PL 96, 59D–60A.
[7] Ibid. 2; PL 96, 61BC.
[8] Ibid. 10; PL 96, 95C.

repented and turned back to the Lord. . . . All men sing to the Lord and Son the new song of their redemption, for he, being born of this Virgin, has done marvelous deeds. The Lord, through this Virgin, "has made known his salvation" (Ps 97 [98]:2).[9]

Further, he asserts that the Virgin herself owes her exceptional calling to the decision God made to come to earth and become man to save all humanity:

To become my Redeemer, he became your Son. To become the price of my redemption, his Incarnation took place from your flesh. From your flesh he took a body that would be wounded, that he might heal my wounds.[10]

Consecration to the Blessed Virgin

In the last chapter of his treatise, the bishop of Toledo renews his own faith in the mystery of Mary's divine and virginal motherhood. In this text, repeated praises of the Mother of God are combined with tones of humble and confident prayer. He invokes the intercession of the Lord's Mother to obtain purification from his own sins, the grace of love for her, the revelation of the sweetness of her divine Son, and the strength to speak in defense of the truth and to witness to his faith in Christ. As a proof of the authenticity of his feelings, Ildephonsus pronounces a genuine act of self-giving or consecration to the Blessed Virgin, in which he closely connects fidelity to God with fidelity to Mary, service to God with service to the Mother of God, obedience to God with obedience to Mary. He calls her "cooperatrix" in her own redemption.[11]

He repeatedly confirms his will to become the slave of the Blessed Virgin, to live according to her commands and under her patronage, in order to serve her Son better. He is absolutely convinced that "what is offered to the Mother redounds upon her Son."[12]

In an ancient biography of Ildephonsus of Toledo, written a century after his death, a story is told that the Virgin appeared to the saint. As a

---

[9] Ibid. 4; PL 96, 67C.
[10] Ibid. 12; PL 96, 105C.
[11] Ibid., PL 96, 105B.
[12] Ibid., PL 96, 108A.

sign of gratitude for everything he did to spread devotion to her, Mary gave the saint a chasuble to wear when celebrating feast days dedicated to her.[13]

Even if this story is legendary, it tellingly expresses the relationship of loving devotion that existed between the faithful servant and his heavenly Lady.

READINGS

A PRAYER INSPIRED BY THE MYSTERY OF THE INCARNATION

O my Lady, my ruler, you who rule me, Mother of my Lord, Handmaid of your Son, Mother of the world's Maker, I pray you, I beg you, I beseech you, that I may have the spirit of my Redeemer, that I may truly and worthily know you, that I may speak truly and worthily about you, that I may say whatever true and worthy thing needs to be said about you. For you have been chosen by God, taken up by God, called by God; you are near to God, clinging to God, joined to God. You were visited by the angel, hailed by the angel, called blessed by the angel, troubled by his words, absorbed in reflection, astonished by his greeting, and you marveled at the words he spoke.

You hear that you have found favor with God, and you are commanded not to be afraid; you are strengthened with confidence, instructed in knowledge of miracles, promoted to a new state of glory, hitherto unknown. The angel assures you that your chastity is not harmed by the Child, your virginity is ensured by the name of the Child, and you will remain whole and chaste after giving birth to the Child. What is to be born of you is holy and will be called Son of God—so the angel evangelizes you—and in a wonderful way you learn how great will be the power of the King to be born.

You ask, "How will this happen?" You enquire about the cause. You seek an explanation. You seek to know by experience. You enquire about how it will be arranged. Then hear his unheard-of oracle, consider the unusual work, note the unknown secret, attend to the unseen deed. The Holy Spirit will come upon you, and the power of the Most

---

[13] Ibid., PL 96, 11C–12A.

High will overshadow you (Lk 1:35). Invisibly, the entire Trinity will accomplish the conception within you. Only the Person of the Son of God is to be born in your body, and he alone will take flesh from you. And so what will be conceived in you, what will be born from you, what will come forth from you, what will be brought forth and delivered from you is holy and will be called Son of God. For he will be great; he will be the God of power; he the King of all the ages; he the Maker of all things.

Behold, you are blessed among women, intact among women in childbirth, mistress among handmaids, queen among sisters. For behold, henceforth all generations will call you blessed; all the powers of heaven recognize you as blessed; all the prophets preach you as blessed; all the nations celebrate you as blessed. Blessed are you for my faith; blessed are you for my soul; blessed are you for my delight; blessed for my heraldings and preachings. I would preach you as much as you should be preached, love you as much as you should be loved, praise you as much as you should be praised, and serve you as much as your glory should be served.

In receiving God alone [into your womb], you remain inferior to God the Son. In giving birth to him as both God and man, you rank first with regard to your Son as man. For when you receive him, God is merely your guest, but when you conceive him, he dwells within you as both man and God. In the past you were pure for God; in the present you are filled with man and God; in the future you will give birth to man and God. Both in being with child and being a virgin you are happy; both in having offspring and retaining your chastity you are joyful; both to your Son and to your spouse you are faithful. You remained so faithful to your Son that he did not know a father of his flesh. You remained so faithful to your spouse that he knew you to be bearing a child without a man. While you are filled with great glory because of your Son, you have glory equally great because you remained untouched by any man whatever. You have been instructed about what you should know, taught what to believe, reassured about what to hope, made strong to choose what you should hold without loss.

—Ildephonsus of Toledo, *De virginitate sanctae Mariae* 1;
PL 96, 58A–59B

CONSECRATION TO THE VIRGIN MARY

And now I come to you, only Virgin Mother of God; I come into your presence, only masterwork of the Incarnation of my God; I prostrate myself before you, the only one found to be the Mother of my Lord; I beg you, only one found to be the handmaid of your Son, that you might obtain the removal of the guilt of my sin, that you might command me to be cleansed from the iniquity of my actions, that you might make me to love the glory of your power, that you might show unto me the manifold sweetness of your Son, that you might give me to speak and defend the truthfulness of faith in your Son, that you might grant me even to cling to God and you, to serve your Son and you, to wait upon your Lord and you—to wait upon him as my Maker and upon you as the Mother of my Maker; upon him as the Lord of might, upon you as the Mother of God; upon him as my Redeemer, upon you as the work of my redemption.

For what he wrought in redeeming me, he formed in the reality of your person. To become my Redeemer, he became your Son. To become the price of my redemption, his Incarnation took place from your flesh. From your flesh he took a body that would be wounded, that he might heal my wounds. He drew forth a mortal body from your mortal body, that he might take away my death. He took from you a body that he assumed without sin, in which he would erase my sins. He humbled himself and assumed my nature from your real body. He was my forerunner, bringing my nature into his kingdom to dwell amid the glory of the Father's throne, establishing it higher than the angels.

Therefore I am your servant, because your Son is my Lord. Therefore, you are my mistress, because you are the handmaid of my Lord. Therefore, I am the servant of the handmaid of my Lord, because you, my mistress, became the Mother of my Lord. Therefore I have become your servant, because you have become the mother of my Maker. I pray you, I pray you, O holy Virgin, that I might possess Jesus from that same Spirit by whom you gave birth to Jesus. Through that Spirit, through whom your flesh conceived Jesus, may my soul accept Jesus. By that Spirit, by whom you were able to know and give birth to Jesus, may I be granted to know Jesus. In the Spirit, you professed yourself, to be the handmaid of the Lord, desiring that it be done to you according to the angel's word; in that same Spirit, may I, a lowly man, speak lofty things of Jesus. In the Spirit, you adore Jesus as your Lord and look upon him as your Son; in that same Spirit may I love Jesus. May I show reverence to Jesus, just as he, though he was God, was submissive to his parents (see Lk 2:51).

—Ildephonsus of Toledo, *De virginitate sanctae Mariae* 12;
PL 96, 105B–106B

2

THE VENERABLE BEDE
(d. 735)

This great Doctor of the Church is a symbol of the growth and vitality of Christianity in the British Isles during the eighth century, when those islands were inhabited by Celts and Anglo-Saxons. Despite her geographical separation from continental Europe, the Church in Britain always preserved an active connection with the rest of Christianity. Nourished by the common treasures of the Western tradition, at the same time she gave witness to the perennial fruitfulness of this inheritance. Marian doctrine and devotion are an integral part of this tradition, which the Venerable Bede studied with faith and handed on with great skill.

He was born in 672 or 673 and, when still a small child, was entrusted to the Benedictines of Wearmouth and Jarrow to be raised by them. He, too, became a Benedictine monk, was ordained priest at the age of thirty, and spent his whole life in study, contemplation, and teaching. He was a man of many-faceted learning. He knew Latin and Greek well and some Hebrew. He was an avid reader of the Church Fathers, especially Jerome, Augustine, Gregory the Great, and Isidore of Seville, who inspired his biblical exegesis. He was attracted to the Christian Latin poets, as well. His love for learning also inclined him to study classical literature. His literary output is enormous. He wrote many exegetical, instructive, and historical works, among which his lengthy *Historia ecclesiastica gentis Anglorum* (*History of the English Church and People*) is most important. Bede died in 735.

Bede's Marian teaching is found especially in his exegetical writings and homilies. Even though there is nothing particularly new in its content, it bears the marks of a deep and intentional fidelity to Christian tradition. It is apparent that Bede wanted to gather together the essential elements of this tradition.[1]

---

[1] Most of his works may be found in Migne, PL 91, 92, and 94. Critical editions of some of his works have been published in CCL 120 and 122. For a study of his Marian

Mary's Greatness

Following the teaching generally presented in the Latin Church, Bede draws a luminous portrait of the Virgin Mary. She is the masterpiece of the Holy Spirit, who acted in her to purify her from concupiscence and make her ready to become the Mother of the incarnate Word. Using terminology that seems to anticipate the doctrine of the Immaculate Conception, he observes:

> No wonder that the Lord, when he was about to redeem the world, began his work with his Mother, so that she, through whom salvation would be put into place for all, would be the first to taste the fruit of salvation from her Child.[2]

Nevertheless, Bede does not go so far as to intuit the mystery of the Immaculate Conception. He holds that Mary was conceived in original sin, like all other human beings. Her glory, instead, shines out fully from the double privilege of her virginal motherhood. Commenting on the angel's greeting, "Hail, full of grace" (Lk 1:28), Bede adds:

> The Virgin was truly full of grace, since by a divine gift it was granted her that she should be the first of all women to offer to God the most glorious gift of virginity. Rightly, then, did she deserve to experience both the vision of the angel and being addressed by him, since she strove to imitate the life of the angels. Truly was she full of grace, since it was given her to bear him by whom she was made grace and truth. And so the Lord was truly with her, for he first lifted her up from earthly things to the longed-for realities of heaven, by a love for a new kind of chastity, and afterward, through the mediation of his human nature, he consecrated her with the fullness of divinity.[3]

It is impressive to see how our author uses the expression "grace and truth", which the Gospel ascribes to Christ (cf. Jn 1:14), to illustrate the extraordinary personal condition of the Lord's Mother.

---

thought, see G. Söll, "Die Bedeutung des ethischen Marienbilds in der lateinischen Kirche des Frühmittelalters für die Entwicklung der Marienlehre und der Marienverehrung von Beda bis Anselm von Canterbury", in CongrZag 2:91–108; TMPM 3:696–717.

[2] *In Lucam*; PL 92, 321B; CCL 120, 36.

[3] *In Annuntiatione B. M.*; PL 94, 11AB; CCL 122, 16.

Virgin and Bride

If the gift of the divine motherhood came to Mary exclusively from God, the gift of virginity is also the result of an initiative on her part. Bede points out how she was the first woman to make a vow of virginity:

> How, she asks, can this be, that I should conceive and bear a son, since I have decided to perfect my life by chaste virginity?[4]

But Mary's vow of virginity did not rule out marriage to Joseph; on the contrary, it demanded it for several reasons. Mary's Davidic origin would be made apparent through Joseph, since Scripture does not indicate the genealogy of women. Moreover, the guarantee offered by a husband allowed Mary to avoid being accused of adultery and stoned to death, by preserving her from false suspicions. In Joseph, Mary found a sure support during the flight into Egypt, a faithful guardian for the Savior, and an authoritative witness to her virginity. Finally, Mary's marriage kept her virgin birth hidden from the devil.[5]

Another divine teaching may be seen in the marriage of Mary and Joseph. The Gospel says that Mary was a relative of Elizabeth; therefore, she had to belong to the priestly tribe of Levi. On the other hand, Joseph, as a descendant of David, belonged to the tribe of Judah, which had become a royal tribe because of King David. This matrimonial union between members of different tribes, contrary to Jewish tradition, is explained by Bede as follows:

> It was necessary that the Mediator between God and man, when manifesting himself to the world, should take the origin of his flesh from both tribes, doubtless because, in the human nature he assumed, he was to possess both roles; namely, both the priestly and the royal.[6]

Eve-Mary

The comparison between the progenetrix of the fallen human race and the Mother of the Savior is part of the plan determined by God to accomplish the salvation of men. It reveals his wisdom and power:

---

[4] Ibid., PL 94, 12C; CCL 122, 17.

[5] See *In Lucam*; PL 92, 316CD; CCL 120, 30–31. The last reason is obviously suggested by a famous text of Ignatius of Antioch, *Letter to the Ephesians* 19, 1, in F. X. Funk, *Patres Apostolici*, vol. 1 (Tübingen, 1901), p. 228.

[6] *In Annuntiatione B. M.*; PL 94, 14A; CCL 122, 19–20.

An angel was sent by God to a Virgin who had to be consecrated by a divine birth, because the first woman [Eve] had been the cause of human ruin, when the serpent was sent by the devil to ensnare the woman with the spirit of pride. Yea, the devil himself, once our first parents had been deceived, introduced himself in serpent's guise to despoil the human race of the glory of immortality.

And so, just as death entered through a woman, fittingly, life reentered the world through a woman. The former [Eve], seduced by the devil through the serpent, offered the man the taste of death; the latter [Mary], taught by God through the angel, brought into the world the Author of salvation.[7]

This parallel, already classic within the patristic tradition, continues to be an obvious favorite of Christian authors. Indeed, it furnishes the clearest and most biblical foundation for the doctrine on the Virgin's cooperation in the mystery of salvation. This collaboration is realized through the exercise of those virtues that appear directly opposed to Eve's sinful errors: faith, obedience, and humility. For Bede, too, the Gospel episode in which Mary is most evidently portrayed as the second Eve is the Annunciation.

Mary and the Church

In Bede's thought, Mary and the Church are closely associated in a single mystery: Mary prefigures the Church, and the Church, in turn, imitates in her own life the mysteries of the Mother of the Lord:

Following the example of the Blessed Ever-Virgin Mary, who was married and at the same time unstained, the Church conceives us as a virgin by the working of the Holy Spirit; she gives birth to us as a virgin without birth pangs; and as a woman married to one person but impregnated by another, throughout her individual parts that make her one and catholic, she remains visibly united to the legitimate Pontiff set over her, but she increases in number by the invisible power of the Holy Spirit.[8]

In writing these lines, our author must have been recalling a famous text of St. Ambrose, in which Mary and the Church are both called Virgin and Bride. Each is united to an earthly husband but fertilized by

---

[7] Ibid., PL 94, 9B; CCL 122, 14.
[8] *In Lucam*; PL 92, 330B; CCL 120, 48–49.

an action of the Holy Spirit, so that their motherhood does not prejudice their virginity.[9]

Bede also exploits the Mary-Church parallel in his exegesis of
Simeon's words foretelling the presence of a sword in the Blessed Virgin's
life. This sword is nothing other than the sorrow and affliction that Mary
would have to face at her Son's Cross:

> Mary could not look upon Jesus crucified and dying without feeling
> bitter anguish, even though Mary did not doubt that Jesus, being God,
> would rise from the dead, still she worried and grieved that the offspring
> of her own flesh was dying.[10]

The Church, too, experiences a sword in the pain she feels because of
the persecution of Christians.[11]

Reflecting on the Gospel scene of the wedding at Cana, Bede sees
there a figure of the marriage between Christ and the Church, a marriage that found "its bridal chamber in the womb of the uncorrupt
Mother, in which God was joined to a human nature".[12]

Witness to Marian Devotion

In one of his homilies, Bede confirms that devotion to the Blessed
Virgin was already firmly established in the Christianity of his time:

> Now a most excellent and salutary custom has arisen in the holy Church:
> daily [Mary's] hymn is sung by all, together with the psalms of evening
> praise, so that a renewed remembrance of the Lord's Incarnation en-
> kindles the hearts of the faithful to feelings of devotion and a more
> frequent meditation on the example of the Lord's Mother makes them
> strong, firmly established in the virtues.[13]

The connection Bede makes between Marian devotion and personal
conduct is particularly significant. Through prayer and meditation, the
example of the Mother of the Lord must be strongly rooted in the hearts
of the faithful, to lead them to a determined practice of Christian
virtues.

---

[9] See *In Lucam* 2, 7; PL 15, 1555; SC 45, 74.

[10] *In Purificatione B. M.*; PL 94, 81D–82A; CCL 122, 132.

[11] *In Lucam*; PL 92, 347A; CCL 120, 69.

[12] *Homilia 13, In Dominica II post Epiphaniam*; PL 94, 68; CCL 122, 96.

[13] *In Visitatione B. M.*; PL 94, 22A; CCL 122, 30.

READINGS

AS IT WAS FULFILLED IN MARY, MAY THE WORD OF GOD
ALSO BE FULFILLED IN US

She says: "Behold the handmaid of the Lord, be it done to me according to your word (Lk 1:38). Indeed, she shows how constant is her humility when she calls herself her Maker's handmaid, even as she is chosen to be her Maker's Mother! The angel's utterance proclaims her blessed; by his words the secrets of our redemption, hitherto unknown to mortals, are brought into the open.

Nor does she extol her uniqueness because her exceptional merit is unique; instead, mindful of her condition and God's condescension, she adds herself to the number of the handmaids of Christ, devoting herself to the service of Christ, as bidden. "Let it be to me according to your word" (Lk 1:38), she says; let it happen that the Holy Spirit come upon me to make me worthy of the heavenly mysteries; let it happen that the Son of God put on the garment of human substance in my womb and thence come forth to redeem the world, "like a bridegroom leaving his chamber" (Ps 19:5).

Dearest brethren! Following her voice and intention as our guide, let us recall that we are the servants of Christ in all our actions and impulses. Let us hand over all the members of our body to his obedience. Let us direct our entire attention toward fulfilling his will. And so let us give thanks for the gifts we have received from him by living rightly, that we might merit to live so worthily as to receive even greater gifts.

With the blessed Mother of God, let us pray diligently, that it may happen to us according to his word; that is, according to that word which he employs in telling the reason for his Incarnation: "God so loved the world that he gave his only-begotten Son" (Jn 3:16).

—The Venerable Bede, *In Annuntiatione B.M.*;
PL 94, 14BD; CCL 122, 20

MARY'S SPIRIT OF HUMILITY AND SERVICE

Mary took care to show to men the same humility she had shown to the angel and to reveal her superior virtue to those inferior to her. For who does not know that a virgin consecrated to God is on a higher level than a woman dedicated to God? Does anyone doubt that the Mother of the eternal King rightly has precedence over the mother of a soldier?

Nevertheless, she is mindful of the teaching of Scripture, "The greater you are, the more you must humble yourself" (Sir 3:18). And so, as soon as the angel who has spoken to her returns to heaven, she arises and goes up into the hills. Carrying God in her womb, she sets out for the dwelling of God's servants and seeks conversation with them.

And it is fitting that she should head for the hills after having seen the angel, for she had tasted the sweetness of the cities of heaven, and by the steps of lowliness she betook herself to the heights of virtue. And so she enters the house of Zechariah and Elizabeth. She knows that Elizabeth is going to bear the servant and forerunner of the Lord. She greets her, not as if she had any doubts about the angel's utterance, but to congratulate her on the gift, which she has learned that her fellow handmaid has received. She does not intend to test the truth of the angel's word by the evidence of the woman [Elizabeth]. Instead, being a diligent young woman, Mary wants to offer her service to a woman advanced in age.

—The Venerable Bede, *In Visitatione B.M.*;
PL 94, 15CD; CCL 122, 22

3

AMBROSE AUTPERT
(d. 781)

This author's writings are extremely important for our knowledge of the theological and spiritual climate of his time, which immediately precedes the Carolingian renaissance. Ambrose was born in the south of France at the beginning of the eighth century. His education, while not skipping over secular learning, strongly stressed the value of the sacred sciences. In 755 he came to Italy and entered the Benedictine monastery of St. Vincent in Volturno, in what is now the Molise region. There he made an in-depth study of Benedictine spirituality and saw the possibility of applying it to the Christian life in general. In 776, he was elected abbot of the monastery, but his election was accepted only by the French monks, while the Italian monks elected another abbot. He died a few years later, in 781, while on his way to Rome in an attempt to find a solution to his monastery's irregular state of affairs.

His Marian doctrine appears to be influenced by nearby Byzantine monasteries, which were then numerous in southern Italy. We can detect in his works the inspiration of the great Fathers of the Eastern Church, whose works were beginning to circulate in the West in Latin translations. To the main lines of Byzantine thought, Ambrose added his own remarkable enthusiasm for the Virgin Mother of God, an enthusiasm whose equal is hardly to be found in earlier Latin authors.

A very large amount of mariological material is found spread throughout Ambrose's works. The writings most abounding in Marian teaching are his two homilies on the Purification and the Assumption[1] and his commentary on the Book of Revelation. His attention was most drawn

---

[1] The complete text of this homily was published under the name of Augustine (PL 39, 2129–34). See J. Winandy, "L'Oeuvre littéraire d'Ambroise Autpert", RB 69 (1950): 105.

to the themes of Mary's final glorification, her spiritual motherhood, and her exceptional holiness.[2]

The Feast of the Purification of Mary

Ambrose Autpert gives us some precious information about the celebration of this feast day (February 2). While tradition, as always, assigned a primarily christological meaning to this celebration, Ambrose presents it as a feast of the Virgin. He writes that it was celebrated with deep respect by many of the faithful in the area around his monastery. He explains:

> On this day, the entire populace of the city is gathered together as one, all aglow with the brilliant light of candles, and together celebrates Holy Masses. And no one may enter the public assembly who does not hold a lit candle in his hands, like one going to offer the Lord in the Temple and, indeed, about to receive him. And by the devotion of their outward offering, they show the light that is burning in their hearts.[3]

According to our author, to "present" Jesus means to unite oneself to Mary's action, while to receive him means to imitate the conduct of Simeon. In handing the heavenly Babe to the saintly old man, his Mother intended to present him to all the elect who live out faith and good works in this life, anticipating events to come:

> Now [the Virgin] offers the Lord to the prophet of prophets; she offers the One to one man, but in offering him to one, she offers him to all, for she gave birth to the one Savior of all.[4]

---

[2] PL 89, 1265–1332, brings together but a small part of the works of Ambrose Autpert. Most of his works were published under the names of other, more famous authors. Studies on his Marian thought include: F. Buck, "Ambrose Autpert, the First Mariologist in the Western Church", in CongrZag 3:277–318; A. Piolanti, "Credentium Mater: Un notevole testo di Ambrogio Autperto", *Euntes Docete* 6 (1953): 49–52; H. Barré, "La Nouvelle Ève dans la pensée d'Ambroise Autpert au pseudo-Albert", EtMar 13 (1956): 1–26; idem, "La Maternité spirituelle de Marie dans la pensée médiévale", EtMar 16 (1959): 87–118; TMPM 3:719–41.

[3] *In Purificatione sanctae Mariae* 1; PL 89, 1291–92; CCM 27/B, 985.

[4] Ibid., 7; PL 89, 1297B; CCM 27/B, 991–92.

Mary Our Mother

Autpert points out that Mary fulfills her mission of uniting the Savior to the elect with characteristically maternal affection, because she is truly their Mother:

> For is she not the Mother of the elect, since she gave birth to their Brother? I mean to say, if Christ is the Brother of believers, why is not she, who gave birth to Christ, the Mother of believers?[5]

This conviction gives rise to confidence and trust in the hearts of the faithful. They express this when they call upon the Mother of the Lord as children call upon their mother:

> Therefore I beg you, my most blessed Virgin, who are never jealous of your children, offer us Christ by your loving favor. Pay no heed to your children's offenses, for they are unable to honor you fittingly. For she, who is bound by the love of childbearing, is tolerant of her children's irreverence. No matter how unworthy they are of your faithful prayers, nevertheless help them, whom you bore in bearing your only Son. Pray to your only Son for the many who go astray.[6]

The Sword of Simeon

The word "sword" is often used in the Bible to indicate the tribulations of this world. Ambrose Autpert thinks that this meaning is well-suited to the sword that the aged Simeon foretold to Jesus' Mother. He explains that the prophecy refers, not so much to the many tribulations that Mary had to suffer in the course of her earthly existence, but more to the tragedy of Calvary:

> [Simeon's words] especially express the suffering that pierced the Virgin's maternal heart as the Lord was dying on the Cross.[7]

However, the sorrow that pierced Mary's soul was not caused by her Son's death alone. She also suffered because of the conduct of his enemies and his friends:

---

[5] Ibid., PL 89, 1297C; CCM 27/B, 992.

[6] Ibid.

[7] Ibid., 12; PL 89, 1301A; CCM 27/B, 997.

And as he hung on the Cross, the Jews present insulted him, calling for him to come down from the Cross, while the apostles, who fled from the Cross, did not believe that he could come down from the Cross. As these things happened, inevitably her maternal and loving heart was pierced through by the sword of suffering because of the Redeemer's Passion.[8]

This exegesis clearly shows our author's understanding of the mutual relationship between the Redeemer and those he came to save. In his redemptive Passion and death, all are united with him, so much so that they contract a spiritual bond with his Mother as well. Thus, his Mother suffered, not only because of her Firstborn, but also because of his brothers.

The Feast of Mary's Assumption into Heaven

Ambrose offers us some precious information about this feast, describing the spirit and solemnity with which it was celebrated in his day:

> Dearly beloved brethren, a day most worthy of honor has arrived, surpassing the feast days of all the saints. Today, I say, is a glorious day, a day of fame, a day in which the Virgin Mary is believed to have passed from this world. And so all the earth, made splendid by the passing of so great a Virgin, sings praises with the greatest exultation.[9]

There is a christological reason for such a solemn celebration: she who has gone up to heaven made it possible for us to receive the Author of life, the Prince of those martyrs whose victories we celebrate.

Ambrose then recalls the essential content of what the Church of his time taught about this mystery. He does not attribute any importance to apocryphal writings that claim to transmit details of Mary's Assumption, for these cannot offer any guarantee of authenticity. He accepts the thesis that God did not want to publish many detailed facts about this event—as shown, inter alia, by the fact that the apostle John, the most qualified to speak of it, made not the slightest reference to it in his writings—and concludes that, according to faith, the Mother of God was assumed into heaven as was her Son after his Resurrection. But it seems somewhat beside the point to pose questions about the destiny of her body:

---

[8] Ibid., PL 89, 1301B; CCM 27/B, 997
[9] *De Assumptione sanctae Mariae* 1; PL 39, 2130; CCM 27/B, 1027.

According to [the teaching of] the Apostle, we believe that Mary was assumed higher than the angels, "whether in the body or out of the body" (cf. 2 Cor 12:2), we do not know.[10]

Thus we must conclude that, at that time, belief in the bodily assumption of Mary was not yet explicitly professed by everyone in Christendom.

Mary, Worthy of Praise

This solemnity offered the faithful a favorable opportunity to give renewed praise to the Mother of the Lord. Our author has handed down to us some examples of this praise, as when he addresses the Virgin in these words:

> O happy Mary, and worthy of all praise! O sublime Mother, to whose womb the Maker of heaven and earth was entrusted! . . . If I call you "heaven", you are higher; if I call you "mother of the nations", you are greater; if I call you "the beauty of God", you are worthy of the name; if I call you "mistress of the angels", you are shown to be so in all things.[11]

Asking himself what the cause of such greatness might be, Ambrose finds no better explanation than the Virgin's humility:

> Oh, truly blessed is Mary's glorious humility! Blessed, I say, because she became the gate of paradise and was made the stairway to heaven! Surely, the humility of Mary is the heavenly stairway by which God came down to earth.[12]

Mary's Heavenly Intercession

Farther on, after addressing a long prayer to the Virgin, our author invites Christians to turn to her intercession:

> Therefore, dearest brethren, let us entrust ourselves to the intercession of the most blessed Virgin with all the ardor of our hearts. Let us all implore

---

[10] Ibid., 3; PL 39, 2130; CCM 27/B, 1028.

[11] Ibid., 5; PL 39, 2131; CCM 27/B, 1029.

[12] Ibid., 10; PL 39, 2133; CCM 27/B, 1033–34.

her patronage with our whole strength, so that while we celebrate her on
earth with humble respect, she may deign to be our advocate in heaven
with her constant prayers.[13]

But we are assured of Mary's intercession on the condition that we
imitate her virtues in our Christian life:

> When the blessed Mother of God looks upon us and finds us adorned
> with virtues, united in charity, firmly established in humility, she will
> more eagerly hasten to assist us in the presence of her Son and Lord, Jesus
> Christ.[14]

Mary, Type of the Church

Ambrose sees the woman who appears in Revelation 12 both as a figure
of Mary and as a figure of the Church:

> Whether we say that it was the Mother and Virgin Mary who gave birth
> to Christ, or bears Christ, or say the same about the Mother and Virgin
> Church, in neither case do we stray from the truth of the matter. The
> former gave birth to the Head; the latter gave birth to the members of the
> Head.[15]

Ambrose Autpert justifies this conclusion by explaining that, in Revelation 12, Mary represents the Church, which daily gives birth to new
members who are added to the Mystical Body of Christ.[16]

READINGS

MARY, IMAGE OF THE CHURCH

Our Redeemer's Mother and relatives brought him from Nazareth to
Jerusalem, to the Lord's Temple, because the primitive Church, driven
out by the Jews in the expulsion of the first disciples, brought the
Redeemer's dispensation [of salvation] to the notice of the Gentiles. For
that Church was made up, not only of Gentiles, but also of Jews.

---

[13] Ibid., 12; PL 39, 2134; CCM 27/B, 1035–36.
[14] Ibid.
[15] *In Apocalypsin* V, 12, 5a; CCM 27, 450.
[16] See ibid., 1a; CCM 27, 443–44.

Jerusalem means "vision of peace", and rightly is she so called. It is said of her through the Psalmist: "Jerusalem is built as a city which is bound firmly together" (Ps 122:3). She is a temple, as Paul says to his faithful, "God's temple is holy, and that temple you are" (1 Cor 3:17). And when the apostles come out of Judea, proclaiming Christ, they come to the Gentiles. In them, Jerusalem comes together with Jerusalem, and the Temple meets the Temple, since all these [both Jew and Gentile] are one city Jerusalem and one Temple. And so, in this city and in this Temple, Christ is presented by the apostles and accepted. Whence the Church, speaking through the voice of the Psalmist, says to God the Father, "O God, we have received your mercy in the midst of your temple" (Ps 47:10 [48:9]); that is, in the midst of the Church, which is your Temple.

—Ambrose Autpert, *In Purificatione sanctae Mariae* 4;
PL 89, 1294–95; CCM 27B, 988

MARY'S GREATNESS

The woman of whom we are striving to speak is higher than the heavens. She whose praises we are attempting to tell is deeper than the abyss. For she carried, contained in her immaculate womb, the God whom all creation cannot contain. Yes, she is the only woman who deserved to be called Mother and Bride; she repaired the damage done by the first mother; she brought redemption to fallen man.

Now, the mother of our race introduced punishment into the world, while the Bearer of our Lord gave birth to salvation for the world. Eve was the authoress of death; Mary was the authoress of merit. Eve, by killing, harmed us; Mary, by giving life, helped us. The former struck a wounding blow; the latter healed the wound. For Mary, in a wonderful and priceless way, gave birth to her Savior and the Savior of all.

Who is this Virgin so holy that the Holy Spirit deigned to come upon her? Who is this woman so fair that God chose her for himself as his bride? Who is this woman so chaste that she could remain a virgin after giving birth?

She is the temple of God, that sealed fountain (cf. Song 4:12), and the closed gate of the Lord's house. Yes, as I have said, the Holy Spirit came down upon her, and the power of the Most High overshadowed her. She is unstained by intercourse, fruitful in giving birth, a nursing Virgin, feeding the Food of angels and men. And so, it is right that we extol her as blessed in a unique proclamation, since she brought the world a unique relationship [with God]. Finally, she lifted herself up to such lofty heights of heaven that the Word, who was with God in the beginning (cf. Jn 1:1), [reached down] from the highest pinnacle of heaven and took her in.

—Ambrose Autpert, *De Assumptione sanctae Mariae* 4;
PL 39, 2130–31; CCM 27B, 1029

4

THE CAROLINGIAN RENAISSANCE

This name is given to the era that, in the West, followed the period of the barbarian invasions. It began around the end of the eighth century, with Charlemagne's rise to power. After the death of Pépin III (the Short) in 768, Charlemagne first divided the kingdom between himself and his brother Carloman. When his brother died three years later, he not only reunited under his command all the territories inhabited by the Frankish peoples but also managed to incorporate nearly all the peoples of Western Europe into a single great empire, characterized by a new and firmly established political stability.

Due to the expansion of the Muslim Arabs into the West and the tight control they exercised over the Mediterranean, the old continent of Europe appeared, as it were, reduced to isolation. And in fact, for all practical purposes, the trade routes joining it to the East were closed, so that its economy had to give up many mercantile initiatives and fall back on predominantly agricultural activity. This economic regression had a great influence on the lives of individuals as well as on the development of cities. In addition, the defense of the political stability achieved by Charlemagne demanded frequent military engagements.

Despite all this, the Carolingian age was particularly fruitful on the cultural level; in this area, a genuine renaissance took place. The compactness of Charlemagne's empire, which came to embrace nearly all of the world's Christian population, favored a process of the spiritual unification of Europe into one single Catholic faith. For this reason the Carolingian empire, under the name "Holy Roman Empire", marked the beginning of a remarkable religious, artistic, and cultural rebirth. This was already a subject of comment during the time St. Boniface was the papal legate to Germany.

In this particularly favorable context, theological science also flourished to an extraordinary degree. This was due to the contribution of particularly well-qualified scholars who again took up the train of thought of the Church Fathers, steering theology toward new goals and perspectives, including Marian doctrine. Thus, Marian doctrine was able to continue penetrating the awareness of the Christian people as a whole as well as that of the individual faithful. This led to noteworthy positive developments for both private devotion and public worship.

Nevertheless, we cannot overlook the crisis that was gripping Western theological thought. This crisis originated from reasons of political rivalry with Byzantium, following the position taken by the Second Council of Nicaea in 787, legitimizing the cult of sacred images. The debates and controversies resulting from this decision in the West led to the revival of ancient heresies. But a positive result emerged from this situation as well. The theological research and doctrinal reflection provoked by these events stimulated Latin theologians to exceptional efforts, and they committed themselves to developing biblical theology and a knowledge of tradition. This helped minimize the seriousness of sporadic heretical outbreaks. Another result was that devotion to the Mother of God flourished to a remarkable degree, especially in the celebration of liturgical feasts.

A considerable contribution to this process of Christian renaissance came from monastic communities, some of which became famous centers of religious and educational activity, such as Tours, Fulda, and Reichenau. This context would produce the best-prepared and most influential men of the age. While Charlemagne himself was not a man of great learning, he pursued his educational objectives with confidence and determination, obtaining the cooperation of the best scholars of his time.

5

PAUL THE DEACON
(d. ca. 799)

Among the figures of the Carolingian renaissance who left a mark on the development of Marian doctrine, Paul Winifred, commonly known as Paul the Deacon, must be numbered among the most outstanding. Born to a noble Lombard family around 720–724, he became a priest and later entered the monastery of Monte Cassino. After the fall of the Lombard kingdom in Italy at the hands of the Franks, Paul was called by Charlemagne to his court at Aachen as a teacher. There he won fame as a great expert in historical studies; he wrote a *Historia Romana* and the even more famous *Historia Langobardorum*, which is the only ancient history of his people.

He also compiled a collection of homilies that must have been used either for preaching or for spiritual reading during the recitation of the Divine Office. In it he collected a large number of homilies, the authors of which are not always easily identifiable. Two are his own homilies for the feast of Mary's Assumption into heaven. These homilies are important because they witness to the growing faith of the people of God in this Marian dogma, which would be solemnly defined by Pius XII in 1950. Paul the Deacon died around 799.[1]

Symbol and Reality in Exalting Mary

Paul thought of the Blessed Virgin in grandiose terms. In exalting her, he often used the language of images. He considers the image of the Temple especially expressive, because of Mary's natural relationship to divinity:

---

[1] See TMPM 3:745–56; T. Gallus, "De cultu mariano apud Paulum Winfridum", in CongrZag 3:319–28; C. Pozo, "El culto de María en las homilías de Pablo Diacono sobre la Asunción", in CongrZag 3:329–38.

What room could there ever have been for vices in her soul or her body if she, like the heavens that contain all things, was made the temple of the Lord?[2]

This kind of figurative language allows the author to recognize the house of seven pillars, of which Solomon speaks, as the house that divine Wisdom (the Son of God) built for himself when he became man. Paul explains that the seven pillars are the seven gifts of the Holy Spirit, with which the Virgin was endowed to be made worthy and able to give the Redeemer his human flesh, which would become the price of human salvation. Our author illustrates Mary's virginal dignity by the image of the lily. The lily is a flower that raises itself high above the earth from which it sprang and opens up toward the sky. This means that virginity tires of looking upon the things of earth, while it yearns for things above. Paul adds that, just as the lily is all white on the outside while showing the color of flame on the inside, so the purity of virginal flesh shines white on the outside while burning inwardly with the burning heat of charity. While these considerations apply to holy virgins in general, they appear all the more correct in the case of the Mother of the Lord, whom Paul views as the pinnacle of human holiness. He writes:

What is of greater worth, brothers, than this Virgin? What holier thing ever arose within the human race? Indeed, none of the patriarchs could be compared to her, none of the prophets, none of the Fathers of old or those to come after; in a word: no one of men.[3]

The Humble Virgin

Seeking for an adequate explanation of Mary's greatness, Paul sees humility at the root of it all:

Always remember this glorious Virgin Mother, who deserved to be raised to the highest heights because she was humble.[4]

By practicing this great virtue, the Blessed Virgin took away from the devil the honor he had lost because of his pride. Paul addresses the devil in these words:

---

[2] *In Assumptione beatae Mariae* 1; PL 95, 1567AB.

[3] Ibid., PL 95, 1567BC.

[4] Ibid., PL 95, 1569A.

Burst with envy, ancient serpent, and let your indignation break you in two, for behold: *a woman, whose heel you threatened to strike, has crushed your head* (cf. Gen 3:15). For she, by the virtue of humility, has drawn to herself the privilege of having the honor you lost because of your pride.[5]

According to Paul, however, the ontological foundation that legitimates the greatness of this humble Virgin and the honors that surround her is her unprecedented role as the Mother of God:

It was right, and in every way fitting, that all things should lie subjected to her at her feet, since she gave birth to the Creator of all things. It was right that she should be the Mistress (*Domina*) of the angels, since she had been worthy to be the Mother of the Lord (*Dominus*) of the angels. It was right that the purity of the angels should be subject to her in heaven, since she had been totally infused with the divine purity on earth.[6]

Mary's Love for Jesus

The mutual love between Christ and his Mother is a theme dear to today's spirituality, which is so attentive and sensitive to interpersonal values and relationships. Paul the Deacon also likes to emphasize this point. He believes that this Mother's love for her own Son exceeds every other human creature's capacity to love:

And who could evaluate, or even imagine, how great was the affection that this Mother had for such a Son? If a bad mother loves a bad son out of mere natural instinct, if a good mother loves a good son out of both natural instinct and virtue, can anyone imagine how much this perfect Mother loved her perfect Son?[7]

Paul emphasizes the fact that Jesus is a unique Son, because in him the nature and dignity of the Son of God, along with the fullness of all the virtues, present unique and very strong reasons that he should be loved in a measure superior to any other love. Moreover, Mary received an exceptional capacity to love from the Holy Spirit. Our author's conclusion is simple and succinct:

---

[5] *Homilia 45, In Assumptione*; PL 95, 1492C; TMPM 3:754.

[6] Ibid., PL 95, 1491CD; TMPM 3:753.

[7] Ibid., PL 95, 1491–92; TMPM 3:753.

The fullness of the Holy Spirit implanted in this Mother the virtue of loving [her Son]. And so what limit could there have been to her love in this case, where no reason for loving was lacking? And so, because the Virgin loved him more than anyone else, rightly did the Lord love and honor her more than any other.[8]

Mary's Assumption into Heaven

Paul the Deacon sees Mary's Assumption into heaven as a mystery, in which the fullness of Jesus' love for his Mother becomes completely manifest. After applying to Mary the words of the Song of Songs: "Who is she that rises from the desert, breathing forth sweet perfumes?" (Song 3:6), our author comments:

> No doubt her Son himself, King of kings and Lord of lords, ran to meet her exulting, with the multitude of the heavenly host, making himself her faithful staff [the prop of her venerable old age]. He bore aloft his Mother, by whom he had been borne about [in the womb], bore her, now full of days and full of every spiritual treasure, higher than the fullness of the saints, right up to the presence of the Throne on high, and gave her a seat on that unspeakably glorious Throne.[9]

That Mary was lifted up to heavenly glory, not only in her soul, but also in her body was considered by Paul more as a possibility than a certainty. This reserve does not prevent him from taking the celebration of this mystery as an opportunity to exalt the glorious status of the Mother of the Lord:

> Applaud and "rejoice over her, all you who love her" (Is 66:10), for she has been greatly exalted; she has been mightily magnified! In wonderment let us sing her glory; let us sing to her a song of gladness.[10]

Paul next explains the meaning of the text from the Song of Songs quoted above. The desert prefigures the chosen people, abandoned by God because of their repeated infidelity. It is from this desert that Mary rises up into heaven:

> From this desert of deplorable misery, our glorious Theotókos, on the day our Lord remembered to free her from the burden of her cries of

---

[8] Ibid., PL 95, 1492; TMPM 3:753.
[9] Ibid., PL 95, 1495C; TMPM 3:754.
[10] Ibid., PL 95, 1490D; TMPM 3:752.

anguish for the absence of her Son, rose up, filled with joy, to a more blessed desert.[11]

The cries of anguish Paul attributes to Mary contrast with the image we have of her today: a woman composed, brave, ready to accept every trial that comes from God with a strong spirit. But our author was part of that school of interpretation that loved to dramatize the Virgin's suffering, making her a woman of sorrows, the sorrowful and desolate Mother, crushed beneath the burden of a real moral martyrdom. In her final glorification, however, Mary is relieved from all her suffering because she is restored to the tangible and infinitely gratifying presence of her divine Son.

The Virgin's Heavenly Mission

For Mary, being in the glory of heaven does not mean being detached from or disinterested in earthly realities. Even in the glory of paradise, she has a mission to carry out: to act as our advocate and Mediatrix. For the believer, this awareness is a reason for joy and hope. Therefore, Paul the Deacon exhorts us:

> Then let us rejoice and be glad in Mary, for she is the faithful advocate of us all in heaven. Her Son is the Mediator between God and men; she is the Mediatrix between her Son and men. And, as befits the Mother of Mercy, she is most merciful. And she knows how to have compassion on human weakness, because she knows of what we are made. For this reason, she never ceases to intercede for us with her Son.[12]

In these words, Paul recognizes the Mother of God's magnificent responsibility to act on behalf of the comfort and hope of all human beings.

READINGS

THE HEAVENLY GLORY OF THE MOTHER OF GOD

At her entrance, all the trumpets of heaven begin to blow, and all the sons of God shout for joy and acclaim her as most blessed, praising her

---

[11] Ibid., PL 95, 1491B; TMPM 3:752.
[12] Ibid., PL 95, 1496B; TMPM 3:755.

victorious hand that so powerfully humiliated the ancient deceiver, throttling him who tripped up Eve. Not so was Eve, not so! She was like dust that the serpent blew out of paradise.

My dearest friends, if the blessed company of angels venerates and praises this glorious Lady and rejoices in her, we have an even greater reason to rejoice in her and to exalt her name with all honor and all praise.

For Mary came forth from us; she is a precious jewel of our race; our honor was perfected in her. In the sight of the angels, we were brought low by a man and a woman in the beginning, but see, both sexes have been lifted up higher than the angels, the male sex in Christ, the female sex in Mary. Now the angels honor both man and woman as their peers and fellow citizens, as they look on the Prince of both [human and angelic] races set over them. The angels gaze upon two great lights, taken from among men and lifted up higher than they: the greater light and the lesser light, Jesus and Mary. [They are such great lights that] it would be completely improper to compare them to the sun and the moon.

—Paul the Deacon, *Homilia 45*, *In Assumptione*;
PL 95, 1496AB; TMPM 3:755

MARY'S MERCY EXTENDED TO HUMAN CREATURES

And so, dearly beloved, let us rejoice with all our heart in our advocate, who is so powerful, kindly, and faithful. She does not deny her help to anyone who asks for it worthily, and for no one does she intercede with her Son in vain. I say it again: Let us rejoice in her and with the holy legions of angels venerate her with worthy deference and worthy praise. With all the inhabitants of heaven, let us send up our prayers before her.

With what kind of deferential service can we give fitting honor to such a great Lady? Certainly, this is the service that most pleases her: that we should imitate her most holy life, loving what she loved and shunning what she shunned. The beauty of chastity pleases her, for it was this beauty that made her pleasing in the eyes of the Most High.

. . . But still, no matter how horrible our [spiritual] weakness, we must never despair of her mercy, as long as we are willing to accuse ourselves in her sight and beg for her intercession [*interventum*] with a repentant heart. There is no doubt that we will experience her help, for many are her mercies, and great mercy is given to all who call upon her.

. . . Blessed be God who, in his great mercy, has given us such a great advocate in the court of heaven, one so powerful, so merciful, so familiar to his Majesty.

> —Paul the Deacon, *Homilia 45, In Assumptione*;
> PL 95, 1496D–1497D; TMPM 3:755–56

6

ALCUIN
(d. ca. 804)

Alcuin was a man of great learning who also possessed uncommon organizational skills. He was considered the soul of the cultural, artistic, and religious movement that has passed into history (as noted earlier) under the title "the Carolingian renaissance".

He was born around 735 in England and was educated at the bishop's school at York. He was ordained a deacon and remained one for the rest of his life. Charlemagne invited him to his court at Aachen and put him in charge of the Palatine school, where he made the acquaintance of the most famous cultural figures of the time.

He also had time to concern himself with the establishment and reorganization of various monasteries, some of which he personally directed. He died at Tours around 804.

Alcuin's literary output, while very diversified, shows that he did not possess any particularly original teaching. His outstanding merit lay in being a formidable sower of ideas and a tireless leader in educational organization.

He did not raise new questions of Marian doctrine. Instead, he gathered together nearly all the threads of earlier tradition, especially Western tradition. His contribution to the Marian theology and piety of his time must be viewed as considerable.

Among Eastern writers, he had a predilection for the earliest Fathers of the Greek Church, which led him to work out a rather sober Marian doctrine. By contrast, on the level of Christian moral practice, Alcuin always professed a sincere and enthusiastic devotion to the Mother of God. In his sacramentary, which is important because of its influence on the development of the Church's liturgical tradition, he introduced some Masses in honor of the Mother of the Lord, meant to be celebrated on Saturdays. In them, Alcuin applied to Mary such scriptural texts as Sirach

24:14 and Proverbs 8:23, texts that the Church would later use in Marian liturgies.[1]

Defender of Christological and Marian Dogma

During the eighth century, one of the most serious dangers threatening the purity of the Church's faith came from Spain. There, a new form of adoptionism had been reborn, according to which Christ was, not the Son of God by nature, but a mere adopted son. Obviously, this error called into question the dogma of Mary's divine motherhood, and Alcuin saw in it a renewed form of Nestorianism. While he uses the Nestorian term *Christotókos* in his writings, along with the Ephesian term *Theotókos*, he uses the first term with a meaning that includes that of the second. Thus he defends the Virgin's true and divine motherhood.

In his anti-adoptionist polemic, he employs, inter alia, an interesting comparison, going back to the fifth-century African monk Arnobius the Younger. Just as wool, to be transformed into royal purple cloth, must absorb the blood of a purple shellfish (*conchylium*), so the Virgin Mary absorbed the purple color of divinity when the Holy Spirit descended upon her and she was covered with the shadow of the Most High. In this way, the human nature born of Mary became worthy to be assumed by the Word of God.[2]

Finally, Alcuin summed up the legitimate Marian teaching of the Council of Ephesus, reprised by the Council of Chalcedon, in a very beautiful and concise synthesis:

> Mary is both the only *Christotókos* and the only *Theotókos*. She is also the only virgin to conceive by the Holy Spirit and the power of the Most High and was so greatly glorified that she gave birth to God, the coeternal Son of God, consubstantial with the Father. Virgin before giving birth, virgin in giving birth, virgin after giving birth.[3]

Commenting on Jesus' words to the Virgin at the wedding at Cana, Alcuin uses the christological doctrine of the two natures in Christ to

---

[1] See B. Susnik, "Mariologia Alcuini respectu ad propagationem evangelicam aquileiensem", in CongrZag 3:339–47; TMPM 3:759–62.

[2] See *De fide sanctae et individuae Trinitatis* 3, 14; PL 101, 46; TMPM 3:760.

[3] Ibid., 47; TMPM 3:760–61.

shed light on the nature of the relationship binding the Savior to his
Mother:

> He who orders us to honor father and mother would not dishonor his
> own Mother. Nor would he deny that she is his Mother, since he did not
> refuse to take flesh from her flesh. . . . But when Christ, just before he
> works a miracle, says: "O woman, what have you to do with me?", he
> means that the principle of his divinity, by virtue of which he would work
> the miracle, is not something that he took from Mary in the world of
> time. To the contrary, eternal divinity is something he always had from his
> Father.[4]

Thus, Alcuin wants to define in no uncertain terms that Mary is the
true Mother of God, because she gave a human nature to the eternal Son
of the Father. On the other hand, he wants to make clear that she had
nothing to do with the Son's divine and eternal origin. Our author puts
into Jesus' mouth words that make this idea even more explicit:

> What is there in common between divinity, which I have always had from
> my Father, and your flesh, from which I took flesh? . . . I must first reveal
> the power of my eternal Godhead by performing works of power.[5]

Alcuin completes his thought by referring to the scene of Calvary as
portrayed in John's Gospel, with Mary at the foot of the Cross (cf. Jn
19:25–27). He proposes a manifestly Augustinian interpretation:

> But the hour will come for him to show what he has in common with his
> Mother. Then, when he is about to die on the Cross, he will entrust the
> Virgin to his virgin disciple.[6]

Alcuin's Deep Personal Devotion to the Virgin

Alcuin had a deep personal devotion to the Mother of the Lord, which
he was able to express especially in his poetic compositions. Here is one
truly touching text:

> To me you are my dear love, my beauty, the great hope of salvation. Help
> your servant, O most glorious Virgin. My voice tells of you tearfully; my

---

[4] *In Joannem* I, 2, 3–4; PL 100, 766–67.
[5] Ibid., PL 100, 767A.
[6] Ibid.

heart burns for love. Give heed as well to the prayers of all my brothers who cry unto you: O Virgin, you are full of grace; through you may the grace of Christ ever preserve us.[7]

The tone of this text, full of intense feeling, shows how much this cultured man of science lived in his soul a spirituality fed by faith, tenderness, and trust toward Mary, and how she allowed him to perceive the comfort of her mysterious presence.

Likewise, his faith in Mary's queenship clearly comes out. He invokes her as Queen of heaven and attributes to her a special merciful readiness to hear the petitions of those devoted to her. These feelings are apparent in some of his *Tituli*, poetic inscriptions composed for the dedication of churches or altars in honor of the Virgin. We reproduce a beautiful example:

> May devotion and honor recall your memory in this place, O Queen of heaven, greatest hope of our life. With your wonted kindness, look upon God's handmaids and servants here who call unto you, O Virgin most mild. In your mercy, give heed in every moment to our prayers, and by your prayers direct our days, always and everywhere.[8]

Requesting Mary's prayers is based on the belief that she has a mission to fulfill as Mediatrix in the Lord's presence. Alcuin shows this belief when he uses the Latin expression *per te*, "through you" or "by means of you". This faith in the Virgin's power of intercession is inspired by observation of Jesus' conduct toward his Mother at the wedding feast at Cana (cf. Jn 2:1–2) and of Mary's reaction, which he does not interpret as opposition to her Son's words. Alcuin explains:

> Nevertheless the Mother knew her Son's devotion, and so she knew that he would not deny her request.[9]

It is surprising to note that, even though Alcuin composed some prayers in prose, whenever a prayer is addressed to the Virgin, it is always in verse. He probably thought that Mary expressed such a great ideal of spiritual beauty that only poetry was able to celebrate and invoke her as she deserved.

---

[7] PL 101, 771B; MGH, *Poetae Latini Aevi Carolini*, 1:313.

[8] PL 101, 749D; MGH, *Poetae Latini Aevi Carolini*, 1:325.

[9] *In Joannem* I, 2, 4; PL 100, 767B.

READINGS

THE VIRGIN MOTHER OF THE INCARNATE WORD

The blessed Evangelist, to show the uniqueness of the single person in Christ, says: "The Word was made flesh" (Jn 1:14): the Word who was with God before the world was, through whom the world was made; the Word, who did not give up his eternity, even though he chose to become man by taking flesh from the virginal womb. This Word wanted the man that he assumed by his almighty power in time to become what the Word was before time began, namely, God's own Son. And so it happened, that it might not be said that there are two Sons of God, one begotten before time and the other born in time, but God's own, only, and perfect Son, our Lord Jesus Christ.

It was this Son whom the Blessed Virgin Mary bore, without loss of her bodily integrity, giving birth to God and man. She was the whitest of wool, the most glorious in her virginity, and incomparable to all other virgins under heaven, so much so that she alone was worthy to receive the Godhead of the Son of God into herself. For just as wool soaks up the blood of a shellfish so that the purple cloth made of the wool becomes so worthy of imperial majesty that no one can wear it unless distinguished by imperial dignity, in the same way the Holy Spirit came upon the Blessed Virgin, and the power of the Most High overshadowed her, and she became like wool dyed purple by divinity. She alone was most worthy to be clothed with the eternal Emperor.

And so the most blessed Virgin Mary became *Theotókos* as well as *Christotókos*. For while, before Mary, there were other women among the people who were *christotókai*, in that they were mothers of christs [=anointed men], these were not virgins, nor had they been overshadowed by the Holy Spirit and the power of the Most High, so as to be found worthy of bearing God. But Mary is both the only *Christotókos* and the only *Theotókos*. She is also the only virgin to conceive by the Holy Spirit and the power of the Most High and was so greatly glorified that she gave birth to God, the coeternal Son of God, consubstantial with the Father.

Mary was virgin before giving birth, virgin in giving birth, virgin after giving birth. For it was fitting that, when God was born, the merit of chastity should increase, lest he who came to heal what was corrupted should by his coming violate what was whole. Nor did the Ruler of heaven, who fills the wideness of all creation, shrink from entering the narrow confines of the virginal womb. And, at his birth, the army of angels came to sing: "Glory to God in the highest, and on earth peace among men with whom he is pleased" (Lk 2:14).

—Alcuin, *De fide sanctae et individuae Trinitatis* 3, 14;
PL 101, 46–47

AN ANONYMOUS PRAYER

Virgin and Mother whose merit is unequaled! O Mary, you alone are the one whom the Lord preserved in such a condition of soul and body as to make you worthy of the mystery in which the Son of God assumed a body from you as the price of our redemption. O most merciful, through whom the whole world has been saved, I pray you, intercede for me, the most unclean of all and stained with every kind of wickedness; intercede for me, for because of my sins, I deserve to receive nothing except eternal punishment. O most glorious Virgin, grant that I, saved by your merits, may reach the eternal kingdom.[10]

—H. Barré, *Prières anciennes de l'Occident à la Mère du Sauveur*, p. 52

---

[10] Wrongly attributed to Ephrem the Syrian by the codex Troyes 1742, this famous Marian prayer, known since the first years of the ninth century, is cited by its first two words: *Singularis meriti*. Its place of origin is to be located within the city of Tours, where Alcuin spent the last years of his life. He undoubtedly knew this prayer, which was composed in the first person singular for private devotional use. The prayer is a fascinating devotional text, uniting praise with the humble and confident petition of a sinner who is aware of his moral responsibilities but equally aware of the Virgin's role in salvation history.

7

RABANUS MAURUS
(d. 780)

The Benedictine monk Rabanus Maurus earned the title "Teacher of Germany" (*praeceptor Germaniae*) because of the enormous influence he had in his native land. He was himself a disciple of such famous teachers as Alcuin, at the school of Tours, and Haymo of Halberstadt, at the school of Fulda.

Rabanus was born at Mainz around 784. Having entered the Benedictine abbey of Fulda, in Germany, he was ordained priest in 814. Some years later, he became director of the abbey school and was abbot from 822 to 842. In 847, he was elected archbishop of Mainz, his native city. He died in 856, leaving an enormous amount of writings, including scriptural commentaries, encyclopedic treatises, collections of homilies, and many hymns, some of which have become part of the Church's liturgical heritage. His works, despite the diversity of their literary genres, share a markedly didactic and expository style, which is nevertheless capable of transmitting a clear, substantial teaching.[1]

In the field of Mariology, Rabanus stands out, among other reasons, for having contributed to the reflowering of the theme "Mary, image of the Church" within the Latin tradition. He also lays particular stress on the divine motherhood, viewing it as the fundamental condition that explains and legitimates the role Mary played in salvation history. He adds his voice to the ever-increasing choir of those authors who write about Mary in tones of boundless admiration, enthusiastic exaltation,

---

[1] The works of Rabanus Maurus are published in PL 107–12 and in MGH, *Poetae Latini Aevi Carolini*, 2:154–258. Among the studies of his Marian thought, see J. Huhn, "Das Marienbild in den Schriften des Rabanus Maurus", *Scholastik* 31 (1956): 515–32.

and deep devotion. In his sermons, he frequently encourages his listeners to venerate the Blessed Virgin worthily and to implore her maternal aid with persistence and confidence.

Mary in Messianic Prophecy

Rabanus' Scripture commentaries show that he pays special attention to the prophetic texts that Christian tradition applies to Mary. He offers two possible interpretations of the woman of Genesis 3:15, who is destined to crush the head of the infernal serpent. She may be viewed as a representation both of the Church and of the Mother of God. This twofold identification is also confirmed by earlier exegetical tradition. For while the Church crushes the serpent's head through the virtuous conduct of her children, it was above all Christ, the Son of the Virgin, who won the definitive victory over the devil. For this reason, the words of Genesis are also applied to Mary, as Rabanus writes:

> Some have understood the saying "I will put enmity between you and the woman" (Gen 3:15) as referring to the Virgin from whom the Lord was born. They understood it in this way because it was promised at that time that the Lord would be born to overthrow the enemy and destroy death, which the devil had introduced.[2]

The bush that Moses saw burning without being consumed (cf. Ex 3:2) is a prophetic sign of the undefiled virginity of the Mother of the Lord:

> The bush, then (as some hold), is a prefiguration of the Virgin Mary, since she made the Savior blossom forth, like a rose growing out of the bush of her human body; or rather, because she brought forth the power of the divine radiance without being consumed by it. Hence we read in Exodus: "The Lord appeared to Moses in a flame of fire out of the midst of a bush; and he looked, and behold, the bush was burning, yet it was not consumed" (Ex 3:2).[3]

Rabanus also mentions Aaron's rod (cf. Num 17:23), which he interprets in a Marian sense, associating himself with an earlier tradition:

---

[2] *Commentaria in Genesim* 1, 18; PL 107, 496A.
[3] *De universo* 19, 6; PL 111, 513C.

Others think that this staff, which brought forth a flower without the presence of moisture, is the Virgin Mary, who bore the Word of God without intercourse. Of her it was written: "A shoot shall come forth from the stump of Jesse, and a flower blossom from his roots" (Is 11:1); in other words, Christ. For Christ the flower, foreshadowing his future Passion, turned purple in the white light of faith and in the red blood of his Passion. He is the flower of virgins, the crown of martyrs, the grace of those who remain chaste.[4]

We do not find anything new in these Marian interpretations of Scripture texts. Rabanus simply reproposes the teaching of the patristic tradition as it had been consolidated in preceding centuries. In one of his liturgical hymns, he expresses his belief that Mary was truly one of the principal references of the Old Testament messianic prophecies:

What once the venerable choir of prophets sang, filled with the Holy Spirit, truly came to pass in Mary, the Mother of God. As a virgin, she conceived, and as a virgin bore the God of heaven and the Lord of earth. And after giving birth, she merited to remain inviolate.[5]

In the second part of the above quotation, there is an obvious reference to Isaiah's prophecy: "Behold, a virgin shall conceive and bear a son" (Is 7:14).

The Name of Mary

Among the different meanings proposed for the name of Mary during the course of centuries, Rabanus selects three: Light-Bringer, Star of the Sea, and Lady [Domina].[6] His preference leans toward the first two interpretations, which are equivalent:

Because it is normal for a star to guide men to a safe haven, Mary, in this world into which Christ was born, is called Light-Bringer and Lady. Christ guides all to life, as long as they follow him, and Mary brought forth for us our true Light and Lord.[7]

The third meaning, "Lady", goes back to ancient Syriac etymology, which was well known to the Fathers of the Church:

---

[4] *Enarrationes in librum Numerorum* 2, 20; PL 108, 688B.

[5] *In Purificatione sanctae Mariae* 12; PL 112, 1658C.

[6] See *De universo* 4, 1; PL 111, 75AB.

[7] *Homiliae in Evangelia et Epistolas* 163; PL 110, 464C.

But in the Syrian tongue the name "Mary" is translated as "Lady"; and beautifully so, since she gave birth to the Lord of heaven and earth and all creation.[8]

These three meanings have very old origins. Jerome knew of them, along with other meanings, which he listed in his study of the Hebrew names found in the Bible.[9]

It appears that in Rabanus' time, the first meaning had the greatest impact on the religious sensibility and piety of the Christian people. For this was when the famous hymn *Ave maris stella* was becoming widely used. This hymn became one of the most popular Marian songs of all Christendom and was even introduced into the liturgy. The oldest manuscript in which the hymn is found, Sangallese 95, dates from the ninth century.[10]

Summary of Rabanus Maurus' Marian Teaching

In the field of Marian theology, Rabanus is not so much an original thinker as an outstanding teacher, concerned with teaching the doctrine of the faith and exhorting the faithful to piety and devotion.

In treating the dogma of the divine motherhood, he expresses himself in terms of absolute fidelity to the traditional Magisterium of the Church. Mary's Son is none other than the Son of God:

"Savior", by which name the prophet called God-with-us (cf. Is 43:3 and many other texts), means both natures in one Person. For he who was born of the Father before time began is God, and in the fullness of time he became Emmanuel, that is, God-with-us, in the womb of his Mother.[11]

Later, he returns to this theme with great emphasis, reiterating the identity between the Son born of Mary and the Son eternally born of the Father:

Mary gave birth to her firstborn Son; that is, the Son who came from her substance. She bore him who, as God, was born of God before any

---

[8] *De universo* 4, 1; PL 111, 75B.

[9] See *De nominibus hebraicis*, PL 23, 886.

[10] See AnHymn 51:140–42; H. Lausberg, "Der Hymnus 'Ave maris stella'", *Abhandlungen der Rheinisch-Westfälischen Akademie der Wissenschaften* 61 (Opladen, 1976).

[11] *Commentaria in Matthaeum* 1, 1; PL 107, 752D.

creature existed. And she bore him who, in the humanity by which he
became man, surpassed every other creature in merit.[12]

On the same topic, the statement Rabanus makes at the beginning of
his homily on the Assumption may be considered conclusive:

> And so this Virgin Mary is called Mother of the only begotten God; she
> is the worthy [Mother] of the Worthy One, immaculate [Mother] of the
> Holy One, one [Mother] of the One [God], [only] Mother of the Only
> [God]. For no other only begotten God came down to earth, nor did any
> other virgin give birth to the Only-Begotten.[13]

Our author frequently calls to mind the eschatological goal of the
coming of the Son of God to earth, as seen in the following text:

> Jesus, then, is the name of the Son who was born of the Virgin. This
> name, as the angel explained, means that he will save his people from their
> sins. The same Jesus who saves them from their sins, that is, from the
> corruption of their mind and body that is caused by sins, will also save
> them from death itself, forever.[14]

When he touches on the theme of Mary's virginity, Rabanus does not
admit doubts of any kind. He holds that the virginal conception of Jesus
was a necessary part of God's plan of salvation. As for Mary's virginity
during the birth of Jesus, Rabanus never intervened in the debate that
broke out within the monastery of Corbie between Paschasius
Radbertus and his disciple Ratramnus, who was criticized for denying
Mary's virginity *in partu*. In fact, the most one can say is that Ratramnus,
for apologetic reasons, stressed the physical aspects of Mary's childbirth
in a highly realistic fashion, going against certain currents of thought
then widespread in Germany, which denied that Jesus was born in the
natural manner, just as any other human being is born. However,
Rabanus never hesitated to show his faith in the virginal character of
Jesus' birth from Mary.[15]

We have already mentioned Rabanus' idea that Mary is the image or
type of the Church. Within the Latin Church this idea is quite ancient,
going back to Ambrose of Milan. Rabanus Maurus frequently brings it

---

[12] Ibid., PL 107, 754A.

[13] *In Assumptione S. M. V.*, PL 110, 55C.

[14] *Commentaria in Matthaeum* 1, 1; PL 107, 754C.

[15] See ibid., PL 107, 752A.

up. For example, he writes that Mary "mystically signifies the holy Catholic Church, which is incorrupt in her faith".[16]

Further, he goes back to the typically patristic image of the Virgin as the bridal chamber in which, in the Incarnation, a mystical marriage was consummated between God and the Church:

> The manner in which the Father brought about the marriage of the King, his Son, was the manner in which he associated the holy Church with himself in the mystery of the Incarnation. And that Bridegroom's bridal chamber was the womb of his Virgin Mother.[17]

Mary's Glorification and Heavenly Mission

In the light of the mystery of the Assumption, Rabanus intuits the privilege of Mary's queenship. We read in his homily for this feast:

> Behold, you have been lifted up above the choirs of angels, seated next to your Son the King. O happy Mother, you will reign as Queen forever. And he, to whom you offered a place to dwell in your womb, he himself has given you the kingdom of heaven.[18]

In heaven, Mary continues her mission on behalf of her children on earth, as their Mediatrix. Thus Rabanus Maurus repeatedly invites them to lift up their invocations to her:

> Brothers, in meditating on these things, let us not despair or fail to praise her; rather, let us lift her up even higher, according to our ability, and exult in proclaiming her, since her goodness will make up for what our abilities lack.[19]

READINGS

MARY'S HUMILITY IN THE MYSTERY OF THE VISITATION

The most blessed Virgin Mary, after becoming aware that she was pregnant with the heavenly Child, did not pride herself on having

---

[16] *De universo* 7, 1; PL 111, 184B.

[17] *Commentaria in Matthaeum* 6, 22: PL 107, 1053D.

[18] *In Assumptione*, PL 110, 85D.

[19] Ibid., 56A.

received heavenly gifts, as if the credit were hers. Instead, she determined in her mind to keep a watch on her humility, in order that she might become more and more fitted to those gifts, mindful of the Scripture that commands, "The greater you are, the more you must humble yourself" (Sir 3:18). And as soon as the angel who had announced the divine birth to her returned to God, she arose and went into the hills, carrying God in her womb.

She headed for the dwellings of the servants of God and sought to speak with them. And when she arrived, Elizabeth, hearing the greeting of the Mother of her Lord, immediately prophesied about her and testified that the Mother of the Lord had come to her and pronounced her blessed among women and pronounced the fruit of her womb blessed (see Lk 1:42). Further, she told how the infant in her womb, filled with the Holy Spirit, had leapt for joy on hearing her voice (see Lk 1:44).

And when Mary heard this, she did not become proud, boasting, or vainglorious. Instead, in humility, she devoted her complete attention to thanking God.

—Rabanus Maurus, *Canticum Mariae*;
PL 112, 1161D–1162A

GREATNESS OF THE DIVINE MOTHERHOOD

A Mother who conceived offspring in her womb and is chaste; she bore a son and is a virgin. An immaculate Mother, an incorrupt Mother, an intact Mother, the Mother of the only begotten Lord and King of all, the Maker and Creator of everything. The Mother of him who has no mother above and has no father on earth. The Mother of him who is in the Father's bosom in his divinity and was in his Mother's bosom on earth, in the body he assumed.

And so this Virgin Mary is called Mother of the only begotten God; she is the worthy [Mother] of the Worthy One, immaculate [Mother] of the Holy One, one [Mother] of the One [God], [only] Mother of the Only [God]. For no other only begotten God came down to earth, nor did any other virgin give birth to the Only-Begotten.

This is why, dearly beloved brethren, as we gaze on her greatness, in such wonder that our hearts are silent, let us cry out in praise and say, "O truly blessed Virgin Mary, recognize your glory; namely, that glory the angel proclaimed to you, that glory John proclaimed through the mouth of Elizabeth. Before he came forth from the hiding place of his mother's womb, he prophesied, "Blessed are you among women, and blessed is the fruit of your womb" (Lk 1:42).

Mary, you even merited to embrace his advent, promised to the whole world for so many centuries past; you became the dwelling place of his immense majesty. For a space of nine months, by a singular privilege, you alone held the hope of the whole world, the honor of the ages, the common joy of all.

—Rabanus Maurus, *In Assumptione S.M.V.*;
PL 110, 55BD

8

PASCHASIUS RADBERTUS
(d. 865)

This famous medieval master held a place of honor among the theologians of the Carolingian renaissance. His Mariology, which reaches a level of significant development, focuses especially on problems regarding the virginity of the Mother of the Lord.

Paschasius was born in the region of Soissons around 790. He entered the nearby Benedictine monastery of Corbie. In 831 he wrote a book on the presence of Christ in the Eucharist (*De corpore et sanguine Domini*),[1] republished in 844, which was the cause of a lively controversy with Rabanus Maurus and, later, with his confrere Ratramnus of Corbie. In this work, Paschasius openly defends the identity between the eucharistic Body of Jesus and his physical body, conceived in the womb of the Virgin Mary. This marks an important step in the history of eucharistic theology.

In 844 Paschasius was named abbot of the monastery of Corbie, but in 851, because of disagreements and discord that had arisen within the monastic community, he left Corbie and entered the monastery of Saint-Riquier as a simple monk. Later he returned to Corbie, where he died in 865.

Among his works, those that offer explicitly Marian content are the *Libellus de nativitate sanctae Mariae*, wrongly published as St. Jerome's *Letter 50*;[2] his *De partu Virginis*;[3] and the letter *Cogitis me*, which passed

---

[1] PL 120, 1261–1550. See J. R. Geiselmann, *Die Eucharistielehre der Vorscholastik* (Paderborn, 1926), pp. 144–70.

[2] PL 30, 297–305.

[3] PL 120, 1367–86. There is a critical edition edited by E. A. Matter, CCM 56C, 1985. See also J. M. Canal, "La virginidad de María según Ratramno y Radberto, monjes de Corbie, nueva edición de los textos", Mar 30 (1968): 53–160. Cf. R. Maloy, "A Correction in the Text of a Recent Edition of Paschasius Radbertus' 'De Partu Sanctae Mariae'", Mar 33 (1971): 224–25.

into tradition under the name of St. Jerome. It was thought to be addressed to two of that saint's disciples, Paula and Eustochium, but was in reality meant for the community of nuns at Soissons.[4] In this work, which strongly influenced later tradition, the author touches on the question of Mary's earthly end. Finally, three homilies on the Assumption of Mary have been identified, published among the works of St. Ildephonsus of Toledo, the authorship of which must be restored to Paschasius Radbertus.[5]

In his writings, Paschasius successfully combines theological reflection with an expression of his affection for and devotion toward the Mother of the Lord.[6] An eloquent example of his inner feelings may be found in the closing exhortations of the letter *Cogitis me*:

> And so, love the Mother of the Lord, who for your sake bore the immortal Bridegroom. She is his sister, and yours as well, because she did the Father's will and so became a mother. Mary is your relative, not in the flesh, but in the spirit, so that the unity of the Church may be appreciated and the fellowship of the body of Christ understood.[7]

Controversy over Mary's Virginity during the Birth of Christ

In the first half of the ninth century, there again arose the question of Mary giving birth while remaining a virgin. The reasons that this question returned were not purely speculative or academic. It seems that a form of neo-Docetism was afoot in certain Germanic circles that, by appealing precisely to this truth of the Mother's virginal birth, denied that her Son had a true human nature. This error was denounced by Ratramnus, who defends Christ's true humanity in one of his works.

---

[4] PL 30, 122–42. The critical edition is by A. Ripberger, *Der Pseudo-Hieronymus—Brief IX "Cogitis me"; Ein erster marianischer Traktat des Mittelalters von Paschasius Radbert*, Spicilegium Friburgense 9 (Fribourg, 1962). See C. Lambot, "L'Homélie du Pseudo-Jérôme sur l'Assomption et l'Évangile de la Nativité d'après une lettre d'Hincmar", RB 46 (1934): 265–82; H. Barré, "La Lettre du Ps.-Jérôme sur l'Assomption est-elle antérieure à Paschase Radbert", RB 68 (1958): 203–25.

[5] PL 96, 239–57. Cf. CPL 1257.

[6] See H. Peltier, *Paschase Radbert, abbé de Corbie: Contribution à l'étude de la vie monastique et de la pensée chrétienne aux temps carolingiens* (Amiens, 1938), 190.

[7] 18; PL 30, 146D; Ripberger 115, p. 112.

Among other points, he repeatedly states that Christ's birth from Mary was a completely normal birth, according to the laws of nature, following the natural way of childbirth and no other way, as the promoters of the aforementioned neo-Docetism would have it. Were this not so, Jesus would not have had a true birth and Mary could not be considered a true mother. However, Ratramnus defines that when Christ's birth took place, his Mother's womb was closed (*clauso utero*), and thus, even while the process remained natural, it happened in an unusual and miraculous way, which preserved his Mother's virginity.[8]

For his part, Paschasius Radbertus, in his *De partu Virginis*, emphasizes this miraculous and supernatural aspect in order better to defend Mary's virginity in giving birth. He excludes from Mary's act of giving birth all the usual steps laid down by the laws of nature. He holds that, had Mary not given birth in such supernatural conditions, she would not have remained uncontaminated, as other virgins are, and thus could not have been considered a true virgin. To the contrary, she was "full of grace, suffered no pain, and did not experience the corruption of her womb".[9]

Obviously we are dealing with a teaching conditioned by the medieval mentality, which considered marital relations to be a corrupting factor for the woman and her unborn child, a corruption that was manifested in the phenomena related to birth (placenta, amniotic fluid, afterbirth). The case of the Blessed Virgin was different:

> Because she remained a virgin in every way, she was not troubled by any pain; in no way was she corrupted. And so she did not contract the filth of afterbirth, nor did she emit a flow of blood, nor did she experience the corruption of her inner or outer parts. For if she had endured these things and suffered birth pangs of this sort, then undoubtedly she would not have been a virgin, because her virginal integrity would have been violated.[10]

In other words, because Radbertus identifies the corruption of the female parts with the corruption of virginity, he forcefully rejects the idea that Mary could have gone through the common experiences of childbirth in giving birth to Jesus.

---

[8] *Liber de Nativitate Christi* 8; PL 121, 96A.

[9] *De partu Virginis* 1; PL 120, 1373D–1374A.

[10] Ibid., 2; PL 129, 1385A; Canal 55, 144.

Some have thought that, in this work, Paschasius intended to take up a polemical position against the ideas of his confrere Ratramnus, but we may be permitted some doubt with regard to this hypothesis. In reality, the basic positions of the two masters do not disagree. The difference lies in different emphases. Ratramnus insists on the human aspects of Jesus' birth, while Paschasius underscores its extraordinary and supernatural aspects. One may ask, then, whether Paschasius knew the work of Ratramnus and whether he really meant to challenge his confrere's statements.

Mary's Assumption into Heaven

The Assumption is the theme of the aforementioned letter, *Cogitis me*, which does not limit itself to being a theological work but also expresses a fervent devotion to Mary. The work is capable of arousing similar fervor in the reader, provided he is able to grasp its doctrinal richness and intense piety.[11]

The author opens his discourse by denying that the famous apocryphal work called the *Transitus Mariae* has any reliability. He considers this work to be full of doubtful stories, even though different Latin authors had accepted them as authentic "out of love of devotion and a zeal for reading".[12] He gives one fact as certain, "that the Virgin, on this glorious day [August 15] left the body".[13] But it is impossible to tell whether her body rose or not. All we know is that her tomb at Jerusalem is empty, but we do not know where her body is. Paschasius has a better solution to propose:

> It would be better for us to entrust the whole matter to God, to whom nothing is impossible, than to want to define rashly, by our own authority, what we cannot prove.[14]

The authority of this work undoubtedly delayed by some centuries the process of development in the Christian people's belief in Mary's bodily assumption. Not until the twelfth century would a pseudo-Augustinian

---

[11] See J. Leclercq, "La spiritualità del Medio Evo", in *Storia della Spiritualità* 4/A (Bologna, 1986), p. 150.

[12] *Cogitis me* 2; PL 30, 123C; Ripberger 7, pp. 59–60.

[13] Ibid.

[14] Ibid., 2; PL 30, 124A; Ripberger 10, p. 61.

work[15] again revive this doctrine, which, seven centuries later, would be solemnly defined as a dogma of the faith.

Paschasius limits himself to speaking of those facts about which we are certain, the only facts that can guarantee spiritual fruit in the life of believers: "For your exhortation, edification, and in praise of the name of God".[16]

He exalts the Virgin in her glorification in heaven, even though this event is shrouded in mystery, and does not hesitate to proclaim her as Queen:

> Today, the glorious and ever-virgin Mary has gone up into the heavens. Rejoice, I beg you, because she has been lifted up (if I may say it) in a way beyond words and reigns forever with Christ. Today, the Queen of the world is taken away from the earth and from this present worthless world. Again I say, rejoice! For she, sure of her incorruptible glory, has now arrived at the heavenly palace.[17]

The Son himself personally welcomed his Mother into paradise and placed her next to himself on his own throne, amid the exultation of the whole court of heaven.[18]

Marian Devotion

Paschasius never worked out a systematic teaching about the cult of Mary and devotion to her, but all his writings reveal a profound openness to being at the service of Mary because of the unique way she is joined to God. This sentiment of devotion is expressed especially in admiration for Mary and in the necessity to praise her and to praise the Author of her greatness and holiness:

> She deserves the greatest possible honor because of the grace she received, which makes her even more worthy of veneration. For to give her honor and glory means to give thanks and praise to the Redeemer.[19]

---

[15] The text in question is one mistakenly attributed to St. Augustine, published in PL 40, 1140–48. It has been studied by G. Quadrio, *Il trattato "De Assumptione B. M. V." dello Pseudo-Agostino e il suo influsso nella teologia assunzionistica latina*, Analecta Gregoriana 7 (Rome, 1951).

[16] *Cogitis me* 3; PL 30, 124C; Ripberger 13, p. 63.

[17] Ibid., 4; PL 30, 126B; Ripberger 23, pp. 67–68.

[18] Ibid., 9; PL 30, 134D; Ripberger 51, p. 80.

[19] *Sermo 3*, 2; PL 96, 255A.

The Christian's commitment to imitate the Blessed Virgin may offer a tangible proof of devotion:

> Imitate the Mother of the Lord and obey the Fathers; humble yourselves among the virginal flowers, because the granting of chastity and the gifts of virtues come from the grace of God.[20]

> Therefore, O most holy virgins, you should imitate such a great Virgin and venerate her who is so outstanding. Finally, it is most appropriate joyfully to speak worthy praises to her, as much as is allowed; for, in a certain way, her dignity is greater than that of the angels.[21]

The one virtue of Mary that ought to be imitated with particular care is her humility. Christian tradition, ever since the time of the Church Fathers, has always attributed great importance for the spiritual life to this virtue:

> You too, O daughters, if you wish to be true virgins, practice humility and try to imitate the Mother of the Lord with all the love of your heart, for she calls herself a handmaid.[22]

Mary has other virtues, which ought to be proposed to the faithful for their imitation. Among these, Radbertus highlights the spirit of prayer and meditation[23] and the theological virtues of faith, hope, and love.[24]

Finally, we ought to recall the Marian interpretation of the Song of Songs. Paschasius Radbertus makes wide use of this interpretation when citing the Song of Songs, anticipating (to a certain degree) those authors who, from the twelfth century onward, will commonly employ a Marian interpretation in their exegesis of this book of Scripture.

---

[20] *Sermo 1*, PL 96, 245C.

[21] *Cogitis me* 7; PL 30, 129BC; Ripberger 43, p. 77.

[22] Ibid., 16; PL 30, 140C; Ripberger 104, p. 108.

[23] Ibid., 13; PL 30, 136C; Ripberger 81, pp. 95–96.

[24] On the theme of Marian devotion in Radbertus, see W. Cole, "Theology in Paschasius Radbertus' Liturgy-Oriented Marian Works", in CongrZag 3:395–431; R. Rosini, "Il culto della B. Vergine nella lettera 'De Assumptione sanctae Mariae Virginis' ('Cogitis me') dello pseudo-Girolamo", in CongrZag 3:433–59.

READING

THE GLORY OF THE BLESSED VIRGIN IN HEAVEN

If there is great rejoicing in heaven over any repentant sinner whatever, we have to think that there is even greater rejoicing over the great exaltation and glory of the Virgin, that there is great exulting in heaven above. Certainly there is a celebration in her honor, and all the citizens of heaven keep festival, especially because this celebration of Mary represents praise and acclamation of the Savior. Therefore we believe, as has been said above, that they do not keep this solemn day in her honor only once a year but that they continually and eternally make merry and are joyful, making an offering of their gladness, honoring her in a solemn dance of love and happiness.

And rightly, then, that whole celestial city celebrates and honors the Mother, whose Son they ever worship as King over them, before whom the powers tremble and every knee bends (cf. Phil 2:10).

Surely, speaking of Mary's ascension into heaven, the contemplator of heavenly things, looking on with great wonder, says, "I saw my beautiful one going up, like a dove by the streams of waters" (Song 5:12).

And truly she is beautiful like a dove, because she showed the appearance and simplicity of that dove who came [to hover] over the Lord and taught John that the Lord is the one who baptizes. And well is it said, "by the streams of waters", because the Lord led her and nourished her "by refreshing waters" (cf. Ps 23:2). From this water many rivers flow, which water the whole earth with delights and are poured into the garden of joy. Watered daily by these rivers, the blessed Mother of God ascends today, most beautiful and admirable; her fragrance is beyond all price and, so, beyond words.

Sensing the fragrance of her perfume, the whole heavenly Jerusalem runs joyfully to meet her.

> —Paschasius Radbertus, *Cogitis me* 14;
> PL 30, 137CD; Ripberger 86–89, 99–100

9

FULBERT OF CHARTRES
(d. 1028)

The writings of Fulbert and the cathedral of Notre-Dame of Chartres, which he rebuilt after the fire that completely destroyed it in 1020, remain as eloquent witnesses to the Marian doctrine and piety of the eleventh century, the great Marian century that prepared for the even more beautiful flowering of the twelfth century.

Fulbert, the most important theologian of the first part of the eleventh century, was born around the year 960. There are still questions about his origin, which some say was French and others, Italian. After having taken the first steps toward learning under the guidance of an Italian bishop, he went to Rome, where he made the acquaintance of the celebrated Benedictine monk Gerbert of Aurillac, the future Pope Sylvester II. Returning to France, after having spent some months in the school of Rheims, he moved to Chartres and directed the school there. Under his guidance, the school of Chartres became famous throughout Europe, and students from every country came to study there. In 1006 he was consecrated bishop of Chartres. We know little about his pastoral activity. Apparently, after some time, he wished to give up his episcopal duties because he considered himself unequal to such a weighty task, but he was dissuaded from taking this step and so died as bishop of Chartres in 1028, leaving behind a reputation for genuine holiness.

In the collection of his works, his sermons on the Nativity and the Purification of the Virgin are of special interest for Marian doctrine. These sermons are a remarkable witness to his intense devotion to the Mother of God and to the extraordinary zeal he showed in celebrating these feasts. His exceedingly well-developed Marian teaching is among the best worked out and most profound of his time. In a sermon, he summarizes Mary's life and mission thus:

The [birth of the] blessed Mother of the Lord and ever-Virgin Mary was foretold by oracles before she was born. And, foretold by miraculous events, she was born of parents chosen by God. She shone brightly by the privilege of her virtues. She gave birth to the Savior, by whom she was glorified in heaven, and she has never ceased to exercise her patronage in favor of the inhabitants of earth.[1]

This text may be considered a very concise summary of the most important themes of his Marian teaching. We shall now attempt to gather together the most original and specific elements of this teaching by referring to his writings.[2]

The Woman of the Prophecies

Probably inspired by Augustine[3] and Gregory the Great,[4] our author sees Genesis 3:15 as an obvious prophecy of Mary. In this text, he sees Mary as a woman free from the influence of concupiscence, who resists the suggestions of the devil and wins a total victory over him:

If someone should ask: "What woman ever won such a victory?" certainly, none will be found in the series of human generations until we come to her whom we consider the holy woman among all holy women. And if someone should object: "But how did she crush the serpent's head?" the answer is: Surely in the fact that she offered her virginity to God together with her humility.[5]

From these brief reflections, it is already apparent how the bishop of Chartres gave an ethical interpretation to the prophecy of Genesis. He affirms that the Virgin triumphs over Satan, not only through the victorious struggle of her divine Son, but also through her life and personal virtues.

---

[1] *Sermo 4 in Nativitate B. V. M.*; PL 141, 320C; TMPM 3:848.

[2] Our author's works are published in PL 141, 189–368. For studies and partial editions, see J. M. Canal, "Los sermones marianos de San Fulberto de Chartres", RTAM 29 (1962): 33–51; idem, "Texto crítico de algunos sermones marianos de San Fulberto de Chartres o a él atribuibles", RTAM 30 (1963): 55–87; idem, "Los sermones marianos de San Fulberto de Chartres. Conclusión", RTAM 33 (1966): 139–46; J. Pintard, "Saint Fulbert de Chartres à l'origine du culte chartrain de la Nativité de Notre-Dame", in CongrZag 2:551–69.

[3] See, for example, *De Genesi contra Manichaeos* 2, 18; PL 34, 210.

[4] *Moralia in Job* 1, 36; PL 75, 552B.

[5] *Sermo 4*; PL 141, 320D; TMPM 3:848–49.

Fulbert sees another prophetic image of Mary in Aaron's rod (cf. Num 17:6–24), with which Moses worked many miracles in the midst of the people of Israel:

> As that rod, without roots, without any natural or artificial assistance, brought forth [almond blossoms], so the Virgin Mary gave birth to the Son of God without conjugal relations. Her Son is marked out as flower and fruit: a flower, because of his beauty; a fruit, because of the benefit he brings.[6]

To understand better the symbolism of Aaron's rod, our author turns to the oracle of the prophet Isaiah:

> The children of Israel were admonished by the presence of this rod to ask carefully what such a wondrous occurrence meant. Its meaning was unveiled, a long time afterward, by the divine Isaiah: "A shoot [rod] shall come forth from the stump of Jesse, and from his roots a bud shall blossom" (Is 11:1). And as if at these words his hearers had said to him, "O father Isaiah, you speak obscurely, please tell us openly what you mean to say", he added a clarification: "Behold, a virgin shall conceive and bear a son, and shall call his name Emmanuel" (Is 7:14).[7]

Mary, then, is the Mother of the Lord, and Fulbert underscores the fact that she was chosen and specifically prepared by God, who arranged that her arrival and mission should be preceded by a series of prophecies, symbols, and prefigurations.

Predestined from the Moment of Her Conception

Even without speaking of the Immaculate Conception of the Mother of God, Fulbert attributes exceptional holiness to the Virgin as well as an extraordinary spiritual beauty. He sees these privileges as having their roots in the moment of her conception. At the very first instant of Mary's life, he identifies a special divine intervention that acted on the generative capacity of her parents:

> There is no doubt that, in this necessary conception, a vivifying and inflaming spirit filled each of her parents with a singular gift and that they never lacked the watchful presence of the holy angels.[8]

---

[6] Ibid., PL 141, 321C; TMPM 3:849–50.

[7] Ibid., PL 141, 321B; TMPM 3:849.

[8] *Sermo 6 in Nativitate B. V. M.*; PL 141, 326C.

Thus, Joachim and Anne were at the center of a mysterious intervention on God's part, which made them able to bring forth an extraordinary creature whose future life would be full of supernatural events. This would also be shown by the presence of angels surrounding the predestined child. For the Lord wished that this creature should appear haloed by a unique splendor, deriving from a wondrous purity:

> O Virgin greatly blessed, and more blessed still! No one may be compared to you in merit, nor can anyone equal you in chastity.[9]

The Star of the Sea

The very meaning of Mary's name expresses the spiritual beauty emanating from her. Fulbert observes:

> This woman, chosen and outstanding among daughters, surely did not receive her name by pure chance or simply because it pleased her parents, as happens with most girls. No, she received her name according to a divine plan, so that the very pronouncing of her name points to something of great importance. For "Mary" means "star of the sea".[10]

But, according to the bishop of Chartres, it is not only Mary's spiritual light that makes the Mother of God the Star of the Sea. She is the Star of the Sea in a special way because she plays an important role as a guide. Just as the North Star is an indispensable point of reference for sailors, who want to maintain the route that will take them to the safe harbor they desire, so Christians must keep their gaze fixed on Mary in order to reach the final goal of their existence:

> Everyone who worships Christ, when rowing through the waves of this world, must keep his eyes fixed on this Star of the Sea; that is, on Mary. She is nearest to God, the highest pole of the universe, and they must steer the course of their life by contemplating her example. Anyone who does this will never be tossed by the wind of vainglory or broken on the shoals of adversity or drowned in the stormy whirlpool of pleasures; but he will successfully reach the safe harbor of eternal rest.[11]

---

[9] Ibid., PL 141, 327A.

[10] *Sermo 4*; PL 141, 321D–322A; TMPM 3:850. Among the various interpretations of Mary's name, Jerome, as has been noted, also expresses a preference for the meaning "star of the sea". See *De nominibus hebraicis*; PL 23, 886.

[11] Ibid., PL 141, 322AB; TMPM 3:850.

Contemplating, following, and imitating Mary has great spiritual advantages for the faithful, because she has been given every kind of virtue. Fulbert especially recalls her strength of spirit, her prudence, and her simple faith, as demonstrated in her dialogue with the archangel Gabriel, the justice with which she promptly observed all the decrees of God's law, the temperance that allowed her "to make the lily of virginity flower in the valley of humility".[12] This marvelous array of virtues creates an attractive psychological and spiritual harmony within her, which God himself delights to contemplate and which moves men to give glory to the Lord and to imitate this splendid summary of holiness and, by so doing, to achieve their salvation.

Mary's Power of Intercession

Following a method widely used in preceding centuries, Fulbert tries to convince the faithful of the reality and efficacy of the Virgin's intercession, recounting stories that witness to the Blessed Virgin's intervention on behalf of men. He recalls the case of St. Basil the Great, who was able to raise a dead man with the help of an angel sent by the Mother of God.[13] In reality, this episode was recounted in a legendary biography of the great Cappadocian Father, falsely attributed to Amphilochius of Iconium and translated into Latin by Anastasius the Librarian.[14]

But Fulbert dwells at some length on the story of Theophilus, a well-known tale in the devotional literature of those days. Theophilus was a sinner who had negotiated and signed a pact with the devil. He subsequently repented and turned to the Virgin in search of her maternal assistance. She snatched the signed document out of the devil's hand and gave it back to Theophilus, who publicly burned it, "lifting up in the Church praises to the loving Mother of God, through whom he had obtained reconciliation".[15] The legendary life of this penitent was translated into Latin by Paul the Deacon and reproduced in numerous tenth- and eleventh-century manuscripts.

---

[12] Ibid., PL 141, 322D; TMPM 3:851.

[13] Ibid., PL 141, 323AB; TMPM 3:852.

[14] PL 73, 293–312.

[15] Ibid., PL 141, 323B–324A; TMPM 3:852–53.

The bishop of Chartres reminds other sinners that the certainty of Mary's intercession is a strong reason to take comfort and trust. He concludes his sixth sermon on the Nativity of Mary with these words:

> The more you see yourselves as guilty before the majesty of God, the more you should look to the Mother of the Lord, for she is full of mercy. You have an advocate with the Father: the Son of the Virgin himself, and he will be so kind with regard to your sins (cf. 1 Jn 2:1–2) that you may hope for forgiveness from him and from his Mother.[16]

READINGS

THE WOMAN WHO CRUSHES THE SERPENT'S HEAD

And now let us recount one of the aforementioned miracles and then explain it briefly. The eternal God said to the ancient serpent, "I will put enmity between you and the woman, and between your seed and her seed" (Gen 3:15). In this text, brothers, what does it mean to crush the serpent's head, if not to conquer the chief suggestion of the devil, that is, concupiscence, by resisting it? If, then, someone should ask: "What woman ever won such a victory?" certainly, none will be found in the series of human generations until we come to her whom we consider the holy woman among all holy women. And if someone should object: "But how did she crush the serpent's head?" the answer is: Surely in the fact that she offered her virginity to God together with her humility.

She preserved her virginity, which shows that she extinguished the concupiscence of the flesh, and she conserved her humility, which makes one poor in spirit, and this shows that she extinguished the concupiscence of the mind. And so, having overcome the chief suggestion of the devil, she crushed his wicked head with the foot of her virtue.

But this was not the only way she triumphed. She triumphed especially in the fact that wisdom became incarnate of her most pure flesh. As Wisdom says, "Prevailing over wickedness, she reaches from end to end mightily, and arranging all things well" (Wis 8:1). This, then, is the

---

[16] *Sermo 6*; PL 141, 331B; TMPM 3:857.

woman to whom the divine oracle referred, and when it intimated her future birth, it made it known in a unique way.

—Fulbert of Chartres, *Sermo 4*;
PL 141, 320C–321A; TMPM 3:848–49

MARY'S GLORY AND INTERCESSION IN HEAVEN

After the birth of Christ, Mary remained with her Son until his Passion on the Cross, when Christ entrusted his Virgin Mother to his virgin disciple, the apostle John. He cared for her after the Lord's Passion, Resurrection, and Ascension, right to the end. Now her most holy tomb was in the valley of Jehosaphat, where a church was built in her honor, and St. John was buried in Ephesus.

But later, when pious Christians wished to look upon the remains of his (that is, the Lord's) Mother, they found her tomb empty. But when they looked inside the tomb of blessed John, they found nothing except manna.

And so Christian piety believes that Christ, who is God and Son of God, raised his Mother gloriously and lifted her up above the heavens, and that blessed John, virgin and evangelist, who ministered to her on earth, merited to share her glory in heaven.

While words cannot tell what great grace and glory the Lord gave to his Mother, nevertheless we do know for certain that whatever the just ask of him, they will obtain right speedily through the intercession of his Mother, and we also know that sinners have quite often obtained mercy through her intercession.

—Fulbert of Chartres, *Sermo 5*;
PL 141, 325AB; TMPM 3:855

10

THE CLUNIAC REFORM
AND MARIAN DEVOTION
(Tenth Century)

We know how much the spread of monasticism contributed to the formation of society and the development of learning in the Middle Ages. But there were phenomena within monasticism itself that turned out to be of considerable historical importance for Christianity as a whole. The Benedictine reform of Cluny, so named from the French monastery where it originated in the tenth century and which was its main driving force, can be considered one of these important phenomena. It led to an impressive flowering of monasteries and of smaller monastic communities and to the foundation of many churches.

Among the incalculable merits of this monastic reform, we must also number the surprising increase in Marian piety, seen both in the extraordinary multiplication of sanctuaries dedicated to the Mother of God, in some of which were venerated Marian images that very quickly became the goal of frequent pilgrimages, and in popular preaching of a tender and confident devotion to the Blessed Virgin. Inter alia, we may observe that it was from Cluny itself that the Marian title "Mother (or Queen) of Mercy" was disseminated. This title was destined to have profound repercussions and to be widely accepted in the hearts of the faithful of later centuries, right up to our own time.

Odo of Cluny (d. ca. 943)

The Cluniac tradition tells how the origin of the title *Mater misericordiae* was tied to an event that featured, among other characters, St. Odo, second abbot of Cluny and the originator of the monastic reform that took its name from his monastery.

This Benedictine saint managed to convert a thief, who then felt called to the monastic life and led an existence marked by intense religious fervor. During the serious illness that led to his death, the monk confided to Odo that he had had a vision of the Blessed Virgin, who showed herself to him as Mother of Mercy and promised to take him with her to paradise. After hearing this story, Odo began to promote a marked predilection for the title "Mother of Mercy". He repeated it often, and it is found in a brief but beautiful prayer he composed:

> O Lady, Mother of Mercy, on this very night you gave the world its Savior. Be a worthy intercessor for me. I take refuge in your glorious and singular birth, O most loving Mary. Do you now incline your kindly ear to my prayers. I am in terrible fear that my life may be displeasing to your Son. But since, O Lady, he revealed himself to the world through you, for your sake, I pray, may he have mercy on me without delay.[1]

Odilo of Cluny (d. 1049)

St. Odilo, fifth abbot of the monastery of Cluny, left an even deeper impression on the history of Marian doctrine and piety than did Odo. Odilo was born in Alvernia around 962. His disciple and biographer Jotsald tells how from boyhood he could not move normally because of infantile paralysis. During a voyage, while visiting a church dedicated to Mary, he laid hold of the altar cloth and was instantly healed. This was the origin of his great devotion to the Mother of the Lord.

Entering the monastery of Cluny in 991, he became its abbot and held that office for more than fifty years. A man of great ability, he consolidated and expanded the Cluniac reform, bringing the number of foundations affiliated with the monastery from 37 to 65. He died in 1049.

His Marian thought is expressed especially in his sermons, and more precisely in his pronouncements on the Marian feasts of the Nativity, the Purification, and the Assumption. To tell the truth, the contents of his homilies do not appear to be very original. Odilo may be considered not

---

[1] *Vita sancti Odonis*; PL 133, 47BC. The author of this biography is another monk of Cluny, John of Salerno, a disciple of Odo, who testifies that his master "consuetudinem tenuit beatam Mariam matrem misericordiae vocare" (PL 133, 72B). See G. Roschini, "L'origine e il primo sviluppo del titolo e del culto della 'Mater misericordiae' (sec. X–XI)", in CongrZag 4:473–86.

so much a creative theologian as an ideal witness to the Marian doctrine that had already become established in previous centuries within Christendom and in the teaching of the Church.

What appears most original and interesting in his writings is his application of Marian devotion to the monastic life. His biographer tells how Odilo, consecrating himself to the Mother of God in the sanctuary of Our Lady of Le Puy, put a cord around his neck and pronounced the following words:

> O most loving Virgin, Mother of the Savior of all the ages, from this day onward take me into your service. And in every circumstance of my life, be with me always, most merciful Advocatrix. Except for God, I place nothing above you, and, as your very own servant, I freely place myself under your command forever.[2]

In speaking these words, Odilo placed one end of the cord on the Virgin's altar, in order to confirm his intention to offer his personal freedom to her, to the point of considering himself, no longer free, but, rather, a slave at her service.

For Odilo, this kind of devoted servitude brought with it very practical commitments: above all, the imitation of the virtues and examples of Mary, whom the Benedictine abbot regarded as the great model of the Christian life, for her unshakeable faith, her sincere humility, her rigorous chastity, and the complete poverty she practiced in her life. Moreover, these are the virtues that make her the unsurpassable prototype of the monastic life, whom religious ought to contemplate and imitate.

Mary, Model of the Monk

Speaking of the extraordinary vocation of the Blessed Virgin, Odilo uses a term that is still in use in the language of religious life today, namely, "profession". In one of his sermons, we read: "As was proper to her profession, Mary was praying and reading."[3]

---

[2] *Vita Odilonis* 2, 1; PL 142, 915–16. On Odilo's Marian piety and doctrine, see O. Ringholz, *S. Odilo der grosse Marienverehrer* (Einsiedeln, 1922); P. Cousin, "La Dévotion mariale chez les grands abbés de Cluny", in *À. Cluny, Congrès scientifique: Fêtes et cérémonies liturgiques en l'honneur des saints abbés Odon et Odilon, 9–11 juillet 1949* (Dijon, 1950), pp. 210–18; G. Bavaud, "La Dévotion de saint Odilon à la saint Vierge Marie", in CongrZag 3:571–82.

[3] *Sermo 12*; PL 142, 1024B.

Appealing to St. Ambrose and St. Jerome, who make the Mother of the Lord the most perfect model for consecrated virgins, the abbot of Cluny makes the following distinction:

> From this same sermon [of St. Jerome], female virgins, and not only female but male virgins as well, can learn how they must fight virginally and manfully for the Virgin of virgins.[4]

Mary, then, is the model who should be imitated, not only by women virgins who have consecrated their lives to the Lord, but also by men and, in a particular way, by monks. Odilo pushed himself to reach this goal. St. Ambrose said of Mary that, while her body rested, her spirit remained in a state of watchfulness.[5] Odilo's biographer Jotsald applies this saying to the prayer life of the holy abbot:

> Although sleep often overtook him while he was singing the psalms in bed, nevertheless the psalm never left his lips as he slept.[6]

The Blessed Virgin and Monastic Virtues

In his writings, Abbot Odilo never proposed an explicit comparison between the Virgin's life and that of the monk, but he did emphasize some virtues of Mary that, as brought out above, present a clear parallel to the monastic vows. The episode of the presentation of the Child Jesus in the Temple gives him the opportunity to stress his Mother's poverty:

> She was poor in earthly possessions but full of heavenly blessing. . . . She was so poor that she did not have a lamb to offer for sin; but she was so rich that she was able to give birth to the Lamb who takes away the sin of the world, without loss of her virginity.[7]

Odilo was convinced that the total poverty of the Mother of God was not absolutely incompatible with her royal descent from David's house, because her poverty was an interior disposition, which, far from impoverishing her soul, gave her incomparable spiritual riches.

Before this kind of poverty, he cannot keep himself from crying out:

---

[4] Ibid., PL 142, 1028A.

[5] *De virginibus* 2, 2, 8; PL 16, 221A; Bibliotheca Ambrosiana 14/1, 172.

[6] *Vita Odilonis* 1, 6; PL 142, 901C.

[7] *Sermo 3*; PL 142, 1000D.

O blessed poverty, which made us rich! O blessed neediness, which made us wealthy![8]

Odilo returns rather frequently to the theme of Mary's virginity, in order to make a connection to the life of the monk:

For him who was coming into the world, she prepared a temple, consecrated by heavenly virtue and dedicated to perpetual virginity.[9]

In particular, the saintly abbot refers to the episode of Calvary, when Jesus entrusted John to Mary as a son and vice versa, to explain how this reciprocal entrustment was motivated by the fact that both Mary and John were virgins.[10]

The obedience of the Mother of God, according to Odilo, is part of her wonderful humility. Commenting on the response she gave to the angel: "Behold, I am the handmaid of the Lord; let it be to me according to your word" (Lk 1:38), Odilo states:

Even though she could recognize herself as the Mistress of all the faithful without losing her most sincere humility, she did not hesitate to proclaim herself the handmaid of her Lord.[11]

But the special commitment of the monastic life consists in the exercise of contemplation, and Odilo has no difficulty recognizing the life of the Blessed Virgin as an outstanding model of contemplation. He is not unaware that Mary also led an active life and proposes her visit to her cousin, Elizabeth, as an example. But he specifies how, in this case, the Mother of God dedicated herself to action with the sole intention of doing good to another and, more precisely, to the aged mother of the future Forerunner of Christ. But his preference was clearly directed to the practice of contemplation. This would be demonstrated by the circumstance that, in the moment she received the angel's proclamation, the angel found her immersed in profound contemplative prayer.[12]

---

[8] Ibid., PL 142, 1001A.

[9] *Sermo 12*; PL 142, 1023A.

[10] See ibid., PL 142, 1027B.

[11] *Sermo 4*; PL 142, 1003A.

[12] Odilo was surely inspired by St. Ambrose's lengthy reflections on the life of Mary in his treatise *De virginibus*. See in particular 2, 2, 10; PL 16, 221BC; Bibliotheca Ambrosiana 14/1, 172–74.

Before preaching the imitation of the Blessed Virgin to his monks, Odilo practiced it himself with supreme seriousness. His biographer Jotsald gives a splendid witness of this in a brief prayer addressed to the Virgin herself:

> O Virgin Mary, how greatly [Odilo] served your honor! In all his prayers, he considered you the kindly Mistress of earth, whom he loved above all others.[13]

READINGS

MARY APPEARS TO THE MONK CONVERTED BY ODO

[The young monk] added, "That night, Father, I was lifted up to heaven in a vision. And a woman of most glorious appearance and exceptional power came to meet me. As she drew near, she said, 'Do you recognize me?' And I said, 'Not at all, Lady.' And she said, 'I am the Mother of Mercy.' To which I responded, 'What do you command me to do, Lady?' And she said, 'After three days, come back here at this same time.'"

And so it happened. But on the third day, at the hour she had named, he died. . . . And that is why our father [Odilo] had the custom of calling blessed Mary "Mother of Mercy".

—*Vita sancti Odonis* 2, 20; PL 133, 72AB

MARY'S POVERTY

She was the offspring of a royal line, but so poor in temporal rewards! She was poor in material things, but replete with divine gifts. She was so poor that she did not have a lamb to offer for sin (cf. Lev 12:8), but she was so rich that she was able to give birth to "the Lamb who takes away the sin of the world" (Jn 1:29), without loss of her virginity.

It was one and the same thing that Christ wanted: to be born of a poor mother and to be born of a betrothed virgin. And this happened so that, by his birth from a virgin, the divinity that was in his humanity

---

[13] *Planctus de transitu*; PL 142, 1044CD.

would be concealed from the devil, the prince of this world,[14] until the time predetermined by God.

—Odilo of Cluny, *Sermo 3*; PL 142, 1000D–1001A

MARY, PERFECT MIRROR OF HOLINESS

Mary's life and her virginity should be like a picture for us, from which you should draw examples of how to live, for in it examples of probity are impressed as in an original model, showing what you ought to correct, what you ought to shun, and what you ought to hold onto. Now, if "the first impulse to learn is inspired by the nobility of the teacher, who could be nobler than the Mother of God? Who more splendid than she, whom Splendor chose? Who more chaste than she, who gave birth to a body without bodily contact? What should I say, then, about all her other virtues?"[15]

—Odilo of Cluny, *Sermo 14*; PL 142, 1029D

r

---

[14] See Ignatius of Antioch, *Letter to the Ephesians* 19, 1; PG 5, 660A; F. X. Funk and K. Bihlmeyer, *Die Apostolischen Väter* (Tübingen, 1970), pp. 87–88.

[15] Odilo quotes Ambrose word for word: *De virginibus* 2, 1, 7; PL 16, 220B; Bibliotheca Ambrosiana 14/1, 168.

II

PETER DAMIAN
(d. 1072)

Echoing what the patriarch Germanus of Constantinople had already taught in the East, Peter Damian summed up his feelings of unbounded admiration and love for the Mother of the Lord in a single phrase: "In your hands are laid the treasures of God's mercy."[1] As an eloquent preacher and authority figure within the Church who was personally involved in the reform movement of the eleventh century, he made a crucial contribution to the spread of devotion to the Blessed Virgin. Moreover, this happened at a time that was experiencing a singular flowering of interest in her, in the areas of both doctrine and piety.

Peter Damian was born at Ravenna in 1007. Because he was orphaned at a young age, his older brother, a priest, assumed care of him and supported him in his studies, first at Faenza and then at Parma, where Peter would later work as a teacher. Around 1035, after gaining some experience of the eremetical life, he went to live in the Camaldolese hermitage of Fonte Avellana. He became an enthusiastic disciple of St. Romuald, founder of the Camaldolese, and a friend of the future Pope Gregory VII. In 1057, he was named cardinal-bishop of Ostia by Pope Stephen IX, notwithstanding his status as a hermit. Some years later, however, he was able to give up his see and return to the hermitage of Fonte Avellana, while continuing to carry out occasional missions entrusted to him. He died at Faenza in 1072, at the age of sixty-five. In 1828 he was proclaimed Doctor of the Church.

His greatest contributions to Marian doctrine are his sermons 45 and 46, dedicated to the Nativity of Mary.[2] But he frequently returns to Marian themes in other sermons, in short theological works,[3] and in his

---

[1] *Sermo 44*; PL 144, 740C.

[2] PL 144, 740–61.

[3] PL 145, 19–858.

hymns and prayers.[4] He touches on nearly all the doctrinal themes regarding the Mother of God that were present in the theological debates of his time, while showing the capacity to develop them with new perspectives.

Meditation on the mystery of the divine motherhood brings him to extol both Mary's exalted holiness and her mediation on behalf of the Church. By the force of his reputation and learning, Peter Damian made a substantial contribution to the further development of Mariology and the cult of the Blessed Virgin. He inspired the motto: "To Jesus through Mary".[5]

Outstanding Dignity and Perfection of the Mother of God

Mary's divine motherhood is an ancient dogma of the Church. For Peter Damian, however, it is also an opportunity to say something original, as he celebrates the spiritual richness that the Mother of the Lord had to receive to make her equal to this lofty role and to give it suitable honor. Taking up a theme dear to the tradition of the Greek Fathers, he defines that it was the Holy Spirit who made Mary a suitable dwelling to receive the Son of God:

> First a house had to be built, into which the King of heaven would come down and deign to be a guest. I mean the house of which it is said through Solomon, "Wisdom has built herself a house, she has set up her seven pillars" (Prov 9:1). For this virginal house is supported by seven pillars because the venerable Mother received the seven gifts of the Holy Spirit.[6]

In his hymn for the feast of the Annunciation, he states the same truth in a more inspired and concise manner:

---

[4] PL 145, 917–86.

[5] "Sicut per te Dei Filius dignatus est ad nostra descendere, ita et nos per te ad eius valeamus consortium pervenire" (*Sermo 46*; PL 144, 761B). For Peter's Marian teaching, see S. Baldassarri, "La mariologia di San Pier Damiani", *Scuola Cattolica* 61 (1933): 304–12; G. Roschini, "La mariologia di S. Pier Damiani", in *San Pier Damiani nel IX centenario della morte*, vol. 1 (Cesena, 1972), pp. 195–237; L. A. Lassus, "Essai sur la mariologie de saint Pierre Damien, précurseur de saint Bernard", *Collectanea Cistercensia* 45 (1983): 37–56.

[6] *Sermo 45*; PL 144, 741BC.

The Son of the Father fills her; the Holy Spirit overshadows her; the all-chaste womb of the holy Maid becomes heaven.[7]

For this reason, Mary is beyond all human praise, since her dignity and perfection confer on her merits so great that they are beyond comparison with those of any other character in the history of salvation:

> But however can human weakness worthily celebrate the feast of her who merited to give birth to the joy of the angels? In what way could the short-lived words of mortal man praise her who brought forth from her [womb] the Word who abides forever?[8]

The greatness of the role played by Mary has its roots, not only in the transcendent divine nature of the Son she bore, but also in the purpose of the Incarnation, the redemption of the human creature. This redemption cannot be realized without Mary's motherhood. It even appears that Peter Damian goes too far in claiming that Mary's motherhood was necessary. Consider his words:

> Just as it was impossible for the human race to be redeemed unless the Son of God were born of the Virgin, so it was likewise necessary that the Virgin should be born, from whom the Word would become flesh.[9]

Clearly, our author wants to say that the necessity of Mary's birth is, by its nature, subordinate to that of Christ; nevertheless, he expresses himself in a rather daring way, revealing his elevated concept of the Blessed Virgin's mission in the economy of salvation. Later in the same sermon, the same idea is illustrated by the more poetic image of a wedding:

> First the bridal chamber had to be set up, which would receive the Bridegroom who was coming to take holy Church as his Bride.[10]

Eve's Curse and Mary's Blessing

While Mary's cooperation in the salvation of the human race is radically tied to her maternal role in relation to the divine Redeemer, obviously the Eve-Mary parallel illustrates this idea with extreme clarity, since in

---

[7] *Carmen 44*; PL 145, 933D.

[8] *Sermo 45*; PL 144, 742C.

[9] Ibid., PL 144, 741A.

[10] Ibid., PL 144, 741B.

both cases a woman gave birth: Eve gave birth to sin, followed by a curse and death, while Mary gave birth to grace and, consequently, to blessing and life. Our doctor writes:

> "Blessed are you among women!" Through a woman, the earth was filled with a curse; through a woman, blessing is restored to the earth. The hand of a woman offered the cup of bitter death; the hand of a woman offered the chalice of sweet life. The abundant stream of the new blessing wiped away the contagion of the ancient curse.[11]

Peter Damian also gives a beautiful poetic interpretation of this doctrine in one of his hymns, where he insists that both women shared a virginal state:

> Through a Virgin, life returns to man, whom a virgin had destroyed. Death, conquered by the blood of the slain, perishes, and life returns through the Virgin. Do you, we beg you, lift up above the stars what Eve buried. She is weighed down with guilt, but do you lift [us] up above the stars.[12]

The Mother of God and the Eucharist

In the light of the Eve-Mary parallelism, Peter Damian describes the relationship between the Blessed Virgin and the eucharistic Body of her Son. He emphasizes the fact that the Body she conceived, bore, nursed, and raised with maternal care and love is the very same Body we receive in the eucharistic banquet, the blood of which we drink as the sacrament that accomplishes our redemption. He repeats that this truth belongs to the Catholic faith and is taught as such by the Church. Regarding this idea, we can recall that our author devoted much of his writing to themes related to the mystery of the Eucharist.

Mary, from her spotless flesh, gave birth to the food for our souls—the food that came down from heaven. Peter closes his reflections with another reference to the sad role played by Eve:

> Because of a food, we were cast out of the loveliness of paradise, but by means of another food we have been restored to the joys of paradise. Eve ate the food by which she condemned us to the hunger of an eternal fast.

---

[11] *Sermo 46*; PL 144, 758AB.
[12] *Carmen 65*; PL 145, 941A.

Mary brought forth the food that opened for us the entrance to the banquet of heaven.[13]

Because of this marvelous act accomplished by Mary, Peter Damian considers it impossible to find human words that adequately express our praise and gratitude to her, to whom we owe so much.

Mary and the Church

Other interesting and original points may be found in the writings in which this great Doctor develops his Marian doctrine; for example, the way in which he understands the relationship between the Blessed Virgin and the Church. He describes Mary as being related to the Church as a mother is related to her child. This relationship passes through the mediation of Christ:

> Mary is a great and happy Mother, as well as a blessed Virgin, from whose womb Christ took flesh; and from Christ's flesh the Church flowed out in the water and the blood. And so in this way, and from Mary, the Church is seen to have come forth. Each of the two is chaste; each is pure; and each is protected by the girdle of perpetual virginity.[14]

Because Christ came among men by means of the Blessed Virgin's motherhood, men find in her the way that leads to him. This principle, which will find important applications in the ascetical and spiritual life of Christians of later generations—even in contemporary Marian spirituality it is summed up in the motto *Ad Jesum per Mariam*—was explicitly formulated by our author, as noted above.[15]

Devotion to the Mother of the Lord

Peter Damian's attitude of profound devotion and tender love toward Mary was born from his great esteem for her and her mission. This is clear from his writings and especially from the many invocations he addresses to her in his prayers with impressive fervor. Moreover, he takes care to recommend to the faithful certain practices of Marian devotion,

---

[13] *Sermo 45*; PL 144, 743C.
[14] *Sermo de sancto Joanne*; PL 144, 861B.
[15] See *Sermo 46*; PL 144, 761B.

such as the daily recitation of the Angelus and of the "Five Joys of Mary".[16] He also composed a daily office "in honor of holy Mary".[17] Further, he explains the reason why Saturday is dedicated in a special way to the Blessed Virgin: it was on this day that Wisdom built herself a house (cf. Prov 9:1) and rested in it in a mystery of humility.[18]

Peter Damian is undoubtedly an important witness to the growing role assumed by the Mother of the Lord in the doctrine and life of the Church in the West. Christians acquired an ever-greater awareness of the efficacy of her intercession and became accustomed to turning to her as Mother of Mercy. Peter Damian invoked her under this title, praying to her in his second sermon on the Nativity:

> O most clement Mary, Mother of pity and Mother of Mercy itself! We, who rejoice to celebrate your great praises on earth, beg you that we might merit the help of your intercession in heaven.[19]

READINGS

THE ENTIRE HISTORY OF SALVATION IS REFLECTED IN MARY

My dearly beloved brothers, I pray you, carefully attend to this your story, yes, even the story of our salvation, and in your hearts draw up in order the plan of human restoration. Let your hearts keep watch and your eyes stay awake.

For since such a man could not be found among the human race, the Creator of men, lest man perish from his sin, taking flesh from the most blessed Virgin, became a man without sin, conceived without sin in the

---

[16] *Opusculum 33*, 3; PL 145, 564BC.

[17] *Carmina 48–65*; PL 145, 935B–941A.

[18] *Opusculum 33*, 4; PL 145, 565D–567B.

[19] *Sermo 46*; PL 144, 761B.

[20] The expression "without sin" can be interpreted in two ways here. If referred to the term "conception", it means that Christ was conceived by Mary without sin; that is, virginally. If referred to Mary's womb, it would mean that Mary was exempt from original sin. Even though Peter Damian never spoke explicitly about the Immaculate Conception, he does make some very strong statements about the Virgin's holiness. See *Opusculum 6*, 19; PL 145, 129BC; Roschini, "Mariologia", pp. 216–19.

Virgin's womb,[20] and lived in the world without sin. O brothers, pay heed, pay heed, I say, and listen attentively to the inexpressible mystery of our redemption.

Behold, brothers, the priest without any sin and so worthy and powerful that, in offering the sacrifice, he cleanses others of sin.

—Peter Damian, *Sermo 45*; PL 144, 744CD

MARY AND JOHN ASSUMED BODILY INTO HEAVEN

Even if we dare not state it categorically, nevertheless it is pious to think that, just as it is believed of the Blessed Mother of God, so too it may be asserted as probable that blessed John rose. Since both shared in virginal integrity, so they may rightly appear equal with regard to an anticipated resurrection. Nor should there be a difference in their resurrection, since they had such a unity in their way of life.

For if both John and Mary were blessed virgins, and did not rise at all, why do their bodies not lie buried in their graves, when the bodies of blessed Peter, Paul, and other apostles and martyrs are known to be buried in their tombs?

—Peter Damian, *Sermo de sancto Joanne*; PL 144, 870CD

PRAISE FOR THE GREATNESS OF THE MOTHER OF GOD

All things on earth rejoice; the stars sound their praises; before the bridal chamber of the Virgin, the praises of their songs alternate.

This Virgin, pregnant with the Word, is made the gate of paradise. She who returned God to the world has opened heaven to us.

Happy this childbearing woman, from Eve's law set free; she conceived without a man, and she gave birth without a cry.

Mary's rich womb gave birth to the price of the world's ransom, and we, the redeemed, rejoice, set free from the yoke of our debt.

The Son of the Father fills her; the Holy Spirit overshadows her; the all-chaste womb of the holy Maid becomes heaven.

—Peter Damian, *Hymnus 44 in Annuntiatione*, ad Nocturnum;
PL 145, 933CD

PART TWO

A Golden Period for Marian Doctrine

(Twelfth Century)

Prologue

The twelfth century has been called a "Marian century", and with good reason.[1] During this period, the Mother of the Lord truly became the center of attention. This was true, not only with regard to doctrinal and exegetical research and development, but also within the wider field of liturgical worship and popular devotion. Authors who touched on Marian themes are numerous, and many of them made a notable contribution to the development of an extraordinarily rich Marian teaching. This created a solid theological foundation for a steadily increasing Marian piety, which was expressed in many new ways, celebrating the mystery of the greatness of the Virgin Mother of God.

This situation may also be seen as the result of a fruitful retrieval of the tradition of the Fathers of the Church. This allowed for new perspectives and approaches, since a thorough knowledge of the past can act as a strong stimulus to look for new and original ideas, encouraging a dynamic and creative reaching out toward the future.

Some historical witnesses to this phenomenon can still be seen today. One thinks of the splendid cathedrals built in Mary's honor, which clearly reflect the Marian faith and devotion of believing communities and continue to encourage today's faithful to practice an authentic and committed Christian life.

The historian of Mariology Theodore Koehler makes some very pertinent observations about cathedrals dedicated to the Blessed Virgin:

> The cathedrals are the manifestation of a system of religious education. They guided the Church in her earthly pilgrimage by means of the catechetical proclamations on their portals, the history of salvation depicted in the windows, capitals, and walls of their naves. The pilgrimage finishes at the altar, within the sanctuary of the sacrifice of Christ, in communion with the God of the Resurrection. This system had a name: "Our Lady, type of the Church". Mary is Mediatrix, Queen, and Mother. The same can be said of the Church.[2]

---

[1] See Theodore Koehler, "Storia della mariologia", in NDM, p. 1394.

[2] Ibid., pp. 1394–95.

Obviously, sanctuaries were the goal of frequent pilgrimages, which in those days assumed great importance and were seen as effective ways to transform the religious life of the pilgrims. They created a sense of fellowship and mutual awareness among different peoples and encouraged the rise of common values and interests. The phenomenon left its mark, not only on the history of the Church of the time, but also on medieval history and civilization in general. It has rightly been observed that Europe was formed by pilgrims:

> In a time when Christianity, enclosed in a world that threatened to collapse in upon itself in a systematic disintegration, was flanked on one side by the pressure of Islam and blocked on the other by unknown lands and oceans, pilgrimages developed an international spirit, keeping alive the relations between different peoples, overcoming the barriers of distance and every obstacle with an incredible vitality, promoting and feeding knowledge, connections, and communion among different churches, conquering the isolation experienced by different regions.[3]

Another conspicuous component of the Marian character of the Church of that time was the ancient religious orders, which had already set apart a special place for the Virgin in their spirituality, their liturgy, and the personal life of their members. This can be said, for example, of the Augustinians, Benedictines, Cluniacs, and Cistercians.

Also in this period, many prayers of praise and invocation of the Mother of God, both in liturgical celebrations and in personal devotion, came into widespread use among the faithful. Marian hymns experienced remarkable growth under the influence of the celebrated *Akáthistos* hymn.[4] We know that, as early as 1135, the *Salve Regina* was sung as a processional hymn in the monastery of Cluny, and the new poetic genre of the *Planctus Mariae* was becoming more widespread. The hymn *Stabat Mater* came into wide use.

The theologians of this period, committed to the study of the classic Marian passages of the Old and New Testaments, worked to develop the principal themes of Marian doctrine. At the same time, additional scriptural passages began to suggest themselves to exegetes as susceptible of a Marian interpretation. A typical example is the Song of Songs.

---

[3] S. Rosso, "Pellegrinaggi", in NDM, pp. 1090–91.

[4] See G. G. Meersseman, *Der Hymnos Akathistos im Abendland*, 2 vols., Spicilegium Friburgense 2–3 (Fribourg, 1958–1960).

The divine motherhood of the Virgin Mary came to the fore with ever-greater clarity. Theologians emphasized not only its physical element, but also its spiritual dimension, considering it as a result of Mary's complete faith in the word of God.

Between the end of the eleventh century and the beginning of the twelfth, an apocryphal text, falsely attributed to Augustine of Hippo, became the object of special attention in theological circles. The work put forth a consistent and convincing teaching about the Assumption, understood as the mystery of the Virgin's heavenly glorification, body and soul.[5] The pseudo-Augustine eventually dissipated doubts raised about the Assumption in a work of Paschasius Radbertus (d. ca. 865), which, circulating under the name of St. Jerome, had met with widespread agreement over the previous two centuries.[6]

The faithful intuitively recognized that faith in the Assumption led to the recognition of other Marian truths implicit in the mystery, such as Mary's queenship, her mediation and heavenly intercession, and her role as paradigm of the heavenly Church, with regard to the earthly Church.

By contrast, the doctrine of Mary's preservation from original sin was still struggling to become part of the belief of theologians. The difficulty remained of reconciling this Marian privilege with the dogma of the universal redemption accomplished by Christ. It would fall to a disciple of Anselm of Canterbury, Eadmer of Canterbury, to indicate the way to a positive solution of the problem using the argument from fittingness. This argument would later be considered by Duns Scotus. He was the one who would suggest the true solution, teaching that being exempt from the sin of Adam does not at all exclude the Mother of God from the redemption accomplished by Christ; to the contrary, this privilege is to be seen as the most perfect form of redemption, and the Son of God wished to apply it to his Mother.

Due to reflection on the presence of the Mother of Jesus at the foot of the Cross, the doctrine of Mary's spiritual motherhood is described in

---

[5] The text, published in PL 40, 1140–48, has been exhaustively studied by G. Quadrio, *Il trattato "De Assumptione B. M. V." dello Pseudo-Agostino e il suo influsso nella teologia assunzionistica latina*, Analecta Gregoriana 7 (Rome, 1951).

[6] The work may be found, presented as a letter by Jerome to Paula and Eustochius, in PL 30, 122–42. The critical edition was published by A. Ripberger, *Der pseudo-Hieronymus—Brief IX "Cogitis me": Ein erster marianischer Traktat des Mittelalters von Paschasius Radbert*, Spicilegium Friburgense 9 (Fribourg, 1962).

increasingly clear outline. Her spiritual motherhood is revealed in Christ's words to his Mother and the Beloved Disciple.

In sum, we may recognize that the twelfth century gave birth to a remarkable treasure of Marian reflection, both in the field of theology and in the practice of the Christian life, where devotion to the Blessed Virgin acted as a powerful incentive to fidelity and generosity.

ANSELM OF CANTERBURY

(d. 1109)

St. Anselm is one of the outstanding figures of European history. He greatly influenced the history of Christian thought in important ways. He had the ability to see that human reason plays a fundamental role in developing theological doctrine, which he understood as the quest to understand the facts of the faith. He is rightly considered to be the forerunner and father of Scholasticism, which built on his brilliant intuitions in developing its grand enterprise of organizing the whole of theological knowledge. Anselm is famous as the author of the so-called ontological argument for the existence of God. Theologian and mystic, he was able to integrate his scientific activity, pastoral commitment, and the interior life.

For him, the Blessed Virgin was more than a simple theme for theological development. He venerated and loved her as a real, authentic person, close to his heart, as a maternal and necessary collaborator in consolidating a saving relationship with Christ the Redeemer. In Anselm's teaching, the mystery of Christ and the mystery of Mary always shed light on each other.

Anselm was born at Aosta in 1033 and received his first education at the Benedictine school in the city. When still very young, he left his family because of strong disagreements with his father and went to France. Having reached Normandy, he became acquainted with the famous Benedictine abbey of Le Bec, and, in 1060, he decided to enter it as a monk. In 1078, he was elected abbot there, succeeding the celebrated abbot Lanfranc of Canterbury, who had been born in Pavia, Italy, but was named archbishop of Canterbury. But then, in 1093, after the death of Lanfranc, Anselm was again called to succeed him, this time as archbishop of Canterbury and primate of the English Church. In his new role, he was able to carry out some truly remarkable pastoral work, notwithstanding the serious difficulties caused by his disagreements with the Crown, especially problems stemming from the secular power's illegitimate interference in the internal life and organization of the Church. Because of this he had to go into exile twice. Once returned definitively to his see, he dedicated himself to his pastoral mission with untiring zeal until his death in 1109.

In the copious body of his work, Anselm concerns himself rather rarely with the Virgin Mary. This conclusion is inescapable, especially following the investigation of the authenticity of some of the works published under his name but not attributable to him. Still, he does speak of the Mother of the Lord, especially in his treatises *Cur Deus homo* and *De virginali conceptu et de peccato originali*. Also, in the large collection of prayers attributed to him by certain tradition, we find three long prayers addressed to the Virgin that are considered authentic. But the theological importance of St. Anselm's Marian teaching must be evaluated in the light of his exceptional genius and the determining influence he had over the future masters of Scholasticism.[1]

The Problem of the Immaculate Conception

In addressing mariological questions, Anselm did not pass over questions arising from the historical and devotional context of his time. A specific problem that came to a head in this context was the English Church's custom of celebrating the mystery of Mary's conception. This feast day was introduced in 1060, abolished in 1066 with the arrival of William the Conqueror, and restored in the first years of the following century. The celebration of this feast did not necessarily support faith in the dogma of Mary's preservation from original sin, as the mystery of the

---

[1] Anselm's works were published in PL 158 and 159. The critical edition was edited by F. S. Schmitt, *S. Anselmi Opera Omnia*, 6 vols. (Edinburgh, 1946–1961). Various studies of his Marian thought have appeared; some of them are: R. T. Jones, *Sancti Anselmi Mariologia* (Chicago: Mundelein Seminary, 1937); J. Bruder, *The Mariology of St. Anselm of Canterbury* (Dayton, Ohio, 1939); H. du Manoir, "La Piété mariale de Saint Anselme de Cantorbéry", in CongrZag 3:597–611; M. Schmaus, "Die dogmatischen Grundlagen des Marienkultes nach Anselm von Canterbury", in CongrZag 3:613–29; A. Krupa, "De Maria matre misericordiae sancti Anselmi Cantuariensis doctrina", in CongrZag 4:487–98; E. Briancesco, "El lugar de María en el discurso cristológico de San Anselmo de Canterbury", *Teología* (Buenos Aires) 18 (1981): 25–30.

Immaculate Conception is understood today. It did involve the belief
that the Virgin's birth was out of the ordinary; in other words, her birth
was preceded by a divine intervention through which she was purified
from original sin in her mother's womb.

In his *Cur Deus homo*, the archbishop of Canterbury denies Mary's
Immaculate Conception.[2] However, in his *De virginali conceptu et de
peccato originali*, speaking of the conception of Christ, he makes certain
statements that in later centuries had a positive influence on the development of teaching favorable to this truth.[3]

In any case, Anselm follows the line of the Augustinian tradition,
which could not exclude Mary from the inheritance of original sin. He
personally shares the idea that Mary was purified in her mother's womb;
however, in contrast to Augustine, he conceives of original sin, not as a
defect of nature, but as an absence of grace and holiness in the human
being's soul. In this perspective, it is easier to understand how, with the
passing of time, the Virgin could have been preserved from Adam's fault
in view of the foreseen merits of Christ, in the sense that the dogma was
understood when defined in 1854. More explicitly, Anselm formulates a
principle that will open the door to the understanding of this revealed
truth:

> It was fitting that this Virgin should shine with a purity so great that,
> except for God, no greater purity could be conceived.[4]

Marian Theology and Prayer to the Virgin

Anselm is interested in Mary for more than theological reasons. Reasons
dictated by his deep inner devotion to her lead him to express sentiments
of sincere veneration and filial love toward the Mother of the Lord. In
addition, there are factors of an ascetical and pastoral nature.

We have a collection of prayers and meditations composed by the

---

[2] See *Cur Deus homo* 2, 16; PL 158, 416B–419B; Schmitt, 2:116–22.

[3] See *De virginali conceptu* 18; PL 158, 451AB; Schmitt, 2:159.

[4] Ibid., 451A; Schmitt, 2:159. This phrasing appears to parallel the a priori proof
of the existence of God expounded by Anselm in his *Proslogion* (see 3; PL 158,
228BC; Schmitt, 1:102–3). He expresses himself in a prayer in analogous terms: "Nihil
est aequale Mariae; nihil, nisi Deus, maius Maria" (*Oratio 52*; PL 158, 956A; Schmitt,
3:21).

archbishop of Canterbury, which includes three long invocations
addressed to the Blessed Virgin. The collection dates from around 1074,
when Anselm was still abbot of the Benedictine monastery of Le Bec.
It was composed at the request of one of his confreres, named Gandolf,
the future bishop of Rochester, who had decided to rededicate himself
to prayer. The prayers are compositions that come from Anselm's heart,
but this does not stop him from illuminating them with an approach
stimulated by faith and intellect. To be better understood and savored,
the three prayers are read in the same order in which they were written,
in order to appreciate their progressive force. One gets the impression
that the author felt dissatisfied by the first text and went on to find a
better formulation to show the Mother of God everything he felt in his
soul. In these texts, the contemplative element and the element of
petition are woven together with a surprising spontaneity.

The first prayer opens with an admiring look at the exalted figure of
the Mother of the Lord. There quickly follows the awareness on the part
of the one praying of his own sinful condition:

> Holy are you, O Mary, and among all the holy ones, you are the most
> holy, after God. Mother of admirable virginity, Virgin of precious fruit-
> fulness, who gave birth to the Son of the Most High, who gave birth to a
> Savior for the lost human race. O Lady, resplendent with such great
> holiness and outstanding with such great dignity, it is certain that you have
> been endowed with power and kindness that are no less than your holiness
> and dignity. To you, O Bearer of life, O Mother of salvation, O Temple
> of kindness and mercy, to you my wretched soul attempts to present
> itself.[5]

As the prayer continues to unfold, it brings out the contrast between
the most holy Virgin and sinful man. This contrast does not preclude
man from turning to her, the most powerful helper for obtaining the
salvation of Christ. What is more, the greater the sin, the greater the
increase of trust in the aid of this powerful and merciful Mother:

> O Lady, the more my sins are filthy in the sight of God and in your sight,
> the more they need your care and assistance. O most clement Lady, heal
> my weakness, and you will wipe away the foulness that offends you.[6]

---

[5] Oratio 50; PL 158, 948C; Schmitt, 3:13.

[6] Ibid., PL 158, 950A; Schmitt, 3:14.

The prayer closes with an appeal to the Son, to whose divine power even his Mother must have recourse to obtain the healing of sinners. The Son himself is addressed as the Mediator with the Father, and thus the author reaches the ultimate font of divine mercy.[7]

In the second prayer, Christ and his Mother are closely associated with regard to how sin offends them:

> When I sinned against the Son, I distressed the Mother; nor could I have offended the Mother without injuring the Son.[8]

However, Anselm does not fail to underscore the positive consequence that accompanies the human tragedy of sin. The Lord, in his infinite goodness, has responded to the human creature's sin with his loving plan of mercy; for this reason, true fear of God, which is born in the soul of the sinner when he becomes aware of his guilt, must always be joined to a serene confidence, which is expressed in prayer:

> [O sinner,] who will reconcile you with the Son if his Mother is your enemy? And who will placate the Mother for you if the Son is wrathful? But even though both of you have been equally offended, are not both of you merciful? If a man is guilty in the sight of the just God, let him fly for refuge to the loving Mother of the merciful God. If he is guilty of having offended the Mother, let him fly to the loving Son of a kind Mother.[9]

The third prayer returns to themes already found in the preceding texts and insists especially on the prayer of invocation for obtaining the gift of love for Jesus and Mary. Toward the end of the prayer, there occurs a double formula, one that has become famous in the history of Christian spirituality:

> O good Son, I pray you for the love with which you love your Mother, that you might grant me to love her truly, as you truly love her and as you wish her to be loved.
>
> O good Mother, I pray you for the love with which you love your Son, that you might grant me to love him truly as you truly love him and as you wish him to be loved.[10]

---

[7] "Domina, sana animam peccatoris servi tui per virtutem benedicti fructus ventris tui, qui sedet in dextera omnipotentis Patris sui" (ibid., PL 158, 950A; Schmitt, 3:14).

[8] *Oratio 51*; PL 158, 951B; Schmitt, 3:16.

[9] Ibid., PL 158, 951C; Schmitt, 3:16.

[10] *Oratio 52*; PL 158, 959A; Schmitt, 3:25.

Mary, Mother of All Believers

While the texts given here are few, we can easily identify in them a clear and comforting awareness of the mystery of Mary's motherhood of believers. This awareness is also evident in the theological reflections of the holy Doctor and in his mystical outbursts. In the third prayer to Mary, he introduces a comparison between the fatherhood of God and the motherhood of Mary. The comparison sheds a remarkable light on Mary's motherhood:

> God, who had the power to create all things from nothing, did not want to restore the fallen universe without Mary. Therefore, God is the Father of the creation of all things, while Mary is the Mother of the restoration of all things.[11]

Obviously, Anselm sees in the divine motherhood the fundamental factor of the Virgin's participation in the restoration of creation wrought by Christ the Redeemer. However, as has been seen, he also explicitly affirms a maternal relationship between Mary and human beings. In a beautiful text, the two motherhoods appear inseparably linked:

> There is no salvation except the salvation whom you bore, O Virgin. Wherefore, O Lady, you are the Mother of justification and of the justified; you are the Bearer of reconciliation and of the reconciled; you are the Parent of salvation and of the saved. O blessed confidence! O safe refuge! The Mother of God is our Mother; the Mother of him in whom alone we hope and whom alone we fear is our Mother.[12]

The Spiritual Inspiration of Anselm's Marian Teaching

Anselm's teaching had a strong impact both within monastic spirituality and on Christian spirituality in general. A Christian who is devoted to Mary draws from his writings a devotion that is theologically solid and genuinely emotional, capable of satisfying the demands of the mind and the impulses of the heart. The holy Doctor preached a true Marian piety, which must bring to maturity in the believer the certainty that reconciliation between God and the human race has happened through

---

[11] Ibid., PL 158, 956A; Schmitt, 3:22.
[12] Ibid., PL 158, 957A; Schmitt, 3:23.

the Mother of Christ. This is the piety that leads to an authentic Christian life.

READINGS

IT WAS FITTING THAT CHRIST SHOULD BE BORN OF A VIRGIN

While it is quite true that the Son of God was conceived by one who was totally virgin, nevertheless this did not happen of necessity, as if reason dictated that a just offspring could not be generated from a sinful parent through a sinful kind of propagation. Rather, it happened because it was fitting that the conception of this human nature should happen in a totally pure mother.

For it was fitting that this Virgin should shine with a purity so great that, except for God, no greater purity could be conceived. And it was to her that God the Father decided to give his only Son, whom he loved as his very self, since he had been brought forth from his own heart, as his equal. God the Father did this so that one and the same [Christ] might be the common Son of God the Father and, on a natural level, Son of the Virgin.

And the Son himself chose to make the substance of his own Mother, in whom the Holy Spirit chose to work, to bring about in her the conception and birth of him from whom he himself proceeds.

—Anselm of Canterbury, *De conceptu originali*, 18; PL 158, 451AB; Schmitt, 2:159

CALLING UPON MARY FOR SALVATION

O Mary, I beg you, by the grace by which the Lord is with you and wanted you to be with him: for the sake of that grace, in accord with that grace, make your mercy be with me; make love of you be always with me, and make concern for my welfare be always with you. Grant that my cry in necessity may be with you, however long my necessity continues; grant that your loving attention may be with me as long as I live; grant that the happiness of your blessedness may be with me always and that compassion for my wretchedness be with you, however much it may help me.

For, O [Mother] Most Blessed, just as everyone who has turned away from you and been rejected by you must perish, so everyone who has turned to you and been recognized by you can never perish. For, O Lady, just as God gave birth to him in whom all things have life, so you, O Flower of Virginity, gave birth to him through whom even the dead come back to life.

And just as God preserved the blessed angels from sin through his Son, so you, O Beauty of Purity (*decus puritatis*), will save wretched men from sin through your Son. For just as the Son of God is the happiness of the just, even so your Son, O Salvation of Fruitfulness, is the reconciliation of sinners.

For there is no reconciliation except the reconciliation you conceived, O Chaste One. There is no salvation except the salvation you bore, O Virgin. Wherefore, O Lady, you are the Mother of justification and of the justified; you are the Bearer of reconciliation and of the reconciled; you are the Parent of salvation and of the saved.

O blessed confidence! O safe refuge! The Mother of God is our mother; the Mother of him in whom alone we hope and whom alone we fear is our Mother. Yes, the Mother of him who alone saves, who alone condemns, is our Mother.

—Anselm of Canterbury, *Oratio 52*;
PL 158, 956B–957A; Schmitt, 3:22–23

2

EADMER OF CANTERBURY
(d. 1124)

This Anglo-Saxon monk was the most famous disciple of St. Anselm of Canterbury, and traces of his master's thought are evident in his writings. To this day, he is considered one of the key figures who laid the foundation for the future development of Marian doctrine and devotion.

Eadmer was born around 1064 and was brought up in the Benedictine monastery of Canterbury, which he later entered as a monk. In 1120, he was named archbishop of St. Andrews in Scotland, but he renounced his see before receiving episcopal consecration. He died at Canterbury in 1124.

He wrote two fairly important Marian works: a treatise on the conception of Mary and another on the excellence of the Blessed Virgin. The central ideas of his mariological thought are the original holiness of the Mother of God and her merciful intercession. Eadmer's approach to the first theme reveals his Anglo-Saxon origin. The Saxons had already introduced the feast of Mary's Conception into England, but our Doctor particularly stands out because of the zeal and conviction with which he defends this truth. His treatise on Mary's conception might appear to be a response to St. Bernard's letter to the canons of Lyons, in which the great Cistercian firmly opposes the celebration of the aforementioned feast.[1] But reasons of chronological order do not allow us to think that Eadmer wrote his treatise with the intention of refuting Bernard's position.

In the second treatise, Eadmer emphasizes Mary's greatness as a person. He considers her superior to all creatures and inferior to God alone. He is greatly attracted by her royal majesty and by the power of her intercession, which is exercised with a motherly sense of mercy. All this

---

[1] *Epist.* 174; PL 182, 332–36.

justifies the legitimacy of her cult and the devotion that believers ought to feel toward her.[2]

Mary Preserved from Original Sin

Considering the theme of Mary's conception, Eadmer reproposes Anselm's principle of her extraordinary holiness and the unique mission for which God destined her. But he does not stop at the conclusion of his famous master, who limited himself to affirming the Virgin's liberation from original sin in her mother's womb. Eadmer goes farther, arriving at a formulation of the dogma practically in the same terms in which it is professed in the Church today.

He starts by affirming his belief in the sanctification of the prophet Jeremiah and of John the Baptist while they were still in the womb of their mothers. He holds that the argument from fittingness acquires even stronger force in the case of the Mother of the Lord:

> If Jeremiah was sanctified in his mother's womb because he was to be a prophet among the Gentiles, and if John, who was to go before the Lord in the spirit and power of Elijah, was filled with the Holy Spirit from his mother's womb, who will dare to say that the one and only mercy seat of the whole world, the most sweet couch of the Son of God Almighty, was deprived of the illumination of the grace of the Holy Spirit from the first instant of her conception?[3]

To explain how the Blessed Virgin, even though conceived by means of a normal human relationship, was exempt from the contamination of original sin, Eadmer uses an example that, while a little odd, is not

---

[2] Eadmer's works have been collected in PL 159. The *Tractatus de conceptione sanctae Mariae*, included among the spurious works of Anselm of Canterbury, was studied and restored to Eadmer by H. Thurston and T. Slater (Freiburg im Breisgau, 1904). There is also an Italian edition of the two tracts cited, to which is appended the Latin text of codex 371, Corpus Christi College, Canterbury: Eadmer, *Sulla concezione di santa Maria e Sull'eccellenza della gloriosissima Madre di Dio*, ed. P. M. Pennoni (Rome: Libreria Mariana Editrice, 1959). Studies of Eadmer's Marian thought include: K. Binder, "Marienkult und Marienverehrung bei Eadmer von Canterbury", in CongrZag 3:665–710; H. J. Brosch, "Die Anrufung Marias als Mutter der Barmherzigkeit bei Eadmer", in CongrZag 4:499–514; H. M. Koester, "Der Beitrag Eadmer zur theologischen Erkenntnis der Unbefleckten Empfängnis", in *Im Gewande des Heils* (Essen, 1980), pp. 61–70.

[3] *De conceptione*; PL 159, 305A; Thurston-Slater, p. 9.

without clarity: the chestnut. This nut is born and grows inside a wrapping that is totally covered with dense and sharp spines. Nevertheless, the chestnut is not stung by these spines, because, when the moment arrives for it to come out of the wrapping, the membrane breaks open and the chestnut comes out unscathed. The conclusion appears to be obvious:

> If God allows the chestnut to be conceived, to grow, and to be formed amid spines without being punctured by them, could he not grant to a human [body], which he prepared for himself as a temple in which he might dwell bodily and from which he would come forth as the perfect man in the unity of his Person, that, though this body be conceived among the spines of sins, it would nevertheless be completely unharmed by their sharp points? He certainly could do it, and he wanted to do it. Therefore, if he wanted to do it, he did it.
>
> And now, O most blessed among women, it is clear that everything worthy that God wanted for someone other than himself, he wanted for you.[4]

We note how much progress was being made by the argument of fittingness, which will receive its classic formulation in three terms: *potuit, decuit, ergo fecit.*[5] A few centuries later, this saying would be made famous by the Franciscan Duns Scotus, who would apply it to the mystery of the Immaculate Conception. Eadmer anticipates him almost to the letter, when he writes: "Potuit plane et voluit; si igitur voluit, fecit."

On the other hand, this very same principle, the so-called principle of "convenience", will also lead to unchecked, exaggerated, and arbitrary statements about the greatness and dignity of the Mother of God. The Christian people, moved by inappropriate zeal and poorly understood Marian devotion, sometimes fails to eliminate such excesses.

Mary as Exalted Creature

Continuing to follow St. Anselm's lead, our author has a very high concept of the Blessed Virgin, thinking that only God is higher than she. In his eternal plan, God lifted her up to make her the Mistress (*Domina*)

---

[4] Ibid., PL 159, 305C–306A; Thurston-Slater, p. 11.

[5] "He was able to do it, it was fitting, therefore he did it."—TRANS.

and Queen of the entire universe. For the Holy Spirit, who made his dwelling in her, made her the sovereign ruler of heaven, earth, and everything that is in them:

> Just as God, who made all things by his power, is Father and Lord of all things, so Blessed Mary, who repaired all things by her merits, is Mother and Mistress of all. For God is Lord of all because he established each thing in its own nature by his command, while Mary is Mistress of all things because she reestablished them in their original inborn dignity by the grace she merited. And just as God generated from his own substance his Son, through whom he gave all things their origin (cf. Jn 1:3), so Mary gave birth from her own flesh to him who restored all things to the beauty of the first creation.[6]

Practically speaking, the Mother of God began to be Mistress and Queen with the Ascension of Jesus into heaven. Then it became clear to her that her place in heavenly glory would be inferior only to that of her Son. When she was gloriously assumed, body and soul, she was received in heaven with great pomp and was placed on a throne, from which she reigns over the entire world, carrying out along with her Son a governance that extends to the whole universe. This happened "by power of her motherly right".[7]

Mary's greatness and power are revealed especially in the role the Lord entrusted to her within the plan of universal salvation. On this point Eadmer offers thoughts and arguments that come close to appearing naive. For example, it seems that he wants to put a monopoly over divine mercy into the Virgin's hands:

> He is our mercy, and you are the Mother of that same mercy. . . . Then do not, do not fail us, for the sake of that mercy, whose Mother you are. For he, who through you became our brother to save us, will not disregard your will with regard to our salvation.[8]

Helping sinners is such a major part of her responsibilities that, if she did not guarantee her help to them, she would fail to fulfill the purpose for which she was exalted. Eadmer asserts:

---

[6] *De excellentia* 11; PL 159, 578AB.

[7] Ibid., 9; PL 159, 574C.

[8] *De conceptione*; PL 159, 314D–315A; Thurston-Slater, pp. 40–41.

Just as your Son is the Savior of the whole world, so you are the one who reconciles the whole world [to God].[9]

While Christ saved humanity by his Passion and death, Eadmer seems to want to say that this redemption is applied to us through Mary and that without her we could not be reconciled:

Look after us, O Mary, lest we perish.[10]

It must be said that some statements of this type could run afoul of the sensitivities of believers who rightly look to Christ as the highest source of mercy and the sole author of salvation. Perhaps these statements are not totally unobjectionable as far as orthodoxy is concerned. Yet we should take into account the fact that, within a context of mystical experience, it is possible to understand and justify a way of speaking that would not survive the scrutiny of pure reason but that alone is able to let us penetrate more deeply the incomprehensible depths of divine mysteries.

Prayer to Mary

The privileged mission God entrusted to his Mother, which she continues to carry out from her dwelling in heavenly glory, allows human beings to turn to her in their material and spiritual necessities, conscious that her power of intercession has a surprising effectiveness. Eadmer states that the divine Judge, faced with the prayer of his Mother, will not deny his favors, even to those who do not deserve them:

If the name of [Mary] is invoked, even if the merits of the one who invokes her do not earn him a hearing, nevertheless her merits will intercede and he will be heard.[11]

In keeping with the tendency to exaggerate that we have already mentioned, Eadmer goes so far as to say that, in danger, it seems more useful to call upon Mary than upon her divine Son:

Sometimes salvation arrives more quickly if we remember the name of Mary than if we call upon the name of the Lord Jesus.[12]

---

[9] *De excellentia* 12; PL 159, 580B.

[10] Ibid.

[11] Ibid., 6; PL 159, 570B.

[12] Ibid., PL 159, 570A.

But Eadmer asks why this is so since, in general, one cannot hold that Mary is more powerful than her Son. Indeed, it is not Jesus who is powerful because of his Mother; to the contrary, it is in Christ that Mary attains the whole power of her intercession. The explanation he presents to support his thesis conceals, beneath a certain anthropomorphism, the existential unease of the creature who feels incapable of plumbing the profound depths of the divine mystery:

> Her Son is the Lord and Judge of all, who weighs the merits of every individual, and for this reason, he does not respond immediately to one who calls upon him but answers only after having made a just judgment. But if the name of his Mother is invoked, even if the merits of the one who invokes her do not earn him a hearing, nevertheless her merits will intercede, and he will be heard.[13]

So it would seem that Eadmer wants to introduce a contrast between Mary's intercessory role and the role of supreme Judge, which is reserved to her Son; in reality, however, this is only the effect of a certain kind of rhetorical taste. He writes:

> If you, then, the Mother of God and thus the true Mother of Mercy, should deny us the fruits of mercy, whose mother you became in such a wonderful way, what would we do when your Son comes to judge all men with fairness?[14]

Behind these questions is found only the certainty that Mary received from Christ the Lord the responsibility of distributing the infinite riches of divine mercy with maternal love.

READINGS

MARY'S ROLE AS OUR MOTHER

O Lady, if your Son became our Brother through you, have you not become our Mother through him? For, when he was about to die on the Cross for us, he said to John, yes, to John, who contained us in his common human nature, "Behold your mother" (Jn 19:27).

---

[13] Ibid., PL 159, 570B.
[14] Ibid., 12; PL 159, 579A.

O sinful man, rejoice! Rejoice and be glad! For there is no reason for you to despair, no reason for you to fear. Whatever judgment will be made in your regard depends totally on the verdict of your Brother and your Mother. So do not turn away the ear of your heart from their counsel. Your Judge—that is, your Brother—has taught you to fly to the aid of his Mother, and your Mother has advised you to take refuge in confidence beneath the protecting wings of her Son, and she has promised that she will be there for you, lest you be overburdened by his justice.

O Mary, what can we say? With what organ of speech or with what joy of heart could we express how much we owe you? Yes, Lady, whatever we may have understood or conceived in our minds or spoken with our mouths, it is insignificant and as nothing compared with what we owe you in fairness. For you were preordained in the mind of God, before every other creature, the most chaste among all women, so that you might give birth to God as true man, born of your flesh, and so that, having become the glorious Queen of heaven, you might rule over all things . . . and prepare for a fallen world the entry into recovery and the prize of eternal life.

—Eadmer of Canterbury, *De conceptione*;
PL 159, 315AC; Thurston-Slater, pp. 41–43

MARY'S GLORY IN THE ASCENSION OF CHRIST

Oh, if she had joy while her Son was still living with her in the flesh, if she had joy when her Son rose from the dead after trampling death underfoot, did she then rejoice with lesser joy when her Son entered heaven in the flesh that, as she knew well, had been taken from her? Who ever said, why, who ever even believed that Mary's joy did not surpass all the joys that came before it?

In this world, good mothers are wont to be very happy when they see their children raised up by earthly honors. Even so, will not this Mother, who was undoubtedly good, not be glad with inexpressible joy when she sees her only Son enter heaven with commanding power and reach the throne of God the Father Almighty? Was a joy like this ever heard of? Was a joy like this ever seen in public, so that the human mind might at least direct its attention toward it in some way?

—Eadmer of Canterbury, *De excellentia* 6; PL 159, 568C–569A

3

RUPERT OF DEUTZ
(d. 1130)

This outstanding theologian deserves to be reckoned among the most distinguished authors of the twelfth century. He appears to have been the first writer to have interpreted the whole book of the Song of Songs in a Marian key.

Rupert was born at Liège around 1075 and became a Benedictine monk in the local monastery of St. Lawrence. In 1120 he was elected abbot of St. Herbert in Deutz, near Cologne, where he died in 1130. He was a particularly prolific writer, who preferred the study of theological and exegetical questions. The special attention he devoted to the Song of Songs and his mariological interpretation of this Old Testament book appear to take their origin from the many verses and passages from this biblical poem that were then widely used in the liturgy of Marian feasts, especially in the Assumption and the Birth of the Virgin. Rupert's Marian teaching, in its essentials, agrees with what was generally being taught in his day.[1] He laid particular emphasis on Mary's condition as the Bride of God and on her relationship with the Church. In her presence at the foot of the Cross, he saw a sign of her mission as Mother of all believers.

---

[1] The Marian thought of Rupert of Deutz has been the object of several studies. We mention some of them: M. Peinador, "El designo divino en la historia de la salvación según Ruperto de Deutz a la luz de Gn 3,15 y Ap 12,1", Clar 4 (1965): 141–72; R. Spilker, "Maria-Kirche nach dem Hoheliedkommentar des Rupertus von Deutz", in CongrLourd 3:291–317; idem, "La mariología de Ruperto de Deutz", EphMar 17 (1967): 121–48; idem, "María y la Iglesia en la salvación según Ruperto de Deutz", EphMar 18 (1968): 337–81; J. M. Salgado, "Les Considérations mariales de Rupert de Deutz (m. 1129–1135) dans ses 'Commentaria in Canticum Canticorum'", Divinitas 32 (1988): 692–702; D. Flores, La Virgen María al pie de la cruz (Jn 19,25–27) en Ruperto de Deutz (Rome, 1993).

The Problem of the Immaculate Conception

In gradually becoming aware of this truth of the faith, the Christian people was inspired by its own *sensus fidei*, that inner light granted by the Holy Spirit to believers who are open to his presence and action and committed to an authentically evangelical life. In the history of Christian truths, as is well known, this sense of the faith stayed alive and sometimes prevailed even over the opinion of famous theologians. Rupert was one of the theologians who denied Mary's exemption from original sin; obviously, he did so for serious reasons, but these will also show how God's logic is superior to human logic.

The abbot of Deutz, imbued with the Augustinian mentality that conditioned all medieval thought, did not perceive the possibility that a human creature "belonging to that mass, which became corrupt in Adam"[2] could be exempt from the common inheritance of original sin. Mary, too, would have had to inherit the fault of our ancestors.[3] Nevertheless, following a belief that had already flowered in the awareness of some ancient Fathers of the Church, he held that there had been a special divine intervention in Mary's case, because of which she was freed from original sin before the mystery of the Incarnation of the Word of God took place in her. Thus, while not accepting the Immaculate Conception, Rupert notes that the Blessed Virgin had to be adequately predisposed to exercise her lofty function as Mother of the incarnate God.

The Mystery of the Blessed Virgin, Bride of the Eternal Father

The inspiring power that the text of the Song of Songs exerted on Rupert's mariological teaching explains why he felt compelled to bring to the fore the concept of Mary as the Bride. He calls her "Bride of the eternal Father" because she contracted a marriage relationship with him. In the Old Testament, God chose to prefigure this relationship in his nuptial bond with the chosen people:

---

[2] *In Canticum Canticorum*, I, 2; PL 168, 841C; CCM 26, 12.

[3] See R. Spilker, "La actitud negativa de Ruperto de Deutz ante la Inmaculada Concepción de la Virgen", Mar 30 (1968): 192–217.

> The Virgin Mary was the Bride of God the Father. And in her was realized the reason why, in the Scriptures, he called the Church of that people [Israel] his wife.[4]

Mary is situated between Israel of old and the new Israel, the Church, as the highest expression of the former and the prefiguration of the latter:

> Therefore the Blessed Virgin, the best part of the first Church, merited to be the Bride of God the Father, so that she might also be the exemplar of the younger Church, the Bride of the Son of God, her son. For the same Holy Spirit, who accomplished the Incarnation of the only-begotten Son of God in her womb, would accomplish the rebirth of many sons of God from the womb of the Church or by means of her womb, in the life-giving bath of his grace.[5]

The analogies between Mary and the Church are bridal by nature. Both Mary and the Church possess a fruitfulness resulting from the mysterious action of the Holy Spirit. Just as the Holy Spirit intervened in Mary to bring about the Incarnation, so he intervenes with his grace to bring about the rebirth of the sons of God.

Mary at the Foot of the Cross

Rupert interprets this emblematic episode, recounted in the fourth Gospel (cf. Jn 19:25–27), in the light of Mary's spiritual motherhood. He connects it to another Johannine passage: "When a woman is in labor, she has pain, because her hour has come" (Jn 16:21). In these words is found the explanation of the birth pangs endured by the Blessed Virgin on Calvary, an obvious reference to giving birth spiritually to the reborn sons of God. Rupert brings out the contrast between the painless birth, by which Mary brought the incarnate Son of God into the world at Bethlehem, and our spiritual birth, which, on Calvary, caused the Virgin to endure real and deep sufferings in her soul.

Therefore he makes a precise distinction: the apostle John must truly be called Son of Mary, and the Virgin must deservedly be considered his true Mother. Then he explains how the words of the above-mentioned Gospel passage, which apply to every woman who gives birth, a fortiori

---

[4] *De operibus Spiritus Sancti* 1, 7; PL 167, 1577D; CCM 24, 1829.

[5] Ibid., PL 167, 1577D–1578A; CCM 24, 1829–30.

were pronounced by Jesus in reference to the woman who would stand by his Cross. There too, she would be like a woman giving birth:

> Because [on Calvary] the Blessed Virgin truly suffered the pangs of a woman in childbirth, and because in her Son's Passion she gave birth to the salvation of us all, she is clearly the Mother of us all. Therefore [Jesus'] statement about this disciple, "Woman, behold your Son" (for he was very rightly concerned for his Mother), and likewise to the disciple, "Behold your mother", could have been said correctly about any other disciple had he been present.[6]

Now we understand how Rupert of Deutz must be considered an important witness to the new perspective in which Mary and her mission within the Church were considered. While, in previous centuries, the attention and interest of believers were focused especially on the Virgin's role in the Incarnation of the Son of God, in the twelfth century there began a persistent consideration of the role she played on Calvary, alongside her Son the Redeemer: "The accent moves from Mother of God to Mother of men and, at the same time, from Mary's role in the Annunciation to her role on Calvary."[7]

Reflection on Mary's presence at the foot of the Cross of Jesus becomes more and more insistent, awakening an increasing response from the faithful, who find in it new aspects of Christian truth, abounding in inspiration and Marian piety. It is precisely within this line of thought that the meaning and value of Mary's participation in her Son's sacrifice on the Cross become better understood, along with the ecclesial ramifications of her unshakeable faith and the import of Jesus' words: "Woman, behold your son. . . . Behold your mother" (Jn 19:26–27).

Not only the apostle John, but all men were seen as included in these words, so that Mary became the spiritual Mother of them all. In this context arises and develops the believer's interest in seeking a personal relationship with the Blessed Virgin, based on love and filial dedication.

Queen of Heaven and Earth

While the ancient Christian writers recognized Mary's royal dignity only implicitly, recognizing that she had been raised up above all creatures, as

---

[6] *In Joannem* 13; PL 169, 790AB; CCM 9, 744.
[7] R. Laurentin, *Maria nella storia della salvezza* (Turin, 1972), p. 67.

the centuries went on, explicit recognition of it became more and more frequent. Rupert was one of the authors who openly proclaimed Mary's queenship. Speaking of her unique greatness, he sees it rooted in and explained by the singular act of election by which God chose her from the beginning of creation. Rupert applies to Mary the words of Scripture: "The Lord created me at the beginning of his work. . . . Ages ago I was set up" (Prov 8:22–23).

He recognizes and venerates her as Queen of the saints in heaven and of men on earth, since she possesses the entire kingdom of her Son. According to the legal mentality of the Middle Ages, this royal possession belonged to her quite legitimately, since she is the Mother of the Church, the Sister of Christ in faith, and his Bride in love.[8]

In his *Vita S. Hereberti*, Rupert tells of an apparition of the Blessed Virgin to St. Herbert, in which she shows him how her royal power is expressed especially in the aid and assistance she offers her sons and in the mercy she shows them. Therefore, Mary is rightly invoked as Mother of Mercy and of eternal salvation.[9]

READINGS

MODEL OF THE CHURCH

And so, as we had already begun to say, the Blessed Virgin Mary was the Bride of God the Father, and before all ages he had decided to bring about in her the reason why, in the Scriptures, he called the Church of the [Jewish] people his wife. That is, he had decided that his Word, which had spoken through the hearts and mouths of the prophets in a way already explained, should take flesh in the womb of this Blessed Virgin.

When this was done, it would happen that this Word made flesh, very God, Son of God made man, would be called and truly be the Bridegroom. And the whole Church, without abandoning the Father (whom she had previously been accustomed to call her husband), would agree to accept the marriage proposal of her Spouse. Therefore the Blessed

---

[8] See In Canticum Canticorum 3; PL 168, 891C; CCM 26, 80.

[9] See ibid. 13; PL 170, 404–5.

Virgin, the best part of the first Church, merited to be the Bride of God the Father, so that she might also be the image of the younger Church, the Bride of the Son of God. For the same Holy Spirit who accomplished the Incarnation of the only begotten Son of God in her womb, or from her womb, would accomplish the rebirth of many sons of God from the womb of the Church, or by means of her womb, in the life-giving bath of his grace.

—Rupert of Deutz, *De operibus Spiritus Sancti* 1, 8;
PL 167, 1577–78; SC 131, 80

THE KISS OF GOD

"Let him kiss me with the kiss of his mouth" (Song 1:2).[10] What is the meaning of such a strong and sudden outburst? O blessed Mary, a flood of joy, an onrush of love, a torrent of pleasure has totally washed over you and taken hold of you; it has made you absolutely drunk; and you have perceived what "eye has not seen, nor ear has heard, nor the heart of man conceived" (1 Cor 2:9), and you have said, "Let him kiss me with the kiss of his mouth" (Song 1:2). For you said to the angel, "Behold the handmaid of the Lord; let it be to me according to your word" (Lk 1:38).

What was that word? What had the angel said to you? "You have found favor with God", he said, "Behold, you will conceive . . . and bear a son, and you shall call his name Jesus" (Lk 1:30–31). And then, "The Holy Spirit will come upon you, and the power of the Most High will overshadow you; therefore the child to be born will be called holy, the Son of God" (Lk 1:35).

Was not this word of the angel the promise of an imminent kiss from the Lord's mouth? For this reason let the prudent ponderer weigh both words in the balance of reason, both the word, "Let him kiss me with the kiss of his mouth", which was spoken by a jubilant heart and soul, and the word, "Behold the handmaid of the Lord; let it be to me according to your word", which was spoken by an exultant mouth. Do not both sayings have the same weight? Is not the same meaning contained in different words or terms?

You have heard and believed [the angel's words]; and you have made a request on your own behalf, saying, "Let it be to me". And so it was

---

[10] The translation of Scripture used in the following passages reflects the Latin version used by Rupert.—ED.

done to you. God the Father covered you over with "the kiss of his mouth". What eye saw this? What ear heard it? Into whose heart did it enter? But to you, O Mary, he revealed himself: the One who kisses, the Kiss, and the Mouth of the One who kisses.

—Rupert of Deutz, *In Canticum Canticorum* 1, 1;
PL 168, 839–40; CCM 26, 10

MOTHER OF US ALL

In the hour of his Passion, the Lord correctly compared his apostles to a woman in labor, saying, "When a woman gives birth, she feels sadness, because her hour has come; but when she has given birth to a child, she no longer remembers her suffering because of her joy, that a man has been born into the world. And so you feel sadness now, but I will see you again, and your heart will rejoice" (Jn 16:21–22). If this is true, then did not this Son correctly consider this Mother, this woman standing next to his Cross (cf. Jn 19:25), to be even more like a woman in labor?

But why do I say "like" a woman in labor, seeing that she is truly a woman and truly a mother and truly felt birth pangs in that hour when she gave birth? For this woman did not feel pain when her Child was born to her, in the sense that she did not give birth in sorrow as other mothers do, but now she does feel pain and is tortured and saddened, because her hour has come; that is, the hour for which she conceived by the Holy Spirit, for which she became pregnant, for which the days were fulfilled for her to give birth, for which God became man entirely in her womb.

But when this hour has passed, when the sword has finished piercing her laboring soul, then she will "no longer remember her suffering because of her joy, that a man has been born into the world", because the new man will have been declared, who will renew the whole human race and acquire everlasting rule over the whole world. When I say "born", I mean made immortal and impassible and the firstborn of the dead, who has passed beyond the narrow restrictions of this life and now lives in the wide freedom of the eternal homeland.

Just so, because [on Calvary] the Blessed Virgin truly suffered the pangs of a woman in childbirth, and because in her Son's Passion she gave birth to the salvation of us all, she is clearly the Mother of us all.

—Rupert of Deutz, *In Joannem* 13; PL 169, 789D; CCM 9, 744

4

BERNARD OF CLAIRVAUX
(d. 1153)

In the twelfth century, Bernard was the author who dominated the field of Marian thought. Even though the Marian contents of his many works are not particularly abundant, he had a remarkable gift for speaking about the Blessed Virgin in a fascinating way. Tradition has named him the "Champion and Singer of the Virgin". With good reason, Dante entrusted to him the task of pronouncing the marvelous prayer of praise and invocation of the Virgin that begins the thirty-third canto of his *Paradiso*.

The great Cistercian master did indeed celebrate the mystery and greatness of Mary in superlative tones. His Marian doctrine recommends itself, if not for its quantity, at least for the density of its substance, the clarity and precision of its formulas, and, at times, for the originality of its conclusions. The mark he left on the process of the development of Marian doctrine and piety is absolutely remarkable.

Bernard was born at Fontaines-lès-Dijon, in Bourgogne, in 1090. When he was still a very young student, he felt an attraction to the Benedictine vocation and spent some time experiencing the monastic life. Finally, in 1112, he was admitted to the monastery of Cîteaux, cradle of the Cistercian order, which, thanks to the impulse he gave it, underwent an impressive expansion. Later, Bernard went on to found another monastery, called Clairvaux, which he placed under the special protection of the Virgin and served as abbot for thirty-eight years.

In the meantime, he had become a leading figure, not only in the Church, but also in the political world of the time. Popes, bishops, abbots, emperors, and princes turned to him to avail themselves of his counsels and to entrust him with delicate missions. Bernard divided his time between the monastic life and this ecclesial and secular service. He died in 1153 at Clairvaux, when the monastery numbered more than seven hundred monks and the Cistercian order included 165 foundations.

Bernard's teaching on the Mother of the Lord and, above all, his personal devotion arose from the core of a strongly religious person, gifted with authentic mystical capacities and a marked habit of contemplation, despite the manifold activities in which he was involved.

For him, love for the Mother of God was inseparable from life itself. Dante puts this tercet on his lips:

> And the Queen of heaven, for whom I burn
> Completely with love, will give every grace,
> For I am her faithful Bernard.[1]

Because of his fascinating and convincing oratory, Bernard was able to communicate his interior Marian wealth, which we too can savor and enjoy by reading his homilies on the Virgin. One of their leading themes is the call to an authentic devotion, solidly based on the providential role played by Mary in the economy of salvation.[2]

One of his biographers, his contemporary Alan of Auxerre, recalling that the saint was buried before the altar of the Virgin, noted that Bernard was Mary's "most devoted minister".[3]

His writings were published in PL 182–85 by Migne, who reproduces the edition of Mabillon. Bernard faithfully follows the thought of the Fathers of the Church, so much so that he has been considered the last of the Fathers. He occupies himself with Mary in various works, but we will list only those in which discussion of Mary is prevalent, especially

---

[1] "E la regina del cielo, ond'io ardo / tutto d'amor, ne farà ogni grazia / però ch'i' sono il suo fedel Bernardo" (*Paradiso* 31, 100–102).

[2] Given St. Bernard's immense importance, the bibliography on him, as may easily be imagined, is virtually beyond counting. His Marian teaching has also been exhaustively studied both as a whole and in detail. We limit ourselves to some of the more complete studies: C. Clemencet, *La Mariologie de saint Bernard* (Brignais, 1909); B. Hänsler, *Die Marienlehre des hl. Bernhard* (Regensburg, 1917); A. van der Kerkhoven, *De Marialeer van de heilige Bernardus* (Brussels, 1922); P. Aubron, "La Mariologie de saint Bernard", RSR 24 (1934): 543–77; A. Raugel, *La Doctrine mariale de saint Bernard* (Paris, 1935); D. Nogues, *La Mariologie de saint Bernard*, 2d ed. (Paris, 1947); G. Roschini, *Il dottore mariano* (Rome, 1953); Conference on the Mariology of St. Bernard, Rome, October 21–24, 1991, acts in Mar 54 (1992): 9–428.

[3] *Vita sancti Bernardi*, chap. 31, n. 88; PL 185, 524A.

his sermons (PL 183): *In adventu Domini* (coll. 40–43); four homilies *Super missus est* (55–88), in which he gives an exhaustive exposition of the dogma of the divine motherhood; the three sermons *In Purificatione Beatae Mariae* (365–72); the four sermons *In Assumptione Beatae Mariae* (415–30); the three sermons *In festo Annuntiationis B.M.V.* (383–98); *Sermo infra Octavam Assumptionis de 12 praerogativis B.M.V.* (429–38), a kind of theological treatise on Mary's mediation; *Sermo in Nativitate B.M.V. de aquaeductu* (437–48), a kind of homiletic treatise on Revelation 12:1ff., in which he returns to the theme of mediation; *Sermo de Mariae purificatione et Christi circumcisione* (673–74). In a famous letter, the *Epistula 174* to the canons of Lyons, he discussed Mary's conception, denying that she was exempt from original sin. While the authenticity of Bernard's sermon *In Assumptione B.M.V.* (PL 184, 1001–1010) was called into question by Mabillon (cf. PL 184, 1001), its authorship was restored to St. Bernard by J. Leclercq.[4]

Mary in the Mystery of the Incarnation

Bernard prefers to focus his admiration for the divine plan of salvation on the mystery of the incarnate Word, in whose divine-human existence the closest possible union between God and man was established. But in order to bring about this union, the Lord foresaw the unique contribution of a creature, who would have to furnish the human nature of the incarnate God:

> God formed a single Christ from his own substance and from that of the Virgin; or rather, he became a single Christ.[5]

The importance of Mary's role stems from the fact that she contributed to bringing man closer to God, to making God more accessible to man:

> God was absolutely incomprehensible and inaccessible, invisible and inconceivable. But now he wanted to be grasped, seen, and conceived. "But how?" you ask. Lying in the manger, reclining in his mother's virginal lap.[6]

---

[4] "Sermon pour l'Assomption restitué à saint Bernard", RTAM 20 (1953): 5–12.

[5] *Super missus est* 3, 4; PL 183, 73A.

[6] *In Nativitate* 11; PL 183, 443D.

Thus it is clear that, for Bernard, Mary's greatness and incomparable dignity are rooted in the mystery of the Incarnation, in which the Son of the eternal God becomes the Son of a mere creature:

> Oh, that you would observe whose Mother she is! How far would your admiration for her wonderful loftiness take you! Would it not lead you to understand that you cannot admire her enough? In your judgment, in the judgment of Truth himself, will she not be lifted up, yes, above all the choirs of angels, seeing that she had God as her own Son? Did not Mary boldly call him her Son, who is God and Lord of the angels? [7]

Therefore the coming of the Son of God to earth and the Virgin's divine motherhood stand at the basis of St. Bernard's theological and mystical enthusiasm. In Mary, he contemplates and exalts the responsibility of the answer she gave the angel, with which she decided to collaborate in God's saving plan, and he imagines the human race living in a state of anxious expectation for her response:

> The whole world is waiting, prostrate at your feet. Not without reason, since upon your word depends the consolation of the wretched, the redemption of captives, the liberation of the condemned; in a word, the salvation of all the sons of Adam, of your whole race. [8]

The Blessed Virgin's greatness is such that it can be understood and appreciated only by comparing it to the greatness of God himself. Her greatness presents a dimension that is not only theological but moral. Bernard praises Mary's virtues and interior disposition, choosing to dwell on her virginity and humility, which he considers the two hinges on which her whole existence turns. We give one of the numerous texts on this topic:

> God wanted her to be a virgin. From her, the immaculate one, would proceed the immaculate Son, who would wash away every stain. He also wanted her to be humble, for from her would come forth the Son who is meek and humble of heart, and in himself he would present an example of these virtues, an example necessary and salutary for all. So God, who had first inspired the Virgin's vow of virginity and given her the merit of humility, granted to her that she should give birth. [9]

---

[7] *Super missus est* 1, 7; PL 183, 59D.

[8] Ibid., 4, 8; PL 183, 83D.

[9] Ibid., 2, 1; PL 183, 61D.

These texts are sufficient witness to convince us that our Doctor's Marian teaching is thoroughly based on Christology and the theology of the Incarnation, with deep biblical and patristic roots.[10]

Mary Stands between Christ and Humanity

Alongside the christological perspective, Bernard contemplates the figure of the Virgin Mary from another perspective, which we may call soteriological, for it considers her openness and willingness to help human creatures. This second perspective is always strictly related to the first, because it was Mary's election to the divine motherhood that gave her responsibilities and duties on behalf of the human race. Our Doctor wrote awe-inspiring pages on this theme. He holds that Mary is the mediatrix of all creation because in her God and humanity met.[11] The Virgin's mediation is located, above all, between Christ and his faithful. Bernard illustrated this in a very convincing manner using the celebrated metaphor of the aqueduct. He expounds this fully in his famous homily on the Birth of the Virgin, usually cited as the homily *De aquaeductu*. His premise is that the divine adoption to which the Christian is called passes through the mystery of the Incarnation, where the Virgin Mother is present and active. This active role continues in her mediation, through which she touches grace at its source and distributes it to human beings.

Mary is like an aqueduct that was able to reach the lofty springs of divine grace and convey it to the faithful on earth by the force of her desire, the fervor of her piety, and the purity of her prayer.[12] It was the Lord himself who so arranged matters that we should receive everything from God through Mary; that is, by means of her intercession.

---

[10] St. Bernard's patristic sources have been studied by F. Solà, "Fuentes patrísticas de la mariología de San Bernardo", EstEcl 23 (1949): 209–26.

[11] Bernard's doctrine on Mary's mediation has been thoroughly studied; there is an abundant bibliography on this theme. See J. M. Humeres, "Quanta polleat auctoritate S. Bernardus in doctrina de mediatione B. M. V. declaranda", EphMar 2 (1952): 325–50; P. N. Lodo, "La mediación de María Santísima según la mente de San Bernardo", *Regina mundi* 6 (1962): 16–22; G. Geenen, "Quare et quomodo S. Bernardus docuit mediationem B. V. M. ad Deum", in CongrRom 4:121–29; J. Polo Carrasco, "La mediación de María en las homilías 'De laudibus Virginis Matris' de San Bernardo", in CongrRom 4:153–80; J. M. de la Torre, "La mediación de María en S. Bernardo", EphMar 40 (1990): 221–43.

[12] *De Aquaeductu* 4–5; PL 183, 440.

In exercising this function, she works under the influence of charity, which, inasmuch as it is holiness, unites her to God; inasmuch as it is mercy, it unites her to human creatures. Hence the applications Bernard makes to the religious and moral life of the Christian. The Christian must foster confidence in and devotion to Mary, honor her with his life, and call upon her in his prayer. Thus Bernard exhorts us:

> Let us venerate Mary with every fiber of our being, from the deepest part of our heart, because this is the will of him who wanted us to receive everything through Mary.[13]

Nevertheless, the Virgin is not a purely material instrument of the transmission of grace. She is a living person, who feels sentiments of goodness, love, and mercy toward us, creatures of God redeemed by her Son. Certainly Bernard attributes a motherly heart and sensibility to her, but he never speaks of her exercising a spiritual motherhood on our behalf. Theodore Koehler points out that Bernard, whom Dante called a contemplative affectionately fixed upon Mary,[14] "never concretized his tender feelings for our Lady in the title 'Mother'".[15] However, in relation to Christ, he sometimes calls her the Mother of Mercy, the ladder by which sinners can ascend to God.

But Bernard does not hold that Mary's mediation is absolutely necessary, as if it were impossible directly to address Christ, who by nature is the Mediator between God and human beings. To the contrary, he encourages us to turn to Christ:

> Are you afraid to approach God the Son? He is your brother and your flesh, tempted in all things except sin, that he might show you mercy. Mary gave you this brother. But perhaps you fear the divine majesty within him, because, even though he was made man, yet he remained God. Do you want to have an advocate in the Son's presence, too? Turn to Mary.[16]

Mary will surely be heard by her Son and, through him, by the heavenly Father. It is a mediation that functions more on the psycho-

---

[13] Ibid., 7; PL 183, 441B.

[14] "Affetto al suo piacer quel contemplante" (*Paradiso* 32, 1).

[15] "Maternité spirituelle de Marie", in Du Manoir, ed., *Maria*, vol. 1 (Paris, 1949), p. 575.

[16] *De aquaeductu* 1, 7; PL 183, 441C.

logical level, because it encourages prayer and recourse to the divine mercy.

Devotion to Mary

If such is Mary's mission on behalf of human beings, then they not only can but must turn to her in prayer. Bernard seems almost to challenge anyone who claims to show that the Virgin did not heed one of his requests:

> O Blessed Virgin, if there be anyone who recalls that he has called upon you in necessity and that you were not there to help him, let him not speak of your mercy.[17]

Bernard exhorts the Christian to turn to Mary and pray to her with absolute confidence, because she is like a star that enlightens the whole world, warms our spirit, nourishes virtues, and dries up vices. The text in which our Doctor warmly and passionately beseeches the faithful to look toward Mary, as sailors look to the star to show them the way, is very beautiful and well known. We will reproduce this passage later on.

Mary and Original Sin

Bernard's attitude toward this Marian dogma appears to be completely negative. In 1138, having found out that the canons of the cathedral of Lyons were continuing to celebrate the feast of Mary's Conception, he sent them a letter in which he bemoans the fact, giving a threefold reason: the celebration is not part of the ancient tradition of the Church; it is unknown to the Church universal of his time; and it is not in conformity with the criteria of reason.[18]

He considered this custom to be the result of an excess of zeal on the part of people who claimed to be honoring the Mother of the Lord but went beyond what was legitimate and fitting. For his part, he held that "the royal Virgin has no need of a false honor."[19] Remaining in Augustine's school of thought, Bernard admits that the Virgin's life was

---

[17] *Sermo 4 in Assumptione* 8; PL 183, 428D.
[18] *Epist. 174*; PL 182, 332–36.
[19] Ibid., 2; PL 182, 333.

without actual sins; but as far as original sin is concerned, it seemed impossible to him that a conception could have happened without being under the influence of sexual desire.

In the final analysis, however, our Doctor justified his rejection of the teaching by the fact that Rome had not yet pronounced on the introduction of this feast. In a passage of the above-mentioned letter, he perfectly summarizes his thought:

> Yes, honor the integrity of her flesh and the holiness of her life; wonder at the Virgin's fruitfulness, venerate her divine Son. Exalt her who did not know concupiscence in conceiving or pain in childbirth. Preach her who is to be reverenced by the angels, desired by the nations, foreseen by the patriarchs and prophets, who was chosen from among all and preferred above all. Magnify her, the finder [*inventrix*] of grace, the mediatrix of salvation, restorer [*restauratrix*] of the ages. Exalt her who has been exalted into the kingdom of heaven, above the choirs of angels. This is what the Church sings of her to me, and the Church has taught me to sing the same. And what I have received from the Church, I safely hold and safely hand on to others. As for what I have not received from the Church, I confess that I would admit it with less ease. . . .
>
> I learned in the Church and from the Church to consider the birth of the Virgin certainly a holy day and worthy of celebration. With the Church, I firmly believe that Mary received, in [her mother's] womb, the grace to be born holy.[20]

We may add that the doctrine of Mary's exemption from original sin was not yet sufficiently developed in Bernard's time, but the controversy over it served to stimulate a gradual theological clarification.

Mary's Assumption into Heaven

Bernard speaks very favorably of the dogma of the Assumption, even though he does not clearly express himself with regard to the fate of Mary's body at the end of her earthly existence. The certainty he feels about the Virgin's ultimate glorification is grounded in the teaching of Christ:

> I have learned from the Church to celebrate with the greatest veneration this day, on which the Virgin, taken up from the wicked world, caused the most splendid and joyful festival in heaven.[21]

---

[20] Ibid.

[21] Ibid.

He is convinced that Mary went before us into heaven and that the reception she received there can encourage her servants to hope to follow her at the end of their life.[22]

Further, it would be difficult to understand the commentary on the name of Mary written by the monk of Clairvaux had he not thought of her as being in the glory of heaven. Later we will reproduce the marvelous text in which he poured out all his faith in the mystery of the Virgin and his love toward her. This remarkable passage should suffice to place Bernard among the number of those devoted servants of the Blessed Virgin who made the greatest contribution to bringing out the importance of her presence and function in the economy of salvation, making known the abundant fruit that Marian devotion can bring in a Christian's life.

READINGS

THE NAME OF MARY

"And the virgin's name was Mary" (Lk 1:27). Let us also say a few words about this name, which means "star of the sea" and is most suitably fitting for a virgin mother. For she is most appropriately compared to a star, because, just as a star emits its rays without being corrupted, so the Virgin gave birth to her Son without any injury [to her virginity]. When the star emits its rays, this does not make it less bright, and neither does the Son diminish his Mother's [virginal] integrity. She, therefore, is that noble star risen from Jacob, whose ray gives light to the whole world, whose brightness both shines forth in the heavens and penetrates the depths. It lights up the earth and warms the spirit more than the body; it fosters virtues and dries up vices. Mary, I say, is the distinguished and bright shining star, necessarily lifted up above this great broad sea, gleaming with merits, giving light by her example.

Oh, if any of you recognizes that he is caught between storms and tempests, tossed about in the flood of this world, instead of walking on dry land, keep your eyes fixed on the glow of this star, unless you want to perish, overwhelmed by the tempest!

---

[22] See *Sermo 1 in Assumptione* 1; PL 183, 415.

If the winds of temptations surge, if you run aground on the shoals of troubles, look to this star, call upon Mary!

If you are tossed by the winds of pride or ambition or detraction or jealousy, look to this star, call upon Mary!

If anger or greed or the allurements of the flesh dash against the boat of your mind, look to Mary!

And if you are troubled by the enormity of your sins, confused by the foulness of your conscience, terrified by the horror of the Judgment, so that you begin to be swallowed up by the pit of sadness, the abyss of despair, think of Mary!

In dangers, in straits, in perplexity, think of Mary, call upon Mary. Let her name be always in your mouth and in your heart, and, if you would ask for and obtain the help of her prayers, do not forget the example of how she lived.

If you follow her, you will not go astray. If you pray to her, you will not despair. If you think of her, you will not be lost. If you cling to her, you will not fall. If she protects you, you will not fear; if she is your guide, you will not tire; if she is favorable to you, you will reach your goal. Thus you will experience personally how rightly it was spoken: "And the Virgin's name was Mary."

—Bernard of Clairvaux, *Super missus est* 2, 17; PL 183, 70–71

THE SWORD OF SIMEON

The Virgin's martyrdom (which, as you may remember, we have reckoned the twelfth star of her crown) is confirmed, of course, both in the prophecy of Simeon and in the story of the Lord's Passion.

"This child has been set up", said the holy old man about the Child Jesus, "as a sign which will be spoken against". And he said to Mary, "A sword shall pierce your soul" (Lk 2:34–35). O Blessed Mother, truly a sword has pierced your soul. Besides, if it did not pierce your soul, it would not pierce the flesh of your Son. And indeed, after your Son Jesus (who belongs to everyone but is your Son particularly) gave up his life, the cruel lance did not touch his soul at all, though it opened his side (not sparing one already dead, whom it could not harm). No, it pierced your soul instead. It is certain that his soul was no longer present, but your soul could not be torn away from that place. Therefore, a violent pain pierced your soul, so that we speak of you as more than a martyr. I am sure that, for you, what you felt in sharing your Son's Passion was even worse than the sensation of physical suffering.

Now, was not the word [your Son spoke from the Cross] worse than a sword for you? Did it not pierce your soul, penetrating even unto the division of soul and spirit (cf. Heb 4:12)? "Woman, behold your son" (Jn 19:26). What an exchange! In place of Jesus, you are handed John, the servant in place of the Master, the disciple in place of the Teacher, the son of Zebedee in place of the Son of God, a mere man in place of true God! How could the hearing of these words not pierce your most affectionate soul, when the mere recollection of them breaks our hearts, though they be made of stone or iron?

Do not wonder, brothers, that Mary is said to have been a martyr in her soul. Let him wonder who does not remember having heard Paul recalling that one of the greatest offenses of the pagans was that they were without affection (cf. Rom 1:31). This lack of feeling was far from the heart of Mary, and let it be far from the hearts of her servants. But perhaps someone will say, "Did she not know ahead of time that her Son was going to die?" Yes, undoubtedly. "Did she not keep on hoping that he would rise?" Yes, faithfully. "And despite this, she grieved to see him crucified?" Yes, greatly. Besides, who are you, brother, or where do you get this knowledge, if you find it more amazing that Mary should share in her Son's suffering by her compassion than that Mary's Son should suffer in the first place? If he could die in the body, why could she not die with him in her heart? It was charity, greater than that of any other man, that made [Christ die], and it was also charity that made Mary die with him in her heart, and, after that charity, no other like charity ever was.

Now, O Mother of Mercy, the moon,[23] humbly prostrate at your feet, devoutly implores you, her Mediatrix with the Sun of justice, begging you by the most sincere feeling of your heart that in your light she might see light and merit the grace of the Son by your procuring. For he truly loves you more than all others and has adorned you, dressing you in a robe of glory (cf. Sir 6:31) and placing a crown of beauty on your head (cf. Ezek 16:12). You are full of graces (cf. Lk 1:28), full of heavenly dew, resting upon your beloved, sated with delight (cf. Song 8:5).

—Bernard of Clairvaux, *Sermo infra Octavam Assumptionis* 14–15;
PL 183, 437–38

---

[23] By this metaphor Bernard signifies the Church.

5

PETER THE VENERABLE
(d. 1156)

When considering the history of devotion to Mary within Western monasticism, we must recall the name of Peter the Venerable. This last of the great abbots of Cluny deserves to be remembered in this connection because of his important initiatives in this area.

He was born around 1094 in Auvergne. In 1109, he entered the monastery of Sauxilange and, after living in various Benedictine abbeys, was elected abbot of Cluny in 1122. He governed that famous monastery until his death in 1156. His activities, both within the monastery and outside it, made him one of the more important and authoritative ecclesiastical personages of his time. He dedicated himself to restoring monastic discipline, acting with firmness and a sense of balance. In 1132, he organized the general chapter of the Cluniac congregation; he visited numerous monasteries of the order in France and beyond. He took advantage of every chance to defend the person and authority of the Supreme Pontiff and several times went on missions to Rome. He was a great friend of St. Bernard, even though in some matters he occasionally disagreed with him.

Peter's writings are packed with dense theological reflection. In them, he confronts various problems of his time, especially in relation to Christology and the sacraments. Some of his works have an apologetic character and aim to defend Christian truth against errors and enemies. His refutation of the Islamic religion is interesting; he worked it out carefully, after having had the Koran translated into Latin so that he would be able to write with an adequate knowledge of the subject. Peter the Venerable did not write works on Marian topics as such; however, passages that speak of the Virgin are to be found in various of his writings. This happens especially in some of his liturgical compositions, in some of his letters, especially in *Letter 94* to the monk Jerome, in a sermon in praise of the Holy Sepulcher, in his treatise on miracles, and in the statutes of Cluny.[1]

His Marian Piety

When speaking of devotion to Mary or the honor that ought to be rendered her, Peter typically insists on practical things; that is, on actions, deeds, and external and interior attitudes through which the faithful express what they experience in their hearts with regard to the Virgin Mother of the Lord.

But his more immediate objective is to increase devotion to Mary within his order. This allows us to understand why he speaks of her many times in the statutes of the Cluniac congregation. Among the various monastic decrees, some directly pertain to the attainment of this goal.

Every day, the monks are supposed to remember the Blessed Virgin in a special way by celebrating a Mass in her honor on the altar dedicated to her.[2]

Also, since the entire monastic community could not sing the Office of the Blessed Virgin Mary every day, because of time restraints, at least the sick monks had to do so in their own special chapel, which was dedicated to the Mother of the Lord.[3]

Another statute laid down that the *Salve Regina* should be sung during the processions on the feast of the Assumption. One procession took place in the monastery itself; the other went from the principal Church of the Apostles to the Church of the Mother of the Lord.[4]

To justify these decrees, Peter appeals to two principal reasons: first, the Virgin needs to receive the special honor that is owed, after God, to

---

[1] The works of Peter the Venerable were published in PL 189, 61–1054. The critical edition of his letters was prepared by G. Constable, *The Letters of Peter the Venerable*, 2 vols. (Harvard University Press, 1967). For studies of his Marian thought, see G. Constable and J. Kritzeck, eds., *Petrus Venerabilis (1156–1956)*, Studia Anselmiana 40 (Rome, 1956); B. Billet, "La Dévotion mariale de Pierre le Vénérable", in CongrRom 4:181–214; idem, "L'Oeuvre mariale de Pierre de Vénérable", *Esprit et Vie* 87 (1977): 465–77; J. Leclercq, *Pietro il Venerabile* (Milan: Jaca Book, 1991).

[2] PL 189, 1040B.

[3] Ibid., 1041D–1042A.

[4] Ibid., 1048A.

her above all other creatures, as Mother of the one who is the Lord and
Maker of the universe;[5] second, the decree serves to obtain that help
which she promises to her special servants.[6]

Faith and Devotion

Far from promoting an arbitrary Marian devotion, the abbot of Cluny
firmly upholds the principle according to which the believer, in venerating the Virgin and showing his love for her, must let himself be guided
by the rule of faith, as proclaimed in the word of God and explained by
theology. On the basis of this principle, he does not hesitate to criticize
abuses and exaggerations.[7]

The distinction between Christ and his Mother must be precisely
maintained in any case. For example, Peter observes that when one
speaks of the fullness of grace in Christ and the fullness of grace in his
Mother, one must not mean the same thing. The fullness of grace resides
by nature only in the incarnate Word (cf. Jn 1:14). The same expression,
applied to Mary, must be understood in the sense that she carried in her
womb Christ, who is full of grace and truth.[8]

Peter the Venerable was one of the first authors to occupy himself
with the problem of Mary's knowledge. He opposes the idea that she
could be considered omniscient, as some were proposing. In fact, the
New Testament proves the exact opposite. If Mary had known all things
and all the events of this world, an angel would not have had to appear to
Joseph to tell him to take the Baby and his Mother and fly to Egypt (cf.
Mt 2:13). Also, the episode of the finding of Jesus in the Temple clearly
shows that Mary did not know everything.[9]

The difference between Mary's condition and that of the angels is clear.
The angels knew many things that she did not, because they already
enjoyed the beatific vision. It would be foolish to attribute angelic
knowledge to the Virgin before she began to partake of the vision of God
in heaven. Instead, the wisdom and beatitude Mary possessed on earth

---

[5] Ibid., 1040 (no. 54), 1048 (n. 76).

[6] Ibid., 1040 (no. 54).

[7] Letter 3, 7; PL 189, 292D; Constable, 1:243–44.

[8] Ibid., PL 189, 292D–293A; Constable, 1:244.

[9] Ibid., PL 189, 291A–292C; Constable, 1:243.

were nothing other than the fruit of her faith, her hope, and her sublime charity.[10]

Finally, Peter distinguishes the situation of the Virgin from that of the apostles. He does not hold that special graces were granted to the Virgin on the day of Pentecost for the purposes of the apostolate. In receiving the Son of God in the mystery of the Annunciation, she had already received the fullness of grace. When the apostles received the Holy Spirit in the upper room, they received specific gifts of the apostolate because they had been sent by Jesus to proclaim the gospel and to preach the doctrine of the faith. But this was not Mary's task. Today, Peter's explanation might appear to have a somewhat anti-feminist tone. In fact, he holds that evangelization is a role reserved exclusively to men. But he adds that women, too, have an important mission to fulfill in the Church: that of lifting up spiritual canticles, following the example of such famous women of the Old Testament as Miriam, the sister of Aaron, Deborah, and Hannah, the mother of Samuel.

The Mother of the Lord, too, after the Lord's conception, rejoiced and lifted up the song of her *Magnificat*. Nevertheless, the fact that she did not receive the graces of the apostolate on the day of Pentecost does not in any way take away from her superiority over the Twelve.[11]

All these reflections bring Peter to conclude that the unique exaltation of the Virgin, willed by God even during her earthly existence, does not authorize the faithful to attribute untrue merits and privileges to her.

Mary and the Holy Spirit

Peter does not fail to underscore the mysterious and unprecedented action of the Holy Spirit in the Virgin:

> It was fitting that she was purified, sanctified, and glorified by the Holy Spirit and the power of the Most High, inasmuch as she was going to conceive, bear, and nurse the almighty Son of God.[12]

Devotion, praise, and prayer addressed to Mary are based on this same dynamic and organic principle. It has been rightly noted that the privileged role of the Holy Spirit, recognized by Peter, is one of the obvious

---

[10] Ibid., PL 189, 296D–298C; Constable, 1:248–50.

[11] Ibid., PL 189, 287C–290A; Constable, 1:238–41.

[12] Ibid., PL 189, 286D; Constable, 1:237–38.

characteristics of his Marian doctrine and devotion. This pneumato-
logical emphasis may be found to a greater or lesser degree throughout
the Benedictine monasticism of his time.[13]

READING

IN HONOR OF THE MOTHER OF THE LORD

> Sing Alleluia! From the earth
> When Christ from Mary's flesh took birth
> The Truth sprang up with gladsome cry.
> Now let new glory fill the sky,
> Now let new joys be sung below.
> Creation's Maker saw its woe;
> He pitied it, about to die.
> To prisoners he then drew nigh
> And stretched out freedom's strong right hand
> To free the foe's imprisoned band.
> So heaven poured down dew to earth,
> And to its Savior earth gave birth.
> The choir of angels needs must sing,
> For Mary's Infant is their king.
> The Spirit made her virgin womb
> Grow fruitful, made it God's own room
> And, like a flower from a stem,
> The Virgin then produced for men
> The world's Redeemer, not in silk,
> But clothed in flesh. On holy milk
> From virgin nurse the Boy God feeds;
> This miracle all else exceeds.
> The One to whom all owe their lives
> On food from someone else survives.
> O peerless wonder! See him thrive
> On fleshly food who keeps alive
> The flesh. The Child in her embrace,

---

[13] See Billet, "Dévotion mariale", p. 213.

She worships as the God of grace;
She owns him as Emmanuel,
Her God, Savior of Israel.
The Christian people you extol,
O Mother, with their heart and soul,
And with their voice, and eyes, and mind.
Their Refuge sure and Helper kind,
They yearn for, born from you in time.
Look down, and melt away our crime,
O Mistress of the world, we pray:
Your loving eyes turn not away.
Let evil flee and yield its place
To justice, through Christ Jesus' grace.

—Peter the Venerable, PL 189, 1017–18

6

ARNOLD OF BONNEVAL
(d. after 1156)

The monk Arnold (also spelled Arnald or Ernald) of Bonneval is a witness to the special interest in Mary and fervent devotion to her within the order of St. Benedict. Arnold was a personal friend and a biographer of St. Bernard, from whom he must have gotten much inspiration and motivation. We know very little about the early years of his life. In 1138, while living as a monk in the abbey of Marmoutier, he was elected abbot of the monastery of Bonneval, near Chartres. His life was somewhat troubled, especially because of unjust accusations made against him. He was cleared of these charges by the intervention of Pope Eugene III. He died after 1156. The *Menologium Cistercense* praises him as "a man famed for his learning and piety".

Arnold composed various exegetical and spiritual works, as well as a biography of St. Bernard, written at the request of the monks of Clairvaux. Two works in which he discusses Marian themes are part 3 of his treatise *De septem verbis Domini in cruce* (PL 189, 1693–98) and, obviously, the short work *De laudibus beatae Mariae Virginis* (PL 189, 1725–34), in which he makes a synthetic exposition of the events of Mary's life, accompanied by personal considerations.

As a writer, Abbot Arnold is convincing, refined, and motivated by a sincere devotion to the Blessed Virgin. His writings are rich in profound learning and reveal a passionate craving for mystical experience. He pays most attention to two Marian themes: the role played by the Virgin in the mystery of human salvation[1] and her lot in the life beyond this world.

---

[1] See R. Struve Haker, "Arnoldo de Bonavalle, primer teólogo de la coredención mariana", *Regina mundi* (Bogotá) 7 (1963): 48–75.

Mary and Redemption

It is commonly held that Arnold was the first Latin author to articulate the doctrine of Mary's cooperation in the salvation of the human race. Earlier tradition, going back to the teaching of the Fathers of the Church, limited itself to expounding and clarifying the doctrine of the Virgin's active participation in the Incarnation, concentrating on its soteriological implications. Arnold does not forget this aspect of the mystery.

Echoing the ancient statements of Augustine, he repeats that Mary's contribution cannot be reduced to biological motherhood. First and foremost, it was a question of free choice, inspired by faith:

> When the Word fills us, we carry in our minds what the Mother carried in her womb. For she conceived the Only-Begotten of the Father in her mind before she conceived him in her flesh.[2]

Arnold, however, considers Mary's function in the mystery of salvation within a wider perspective. He perceives that she had an important role on Calvary, and this intuition allows him to make an important step forward in the development of the doctrine of the Virgin's cooperation in human salvation.

In running through the Gospel narrative, one cannot ignore the fact that, on Calvary, Jesus' Mother truly shared in the Passion of her Son. This happened by the will of the Son, who recognized his Mother. Our author states this in the form of a dialogue:

> See, O good Jesus, your Mother is here before you. Why do you not just say, "Who is my mother, and who are my brothers?" (Mt 12:48). Not only do you not reject your Mother, or ignore her, but you entrust her to your disciple and lay the responsibility of caring for her in your stead upon the disciple whom you especially love.[3]

We have to recognize that Arnold uses very bold language to express his beliefs about Mary's cooperation in the redemption. Sometimes it seems that he wants to put the Mother on the same level as the Son:

> Standing before the Father, the Mother and the Son divide the responsibility of extending pity [to us], and, with extraordinary missions of

---

[2] *De laudibus B. M. V.*; PL 189, 1726C.

[3] Ibid., 1731C.

mediation, they pave the way for the task of human redemption. Between them, they compose the inviolable testament of our reconciliation.[4]

Arnold is aware of the position of St. Ambrose, whom he quotes without naming, according to which Jesus needed no assistance in the work of the redemption.[5] Clearly, the Redeemer did not want his Mother to contribute anything to his physical suffering. But Mary made a moral contribution to her Son's martyrdom, which Arnold defends without hesitation:

> Mary immolates herself to Christ in her spirit and begs God for the salvation of the world; the Son obtains the salvation of the world, and the Father refrains from punishment.[6]

It is as if there were two altars on Calvary; one in Mary's heart and the other in Christ's body.[7]

This cooperation is based on a total union of will between Mother and Son; for this reason there are not two distinct offerings to God for the salvation of humanity but one single oblation:

> Love for his Mother moved Christ. At that moment, Christ and Mary had but one single will, and both were equally offering a single holocaust to God: she with the blood of her heart; he with the blood of his body.[8]

The union between Mother and Son goes so deep that it almost involves the Virgin in the inexpressible dynamism of trinitarian love:

> The Father loved the Son, and the Son loved the Father; and the Mother, after these two, was burning with love. The different offices each one exhibited were one reality, one single intention of the good Father, of the faithful Son, and of the holy Mother; one reality, which love performed in common, as piety, charity, and goodness were all joined together.[9]

But, such daring statements notwithstanding, it appears that Arnold kept Mary's action on the level of moral collaboration, since he insists on

---

[4] Ibid., 1726D.

[5] See *Expositio in Lucam* 10, 132; SC 52, 200.

[6] *De laudibus B. M. V.*; PL 189, 1727A.

[7] See *De septem verbis Domini in cruce*; PL 189, 1694B.

[8] *De laudibus B. M. V.*; PL 189, 1727A.

[9] *De septem verbis Domini in cruce*, PL 189, 1695A.

declaring that a bodily oblation remains a prerogative of the High Priest.[10]

Mary in the Glory of God

In the works of the abbot of Bonneval, we do not find an explicit teaching in favor of Mary's bodily assumption into heaven. In fact, he raises some questions about it:

> She went to the Son, and, as the angels came to meet her and bore up her distinguished soul, she was assumed into heaven. Whether this happened with her body or without is not defined by any authority of the canonical Scripture; but however it may have happened, there is no doubt that she is with Christ.[11]

In any case, Arnold maintains that the Mother's heavenly situation is inseparable from the glory of her Son, with whom she reigns "in heaven, at his right, girded about with diadems, in vestments of gold".[12] For she has reached such a peak of blessedness that she is able to share with her Son, in a total and definitive manner, the effects of the salvation of the world:

> Christ is the Lord, and Mary his Lady, and inasmuch as she professed herself to be the handmaid of Christ, she fully understands that this kind of service is more sublime than any kingdom. For she is placed above every creature, and whoever bends the knee before Jesus is inclined to bow down before his Mother as well. In the spheres above and in those below, the Virgin Mother is an object of admiration. . . . The Mother cannot be separated from the Son's dominion and power. Mary's flesh and that of Christ are one; one is their spirit; one their charity.[13]

But what is even more interesting about our author's thoughts on the Virgin's heavenly life is his belief that Mary continues to exercise in heaven the same function she already carried out on earth, especially on Calvary. She makes her own contribution to human salvation:

---

[10] Ibid., 1694B.
[11] *De laudibus B. M. V.*; PL 189, 1733A.
[12] Ibid., 1727B.
[13] Ibid., 1729AB.

Both she and her Son stand before the face of God asking for mercy, not justice, to be shown to us. And they obtain the remission of sins for all who are repentant.[14]

In heaven, Christ and Mary carry out this function of mercy, the former with the fruit of his Passion, the latter with her motherhood:

Now man can approach God with confidence, since in the Son he has a mediator of his case with the Father, and with the Son he has [a mediatrix] in the Mother. Christ, his side laid bare, shows the Father his side and his wounds; Mary shows Christ her womb and her breasts; and there is no way man's case can be rejected where these monuments of clemency and tokens of charity are found together, making a request more eloquently than any tongue.[15]

In this text, Arnold introduces an idea that some theologians will frequently take up in their writings, not without giving rise to a certain amount of perplexity: he seems to want to place Mary between us and Christ. Yet he does not say that she is a required and indispensable means of access for the believer who wishes to address his prayers and supplications to the Savior.

Thus we see Arnold of Bonneval formulating two doctrines: Mary's cooperation in the redemption and her heavenly mediation. In the theological development of later centuries, these two doctrines will become more and more developed and lead to a visible increase in the Marian devotion of the Christian faithful.

READINGS

MARY AND THE MYSTERY OF THE INCARNATION

If I should speak with the tongues of men and angels, I would not be able to speak worthily and properly about the glory of the holy and ever-virgin Mary, the Mother of Christ. For in singing her praises, no suitable instrument may be found, and the creativity of the most subtle will be found dull-witted. And since the high point of veneration is that owed

---

[14] Ibid., 1733A–1734A.
[15] Ibid., 1726 CD.

to Christ, from whose fullness it rained down from above, so that Mary is called "full of grace", it is plain that the glory of the Mother and that of the Son are one and that they have in common a praise that is beyond the power of all our understanding to define.

Because, even if that ancient plan concerning the Word, who was God with God (cf. Jn 1:1), becoming incarnate in the holy Virgin, had been revealed openly to the world, nevertheless our human understanding fears to come into contact with such an unusual occurrence (for it is a miracle and does not follow the natural order of things). Our understanding does not know what to feel, because the majesty of the miracle is a thing of wonder, but one would be an ingrate not to go beyond silence and praise the Miracle-worker.

Unheard-of wonder! The Virgin becomes a mother; the Word becomes flesh; God becomes man: In the face of such a great miracle, who could remain silent? At the same time, who would have the ability to proclaim these wonders? Indeed, we know that his miracle is beyond our grasp, but she, in whose most holy womb the Word was made flesh, provides the word for those who will speak of the Word.

Nor is it right that the Church's joy remain mute, because, when the Word fills us, we have in our minds the same Word that the Mother had in her womb. For she conceived the Only-Begotten of the Father in her mind before she conceived him in her flesh. When the angel greeted her, she believed that her vow of virginity would remain unbroken and that the Holy of Holies would be born from her, because she had also received from heaven the assurance that no word was impossible with God (cf. Lk 1:37).

—Arnold of Bonneval, *De laudibus B.M.V.*; PL 189, 1725C–1726C

MARY ON CALVARY

While the apostles fled, the Mother placed herself opposite her Son, and, the sword of pain being fixed in her heart, she was wounded in her spirit and crucified with Christ in her emotions. And what nails and spear did to the flesh of Christ, Mary's natural compassion and the anguish of her motherly affection did to her spirit.

She stood before the Cross, as was fitting for the Mother of Christ. Perhaps she understood that the death of her Son was the world's redemption and was already thinking that, by her own death, she would add something to what her Son was doing for all. But Jesus did not need the help of another, for he said: "I have become like a man without help, at liberty among the dead (Ps 87:4–5, LXX). He accepted his Mother's love, but he was not looking for help." [16] Rather, he included her among the others for whom he was offering the sacrifice of his blood to the Father, including her in that universal benefit.

—Arnold of Bonneval, *De laudibus B.M.V.*; PL 189, 1731B–C

---

[16] Arnold is repeating St. Ambrose almost word for word. Cf. *Expositio in Lucam* 10, 132; SC 52, 200; *De institutione virginis* 49, CPSal, series latina 6, pp. 345–47; *Epist.* 63, 110; PL 16, 1271.

7

AMADEUS OF LAUSANNE
(d. 1159)

Amadeus of Lausanne is remembered as the author of eight homilies on the Mother of God. These homilies faithfully reflect the atmosphere of the Marian piety found in the Cistercian monasteries of his time. From his youth, he himself had been formed in Cistercian spirituality, which was a strong motivating force behind the religious renewal then underway in the Church.

Amadeus was born around 1110 to the family of the Clermonts, at Chatte, in the Isère valley. Around 1119, he followed his father in entering the abbey of Bonnevaux, where he was taught by the Cistercian monks. But because they had little opportunity to dedicate themselves to educating him, his father brought him to Cluny. Later he spent some years at the court of his cousin, Conrad of Franconia. Finally, in 1125, he decided to enter the monastery of Clairvaux. In that famous Cistercian monastery, he began his novitiate under the guidance of St. Bernard, and there he spent the first fourteen years of his religious life. In 1139, he was called to be abbot of the monastery of Hautecombe, a responsibility he discharged until 1144, when he was elected bishop of Lausanne. Being deeply attached to the monastic life, he first attempted to refuse the episcopal throne, but after Pope Lucius II intervened, Amadeus had to accept. He died in 1159 in the odor of sanctity.

His Mariological Legacy

Our author left behind very few writings. His eight Marian homilies[1] have the characteristics of theological treatises—in reduced form—on

---

[1] Hilda Graef, *Mary: A History of Doctrine and Devotion* (New York, 1964), pp. 244–47; F. Buck, "The Marian Interpretation of the Song of Songs in the Middle Ages", in CongrRom 4:87. PL 188, 1303–46. The critical edition of the homilies has been published in SC 72.

the greatness of the Lord's Mother. In them, Amadeus gives an elegant and delicate analysis of Mary's heart; he contemplates the mysteries and events of her life, from the Annunciation up to her glorification in heaven. He enters into a prayerful dialogue with Mary that is marked by simplicity and openness.

His style, full of freshness and a certain naivete, never lapses to the point that it appears contrived. Sometimes, however, it reveals such great sensitivity and affectivity that it verges on becoming the sort of religious sensuality that would characterize popular religiosity in the following centuries, especially in certain of its more refined expressions, such as literature and sacred art.[2]

In his homilies, we may recognize themes that will become classic in the Marian doctrine of later centuries and that have their roots in the tradition of the Church Fathers: divine motherhood, virginity, new Eve, Mary as Bride, holiness, assumption, queenship, mediation. But Amadeus follows his own path and method in expounding his Marian doctrine. While the language he uses to talk about the Blessed Virgin is laudatory and highly emotional, it is nevertheless convincing and not without a certain attractive quality.

Mary between the Two Testaments

In his first homily, Amadeus sets out to identify the place God set apart for the Virgin within the economy of salvation. He thinks that she occupies the place where the Old and New Testaments meet. He compares the two Testaments to two golden baskets, adorned with flowers and full of fruit. The first basket sits on the Virgin's left, the second on her right. The Old Testament foretells future events; the New Testament praises the omnipotence of the One who brought them to fulfillment:

> In the former is the sign of things to come; in the latter is found the reality signified. We notice that these same baskets represent Christ's glory and his birth from the Virgin, for everything found in the two Testaments is

---

[2] See R. Thomas, "Cîteaux et Notre Dame", in *Maria* 2:616–17. For the Marian teaching of Amadeus of Lausanne, see A. Louf, "Marie dans la parole de Dieu selon St. Amédée de Lausanne", CollOrdCistRef 21 (1959): 29–62; M. A. Gómez, "Las homilías marianas de San Amedeo de Lausana", *Cistercium* 11 (1959): 123–29.

there in order to foretell Christ, to show forth Christ, to proclaim Christ, and the Virgin Mary as well.[3]

The first Testament foretells, and the second Testament reveals. Thus, by scrutinizing the signs and figures of the first Testament, it will be possible to perceive allusions or clues concerning the coming of Jesus and of his Mother. Most of all, however, we will observe how Christ and Mary are closely joined in God's plan:

> Every tree is distinguished by its fruit and valued because of its own specific fruitfulness. Just as the palm tree is appreciated for the sweetness of its dates, the vine for the juice of its grapes, the olive for the fatness of its oil, so it is certain that the praise of the Son redounds upon his Mother, and the divine birth fills the Bearer with glory.[4]

Amadeus wants to convince his audience that everything Mary received is simply the consequence of her unique and unprecedented relationship to the Son of God.

Mary and the Gifts of the Holy Spirit

In expounding the plan of the other seven homilies, Amadeus explains how the Virgin's spiritual progress depends on the action of the Holy Spirit; more specifically, on the action of his seven gifts, as listed in Isaiah 11:2.

The gift of the *fear of the Lord* is the factor that brought about Mary's justification, as manifested in the beauty of her person and the costliness of her garments, images that our author borrows from Old Testament figures. To the question of the angelic hosts: "Who is she that arises all in white?" (Song 8:5, LXX),[5] he responds:

> What does it mean to be all white if not to be clothed in white garments; that is, adorned in a garment of beauty and purity, of justice and holiness?[6]

---

[3] SC 72, 58.

[4] Ibid., 72, 64.

[5] On several occasions, Amadeus of Lausanne applies certain verses of the Song of Songs to the Mother of the Lord. Cf. A. Molina Prieto, "Interpretación mariológica del 'Cantar de los Cantares' en las homilías de San Amedeo de Lausana", EphMar 41 (1991): 207–45.

[6] SC 72, 72.

Mary's greatness and holiness explain her preeminent role within the people of God:

> She joins the Head to his Body, in that she unites Christ to the Church and pours into the other members the life that she was the first to receive. For it was fitting that, as death entered the world because of a woman, so life should reenter the world through a woman. And it was fitting that, just as all were dying in Eve, so all should come back to life in Mary. The former, having unhappily believed the serpent's words, prepared the venom of death. The latter, crushing the serpent's head, administered the antidote of life to all, to slay death and restore life.[7]

The Eve–Mary parallel is a classic theme in Christian tradition, going back to the Fathers of the Church. Amadeus somewhat overemphasizes Mary's role, making her the distributor of life. This statement is correct, as long as it is meant in a christological sense.

With the gift of *piety*, the Holy Spirit joined Mary to himself in a true marriage covenant, the result of which was the virginal conception of the Lord:

> Rejoice, because you will be found with child by the work of the Holy Spirit. Of course, you are Joseph's bride, but the Holy Spirit will be the first to approach you. [God] who created you has also marked you with his seal, has reserved you for himself. Your Creator himself has become your Husband; he has fallen in love with your beauty.[8]

Mary's motherhood, experienced in a miraculous—that is, virginal—birth, has extended the light of divine wisdom into the world. Only this wisdom has the power to analyze phenomena that are above the law of nature:

> Then believe in God, O human littleness—nay, human nothingness—and let your reasoning rest on the solid support of his omnipotent wisdom. . . . Believe, then, that all those who unfailingly cling to their Creator will not be limited by the law of nature but will be above nature, because they will be upheld by the Author of nature.[9]

In the mystery of the sword that pierced Mary's heart as she contemplated her dying Son, the gift of *fortitude* is revealed. Amadeus portrays

---

[7] Ibid., 72, 80.

[8] Ibid., 72, 102.

[9] Ibid., 72, 120.

Mary at the foot of the Cross in an attitude of great courage and interior strength. Taking his inspiration from St. Ambrose, he writes:

> To stand [by the Cross] amid such heartfelt bitterness is a sign of great constancy; to refrain from tears denotes supreme self-control. She held back her tears out of a sense of delicacy; she remained standing because of her sublime greatness of spirit. And so sorrow did not force tears out of her, nor did pain beat down her spirit.[10]

In experiencing the mystery of her Son's Resurrection and glorification in heaven, Mary is filled with rejoicing; and this is the effect of the gift of *counsel*:

> O Blessed [Virgin], you have your joy. Your desire has been fulfilled, and Christ, the crown of your head, has given you the sovereignty of heaven through grace, the governance of the world through mercy, and dominion over the underworld through vengeance.[11]

In the mystery of her Assumption into heaven, Mary perceives the glory of God with full *understanding*, and in this consists her immense beatitude. Still, even in heaven, she is concerned for us mortals:

> From heaven the all-glorious Virgin comes to the aid of us below, and with her all-powerful prayer she drives out all evils and obtains all goods. For all those who ask her from the bottom of their hearts, she makes herself a protection in this present life and in the life to come. Recalling the purpose for which she became the Mother of the Redeemer, she gladly receives the prayers of every sinner and intercedes with her Son for all the faults of the repentant.[12]

Finally, the gift of *wisdom* brings the Virgin to the perfection of heavenly glory, which will be full when the full number of the elect reaches salvation:

> For she rejoices in the salvation of all the elect, beyond everything that may be expressed or believed, knowing that it was for their sake that the Son of God took flesh from her. Then Mary will be made perfect, because God has considered it best that she not be brought to perfection without us.[13]

---

[10] Ibid., 72, 156.

[11] Ibid., 72, 162.

[12] Ibid., 72, 202.

[13] Ibid., 72, 70.

Mary's Role in the Glory of God

Amadeus, following an already established tradition, is fond of emphasizing the mission that Mary continues to fulfill in heaven for the good of men. She works, not only for the salvation of souls, but also for the material needs of those who are devoted to her. Amadeus recalls that many miracles are worked through her intercession in places consecrated to Marian devotion.[14]

Mary's motherly and active care for us calls forth trust from the hearts of the faithful; this trust is expressed as prayer:

> O clement, O loving, O sweet Mary, when the day of wrath, tribulation, and anguish comes, may we not be punished according to our guilt, but through you, O Lady, may we be found worthy of the mercy of him who ascended to the Father to prepare a place for his servants.[15]

READINGS

MARY IN THE GLORY OF GOD

Therefore with unfailing reverence let us honor the Queen of heaven, the Mother of life, the Font of mercy, overflowing with delights and resting upon her Beloved, and let us proclaim her, even though our praise be less than adequate. . . .

The all-glorious [Virgin Mary], completely unsullied in her body, all-peaceful in her spirit, the most mild of all the living, is more humble and holy than all others. She has been lifted up above all and received into paradise by the inhabitants of heaven with the greatest honors, like an empress, and by the supreme Father bidden to take her seat in the kingdom of eternal splendor, on the throne of the most excellent glory, first after the Son, whom she brought forth in his Incarnation.

O great, terrible, and mighty God of inexpressible goodness, you lift up and exalt your humble handmaid to the place from which you once drove out the envious foe, that humility might triumph, enriched by an increase of graces and an august crown bestowed by you, while empty and dark pride dissolves into dust!

---

[14] Ibid., 72, 216.
[15] Ibid., 72, 220.

The all-blessed [Virgin], outstanding for her singular merit, stands in the presence of the Creator, always interceding for us with her mighty prayer. For, taught by that light, in which everything stands naked and revealed, our sweet and kind Lady sees all our dangers, and has mercy on us with a motherly heart. . . .

—Amadeus of Lausanne, Homily 8; SC 72, 206–10

OUR HELPER AND MEDIATRIX

In God's provident design, she was called Mary, that is, "Star of the Sea", that by her name she might declare what she shows even more clearly in reality. For because she has gone up to heaven to reign with her Son, robed in beauty, and so equally robed in strength, *she has girded herself* [with strength] to calm the *mighty raging sea* with a mere nod of her head (cf. Ps 92:1, 4). Those who sailed on the sea of the present world and called upon her with full confidence she has rescued from the blowing of storm and winds and led them, rejoicing with her, to the shores of the blessed homeland. . . .

In her loving vigilance, she anticipates and heals, not only the needs of spiritual salvation, but what is needful for the physical health of the human body. In places dedicated to the memory of her holiness, she obtains mobility for the lame, sight for the blind, hearing for the deaf, speech for the mute, caring for all kinds of diseases, and she offers the blessing of healings beyond number.

The guilty come to her threshold, beating their breasts, confessing their crimes, and, having received forgiveness, return home full of joy. . . .

Willingly she hears their prayers and the prayers of all who cry to her about whatever troubles them, and, by begging her Son, this merciful Mother turns aside every evil from them. . . .

But we need to observe and carefully consider with what great affection, with what great kindness she embraces and loves those joined to her in purity of spirit while, as has often been said, she never ceases by her intervention to deliver wicked and criminal men from the death of sin and from eternal suffering.

—Amadeus of Lausanne, *Homily 8*; SC 72, 212–16

8

AELRED OF RIEVAULX
(d. 1167)

This author, who was canonized by the Church, owes his fame to his solid theological and ascetical works.[1] Because of his writings, he was put almost on the same level as St. Bernard, and in fact Aelred assimilated Bernard's spirituality to a remarkable degree. He is undoubtedly the best-qualified representative of Cistercian monasticism of his time in England.

Aelred was born in Hexham in about 1100. After serving as a young page in the Scottish court, he entered the Cistercian abbey of Rievaulx in 1133. In 1142, he was transferred to the monastery of Revesby, in Lincolnshire, where he had been named abbot. Then, in 1147, he returned to Rievaulx to take the same position there. He spent the rest of his life there, apart from a brief period in which he returned to Scotland on a missionary voyage. He died in 1167, after spending his last years in suffering brought on by ill health and borne with exemplary serenity and abandonment to God's will.

To the end of his days, he was an expert and untiring guide of souls as well as a wise and experienced administrator of monastic life. In the list of his works, made up chiefly of treatises, short works (*opusculi*), and sermons, those that pay the most attention to the Blessed Virgin are the Marian sermons, especially those composed for the feasts of the Nativity of the Virgin, the Annunciation, the Purification, and the Assumption.[2]

---

[1] His works are published in PL 195 and in *Aelredi Rievallensis Sermones inediti*, ed. C. H. Talbot, Series Scriptorum S. Ordinis Cistercensis, 1 (Rome, 1952). Already in his own time there was special praise for his *Speculum charitatis*, a treatise on Christian perfection, and the brief work *De spirituali amicitia*, written in the form of a Ciceronian dialogue discussing Christian existence.

[2] Bibliography: A. Agius, "St. Aelred and Our Blessed Lady", *Downside Review* 64 (1946): 32–38; C. Dumont, "St. Aelred and the Assumption", *The Life of the Spirit*

His vision of the personal relationship between God and the Virgin is so full of love and expressed in a language so charged with affectivity that one author has called it "erotic".[3] Aelred is heavily inspired by the Song of Songs. In the Annunciation, he sees the celebration of a true marriage between God and Mary,[4] a marriage with extraordinary results:

> The Virgin did not lose her virginity in this marriage; God did not lose his divinity in this marriage; the angel did not lose his dignity in this marriage. But there is an even greater miracle in this marriage. The Bridegroom is the Son, the Bride is the Mother, because the Son has joined the soul of that most blessed Virgin to his divinity, since God himself, made man, came forth from her womb "like a bridegroom leaving his chamber" (Ps 19:5).[5]

This spiritual marriage means that Mary entered, not only into a maternal relationship with the incarnate Word, but into a spousal relationship as well.

Mary, the Ideal Creature

The Bible witnesses to the physical beauty of Rachel (cf. Gen 29:17), and this makes Aelred think that Mary, too, must have been exceptionally attractive. Nevertheless, it was above all her purity, charity, humility, and all her other wonderful virtues that literally caught the Lord's attention. In fact, the Lord came down to earth, not only to live in her soul, but also to become incarnate in her womb:

> While it may be pleasant to hold the opinion that blessed Mary was very fair and very beautiful in her body as well, nevertheless we should apply these words to her inner beauty. But who could speak suitably of her inner beauty? Only he, who is "the fairest of the sons of men" (Ps 45:2).

---

8 (1953): 205–10; idem, "Aspects de la dévotion du Bx. Aelred à Notre-Dame", CollOrdCistRef 20 (1958): 313–26; A. Haller, Un éducateur monastique: Aelred de Rievaulx (Paris, 1959); M. Garrido Bonaño, "La Virgen María en las reglas monásticas y en las constituciones religiosas hasta el siglo XVIII", in Virgo Liber Verbi (Rome: Edizioni Marianum, 1991), pp. 393–94.

[3] Hilda Graef, Mary: A History of Doctrine and Devotion (New York: Sheed and Ward, 1964), p. 249; F. Buck, "The Marian Interpretation of the Song of Songs in the Middle Ages", in CongrRom 4:87.

[4] Sermo in Annuntiatione; PL 195, 253D–254A.

[5] Ibid.

More than any other creature, he loved her, desired her, hallowed her, so
that he might not only inhabit her mind but prepare himself a dwelling
place in her womb as well. . . . Surely, when he was in the bosom of the
Father, even then he smelled the fragrance of her virginity and regarded
the beauty of her soul.[6]

Mary's soul must have possessed such a richness of perfection that any
sort of moral shadow whatever was excluded, and she was raised up
above every other creature:

"Many daughters have gathered up riches, but she alone has surpassed all
the others"(Prov 31:29), because, just as her virginity was unique and her
chastity beyond compare, just so her holiness exceeded that of all others.
She was the only woman in the world to whom it could truly be said,
"You are all fair, my love; there is no flaw in you" (Song 4:7).[7]

Sometimes Aelred will even apply to Mary scriptural statements that
refer to Christ, as in the following example:

"Hail, full of grace" (Lk 1:28). Yes, full, [of the grace of him] "from
whose fullness we have all received" (Jn 1:16). No one else has a truer
humility, a more powerful obedience; no one has a purer justice, a more
abundant mercy, a more fruitful purity, a richer charity.[8]

Obviously, this statement does not deny the uniqueness of the fullness
of grace in the incarnate Word, from whom the Virgin herself received
the grace she possessed. In another text, we see Aelred apply to Mary the
words Isaiah spoke about the Messiah to come:

The Spirit of the Lord truly rested upon Mary, the Spirit of wisdom
and understanding, the Spirit of counsel and fortitude, the Spirit of
knowledge and piety, and the Spirit of the fear of the Lord filled her
(cf. Is 11:2).[9]

Assumed into Heaven

In a sermon that may have been composed during the early years of his
preaching career, Aelred considered Mary's bodily assumption into heaven

---

[6] Ibid.

[7] *Sermo in Assumptione*; Talbot, 162.

[8] *Sermo in Annuntiatione Dominica*; Talbot, 80.

[9] *Sermo in Assumptione*; Talbot, 165.

questionable,[10] no doubt because of the influence of St. Bernard's teaching. But later, he accepted the argument of the famous tenth/eleventh-century text of the pseudo-Augustine[11] and affirmed this Marian mystery without hesitation:

> No wonder that the holy Mother of God, who from his infancy stayed with him in his trials, should also be taken up to heaven in her body and lifted up above the choirs of angels.[12]

Mary's Mediation

Aelred expresses himself extremely clearly and even boldly when speaking on this theme. He compares the Virgin to a ship, which enables us to cross the stormy ocean of this world to reach Jesus. She is the way that leads to him. Her fullness of grace is seen as an important factor in restoring the order of salvation:

> By means of this grace, the elements [of the world] are renewed, the infernal regions are destroyed, and the heavenly regions are restored; men are set free, and demons are trampled underfoot.[13]

This mediation makes its effects felt on individual believers, in the context of their saving relationship with God:

> Observe that whoever is praised in the Lord (cf. Ps 33:3) merits to be praised only through the mediation of Mary's merits.[14]

The effectiveness of Mary's mediation depends on her maternal relationship with her Son, while her readiness to help is understandable because of her merciful feelings for us:

> For it is not right that the Son should deny her anything. . . . She is the Mother of Mercy and so gladly stands ready, prepared to hear the desires of those who call upon her, and for them all, she obtains the result they hoped for.[15]

---

[10] Ibid., PL 195, 315B.

[11] PL 40, 1140–48. Cf. G. Quadrio, *Il trattato "De Assumptione B. M. V." dello Pseudo-Agostino e il suo influsso nella teologia assunzionistica latina*, Analecta Gregoriana 7 (Rome, 1951).

[12] *Sermo in Assumptione*; Talbot, 162.

[13] *Sermo in Annuntiatione Dominica*; Talbot, 90.

[14] *Sermo in Assumptione*; Talbot, 162.

[15] Ibid., Talbot, 166.

Mary exercises her mediation in concrete circumstances, which our author is fond of listing in detail, albeit in language that cannot be taken literally:

> So great is her love for the human race that, just as her Son is recognized as the Mediator between his Father and man, so she stands as Mediatrix between us and her Son; she turns away his wrath, calls forth his mercy, begs his favor, defers punishment, so that she has often put back into its sheath the sword of rage that had already been drawn from its sheath to be used against the human race.[16]

We may observe that the first statement in this text resolves, in absolutely precise terms, the problem of the relationship between Jesus' mediation and his Mother's mediation. Aelred does not place Mary between us and her Son, as a kind of obstacle. Christ exercises his mediation on our behalf directly, while Mary's mediation is added to it, so that it may be termed a contributory mediation.

Spiritual Mother

In understanding the mystery of Mary's spiritual motherhood, Aelred made great progress, surpassing the thought of his own master, St. Bernard. He believes that Christians are truly born from Mary, in the sense that Mary is at the head of a line of descendants that stands in contrast with Eve's descendants:

> Through Mary, we were born in a better way than through Eve, since Christ was born from Mary. . . . She is our Mother, . . . the Mother of our light. . . . Therefore she is more our Mother than our mothers in the flesh, because our better birth comes from her.[17]

The motherhood Aelred is speaking of here derives, not from nature, but from the divine motherhood by which Mary brought Christ our light into the world. The fact that it was a spiritual, not a natural, motherhood takes nothing away from it, so that Aelred can justly write:

> Certainly, brothers, she is truly our Mother. For we were born through her; by her we are fed; by her aid we grow.[18]

---

[16] *Sermo in Annuntiatione Dominica*; Talbot, 81–82.

[17] *Sermo 2 in Nativitate*; PL 195, 323C.

[18] Ibid., PL 195, 323A.

Devotion to Our Lady and Queen

It is not enough to love and honor Mary as our Mother. She is also our Lady and Queen and so deserves our homage and service:

> We also owe her our service, because she is our Lady. For the Bride of our Lord is our Lady; the Bride of our King is our Queen; so let us serve her.[19]

Clearly, this approach is inspired by the medieval concept of the relationship between man and woman and formed in the spirit and according to the rules of the chivalry of Aelred's time.[20] The monk whom the preacher addressed in this sermon was supposed to serve the Virgin, just as a knight would place himself at his lady's service.

Devotion to Mary is no excuse for a lack of commitment to the duties of the Christian life, nor is it an excuse to abuse Mary's goodness:

> Let no one say: Though I should do this or that against the Lord, I don't much care; I will serve Holy Mary and will be safe. It is not so. As soon as a man offends the Son, he surely offends the Mother, as well.[21]

True devotion also includes imitation.[22] Whatever level of the Christian life one may have reached, he can always look to Mary as his model. It is also necessary to pray to Mary because she is the way that divine mercy reaches us. She has a powerful influence over her Son, and she is merciful to us; therefore, she hears the prayers addressed to her: "Never can he fail who is helped by such assistance."[23] Prayer to Mary should lead to spiritual communion with her.

To nurture the devotion of the many women who led an eremetical life in England during his day, Aelred inserted into the rules compiled for them some reflections on Mary's life, in which he invites them to identify with the events that the Lord's Mother experienced. For example, the hermitesses were exhorted to enter Mary's room in Nazareth, in spirit, together with the angel; to greet her with him, repeating over and over "Ave Maria!"; to try to experience the same feelings she felt as she heard the angel's words. Then they were supposed to follow along

---

[19] Ibid., PL 195, 323D–324A.
[20] See Graef, *Mary*, pp. 249–50.
[21] *Sermo 2 in Nativitate*; PL 195, 323C–324A.
[22] Ibid.
[23] *Sermo 3 in Assumptione*; PL 195, 336A.

with the Virgin as she went to visit Elizabeth and follow her to Bethlehem when she gave birth to Jesus. At the moment of the Passion, he asks them to join their tears to those of the sorrowful Mother:

> But you, virgin, whose confidence in the Virgin's Son is greater than that of the women who stand far off, go up to the Cross with the Virgin Mary and the virgin disciple, stand close and look upon his face, awash in pallor. How now? Will your eyes be without tears when you see the tears of your dearly beloved Lady? Will you remain dry-eyed when the sword of sorrow has passed through her soul? Will you not sob when you hear him saying to his Mother, "Woman, behold your son", and saying to John, "Behold your mother", as he entrusts his Mother to his disciple and promises paradise to the thief? [24]

Aelred is proposing a kind of meditation on the episodes that will later become the mysteries of the Rosary.

READINGS

SORROW AT THE LOSS OF JESUS

Show me, O my sweetest Lady, Mother of my Lord, what was in your heart then, what wonder, what joy, when you found your sweetest Son, the boy Jesus, not among the other boys, but among the doctors. What did you feel when you saw that every eye was intent upon him, that every ear was pricked up to hear him, when everyone great and small, learned and unlearned alike, was speaking about his judgment and his answers?

"I found", she says, "him whom my soul loves. I held him, and would not let him go" (Song 3:4). Hold him, O sweetest Lady; hold the one you love; fall upon his neck; hug him; kiss him; and so make up for his three-day absence with multiplied delights.

"Son, why have you done this to us? See, your father and I were looking for you sorrowing" (Lk 2:48). Again I ask you, O my Lady, why were you sorrowing? I believe that you were not afraid that the boy would be harmed by hunger or thirst or not eating, for you knew that he was God. Rather you were simply bemoaning the loss of the inexpress-

---

[24] *De institutione inclusarum* 31; CCM 1:671.

ible delights of his presence, if only for a little while. For the Lord Jesus is so sweet to those who taste him, so beautiful to those who see him, so lovable to those who embrace him that his absence, though it be short, provokes the greatest possible suffering.

—Aelred of Rievaulx, *Cum factus esset Jesus annorum duodecim*;
SC 60, 64

MARY, THE BRIDE OF CHRIST

"While the king was on his couch, my nard gave forth its fragrance" (Song 1:12). Surely, when he was in the bosom of the Father, even then he smelled the fragrance of her virginity and considered the beauty of her soul. And so today his angel was sent to announce his coming, not only into her heart, but even into her flesh. See, brothers, what kind of marriage this is and how heavenly, in which the bridegroom is God, the bride is the Virgin, and the groomsman is an angel. The Virgin did not lose her virginity in this marriage; God did not lose his divinity in this marriage; the angel did not lose his dignity in this marriage.

But there is an even greater miracle in this marriage. The Bridegroom is the Son, the Bride is the Mother, because the Son has joined the soul of that most blessed Virgin to his divinity, since God himself, made man, came forth from her womb "like a bridegroom leaving his chamber" (Ps 19:5). Rightly, therefore, did the angel greet her, saying, "Hail, full of grace, the Lord is with you; blessed are you among women" (Lk 1:28 and 42).

—Aelred of Rievaulx, *In Annuntiatione, sermo 9*, 15–16;
PL 195, 254A–B

9

ISAAC OF STELLA
(d. ca. 1169)

Isaac was an enthusiastic spiritual disciple of St. Bernard. He felt a strong attraction to Bernard and his teaching throughout his life, following in the line of his Marian doctrine and devotion. In addition to his affectionate attitude toward Bernard, however, he was also able to make his own contribution, which was original in content and built on a sound theological basis. We can easily place him among the best theologians of his time.

Isaac was born in England at the beginning of the twelfth century. He received a good education that eventually led to his great interest in theological speculation and allowed him to compose powerful and profound works of theology.

He loved to work in the fields and kept up this passion even later in life, letting it become part of his spirituality, making it an occasion of obedience to the law of God, a way to expiate his own sins and to practice charity toward his neighbor, since his agricultural work allowed him to practice almsgiving and hospitality toward the needy.

Following a vocation to the Cistercian religious life, he lived in various monasteries, finally entering one near Poitiers called Stella ("the Star"), in 1145. Two years later he became its abbot. He died around 1169.

The best of his thought is found in his sermons, which are theologically rich, logically well-structured, and convincing in their argumentation. They also reveal a subtle intuition into the psychology of his listeners and a capacity to strike a chord in the deepest places of their hearts and minds. In this collection, we find four sermons dedicated to Marian themes: three celebrating the mystery of Mary's Assumption and one on her Nativity.[1]

---

[1] The works of Isaac of Stella are published in PL 194. His sermons were published in a critical edition in SC 130, 207, and 339. Bibliography: G. Raciti, in DS 7:2011–38;

The development of Isaac's Marian thought is strictly connected to that of his ecclesiology. The famous text in which he proposes the Mary–Church parallel is mentioned in a footnote in *Lumen Gentium*.[2]

An Ecclesiological Mariology

Isaac's clear insight into Mary's function within the mystery of the Church made him one of the forerunners of contemporary Mariology. During the lifetime of the abbot of Stella, the mutual symbolic relationship between Mary and the Church, that appealing intuition of the Fathers, had already become part of the Cistercian tradition.[3] Isaac produced, as it were, its classic formulation, based on the principle of the distinction between universal, particular, and special.

According to this principle, which (among other sources) is inspired by Sacred Scripture, what is said in a general sense of the Church can be applied in a particular sense to the individual Christ and in a special sense to the Blessed Virgin. Obviously, the converse is also true.[4]

While reflection on the mystery of the Church is needed to achieve an exact knowledge of Mary and her mission in the plan of salvation, it is also true that contemplating the mystery of the Virgin Mother of God opens up perspectives for a deeper vision of the mystery of the virgin mother Church. Indeed, what is difficult to understand in a reality that is both spiritual and physical, such as the salvific community of believers, can become more clear when seen in the light of a single person, such as Mary. The Church and Mary, then, are two realities that become understandable when they are considered together.

Mary, the Virgin Earth

From the ancient tradition of the Church Fathers, Isaac draws a parallel between the virgin earth of paradise, from which Adam was formed, and Mary Ever-Virgin, in whose womb the second Adam took flesh:

J. Beumer, "Mariologie und Ekklesiologie bei Isaak von Stella", *Münchener Theologische Zeitschrift* 5 (1954): 48–61.

[2] LG 64, 8.

[3] Suffice it to recall the explicit statement of Serlo of Savigny, who wrote, "The same [Mary] is represented by the Church, and the Church by Mary" (*Homily on the Nativity of the B. V. M.* 1, in BiblPatCist. 6 (Paris: L. Billaine, 1664), p. 117.

[4] *Sermo 51 in Assumptione*; PL 194, 1863A; SC 339, 202–4.

There man was brought forth from earth; here God is brought forth from Mary. There, from earth still incorrupt and virgin, comes an upright man, himself a virgin; here from Mary, always incorrupt and virginal, comes the just God, himself making virgins. There, from the side of the man, woman was created without a woman [to act as mother]; here, from a woman's womb, a man is generated without a man [to act as father]. There, from the rib of a sleeping man, a woman is built up to be a helpmate; here, from the side of the dying Christ, a Bride is consecrated. There, flesh is supplied in place of the rib [that was taken]; here, in exchange for the power that is given, weakness is assumed. There, we see two in one flesh; here, there are no longer two but one in one spirit.[5]

Mary in the Mystical Body

Under the influence of St. Augustine's thought, the Abbot of Stella notes that certain scriptural expressions cannot be understood except in reference to the whole Christ, whose Body is made up of Christ himself and all believers.

Christ, as God, is born of the Father in an eternal generation; as the incarnate Word, he was brought into the world by Mary in a temporal generation. As Head of our Body, he is born together with the Body from the Holy Spirit and the Church in a mystical generation that is prolonged over the centuries.

We must consider that there is simultaneously one Son and a multitude of sons, so that both Mary and the Church are true mothers of Christ. But each of the two, taken separately, is not mother of the whole Christ. In this view, Mary shares the mystery of her motherhood with the Church.

Conceiving by the power of the Holy Spirit, Mary gives birth physically to the Son of God; the Church, also conceiving by means of the Holy Spirit, gives birth spiritually to sons of God, who form a single Body with Christ the Head.

Thanks to the intervention of the Holy Spirit, the Son of God had a generation without sin; the other sons of God, instead, are reborn in the baptismal font, where they received the remission of their sins, by the power of the Holy Spirit. The Spirit is the mysterious agent of both births. Isaac writes:

---

[5] *Sermo 54 in Nativitate*; PL 194, 1873CD; SC 339, 252–54.

It was by the Spirit that the Son of Man, our Head, was born from the Virgin's womb. And by that same Spirit, we, the sons of God, his Body, are born again from the font of baptism. And just as he was completely without sin, so we too are [baptized] unto the remission of all sins.[6]

The Motherhood of Mary and the Motherhood of the Church

While Mary's motherhood and that of the Church have a single reality as their goal: Christ the Head and his members, or "one single Son and many sons", Mary and the Church are simultaneously one single Mother and two distinct Mothers. Neither of the two Mothers, taken separately, is able to give birth to the whole Christ. Isaac repeats this:

Both are Mothers of Christ, but neither of the two gives birth to the whole Christ without the other.[7]

Not only the universal Church, but also her individual members exercise this motherhood along with Mary. Our author maintains this by appealing to the principle of the universal and the particular:

"I will dwell in the Lord's inheritance" (Sir 24:11). The Lord's inheritance, in the universal sense, is the Church; in a special sense, it is Mary; in an individual sense, it is every faithful soul. Christ dwelled for nine months in the tabernacle of Mary's womb; in the tabernacle of the Church's faith, he will dwell until the final consummation of the world; and in the knowledge and love of the faithful soul, he will dwell forever and ever.[8]

For the faithful soul, however, this motherhood is not a preexistent reality but, rather, a commitment involving one's whole life. Through an unceasing progress in faith, hope, and generosity, the faithful soul is called humbly to draw nearer to the unattainable dignity and holiness of the Mother of God.

Mary in Heavenly Glory

While Isaac may have left us three sermons on Mary's Assumption, he expresses himself with a certain caution when speaking of this mystery, especially with regard to the fate of the Blessed Virgin's earthly body:

---

[6] *Sermo 42 in Ascensione*; PL 194, 1832B; SC 339, 50–52.

[7] *Sermo 51 in Assumptione*; PL 194, 1863A; SC 339, 204.

[8] Ibid., PL 194, 1865C; SC 339, 214–16.

Today—whether with her body or without, I do not know; God knows!—she has been taken up, not snatched up for a time or to the third heaven only—if there is more than one heaven—but to an everlasting and blessed dwelling, in the highest region of the heavens.[9]

Apart from this hesitation about the bodily aspect of the mystery, Isaac proclaims the Virgin's extraordinary glorification in heaven:

Once, Queen Esther rose from her couch among the women in the palace of King Ahasuerus and rested in her beloved's embrace (cf. Esther 15). Today, this woman, the Queen of the world, is snatched away from the wicked world; she leaves the couch of the earthly Church, ascending above all the wives and widows, and with the virgins she is bathed and adorned. Yet she outshines all the virgins. For "even though many daughters have piled up treasures", she "has surpassed them all" (Prov 31:29).[10]

The abbot of Stella also considers Mary's heavenly glorification in terms of the role she is called to play on our behalf before God's throne:

Today she enters the presence of the King, her Son and Bridegroom, to intercede for her people (cf. Esther 5:1). Even this King's own Mother would not be able to bear the sight of his majestic face, "unless in sign of clemency the King should extend his golden scepter toward her" (Esther 4:11). . . .

Nevertheless, the Mother enters her Son's presence more confidently than all the rest, not so much because she alone gave birth to him as because she loved him in a unique way.[11]

Faithful to Cistercian tradition, which was nourished on the doctrine of St. Bernard, the abbot of Stella does not neglect to admire and exalt the goodness and mercy of this glorious Queen, who, standing before God's throne, never ceases to help her many children in every way.

---

[9] Ibid., PL 194, 1862B; SC 339, 198–200.

[10] *Sermo 52 in Assumptione*; PL 194, 1867B; SC 339, 222–224.

[11] Ibid., PL 194, 1867BC; SC 339, 224.

READINGS

MARY AND THE CHURCH ARE ONE AND THE SAME MOTHER

There is but one Christ, one single and whole Christ, Head and Body. He is the one [Son] of the one God in heaven and of one Mother on earth. He is both many sons and one Son. For as Head and members are one Son and many sons, so Mary and the Church are one Mother and many mothers, one Virgin and many virgins. Both are mothers, both are virgins; each one conceived by the power of the same Spirit, without carnal desire; each one brought forth offspring to God the Father without sinning.

Mary gave birth to a Head for the body without any sin; the Church brought forth a body for the Head in granting the remission of all sins [in baptism]. Both are Mothers of Christ, but neither of the two gives birth to the whole Christ without the other. Whence what is said in the divinely inspired Sacred Scripture in a universal sense about the virgin mother Church is said in an individual sense about the Virgin Mary. And what is said in a special sense about the Virgin Mother Mary is rightly understood to apply to the virgin mother Church in a general sense. And when a text speaks of one or the other, its content may be applied almost without distinction to either one.

Every faithful soul, in the way suited to each, is understood to be the bride of God's Word, as mother, daughter, and sister of Christ and as a fruitful virgin. Therefore, what is said by the very wisdom of God, which is the Word of the Father, is said in a universal sense in reference to the Church, in a special sense in reference to Mary, and in an individual sense in reference to the faithful soul.

—Isaac of Stella, *Sermo 51 in Assumptione*;
PL 194, 1863AB; SC 339, 202–4

MARY ASSUMED INTO HEAVEN

Today, Mary has ascended from the desert of this world, not without the wonderment of the heavenly powers, who never saw anything like this before, that someone should escape this world and take up her seat above the thrones and choirs of them all. Whence it was said, "Who is she, that comes up out of the desert, full of delights?" (Song 8:5). Delights are the fruits of virtues. Now virtues, while they are still sprouting or beginning to blossom or forming fruit that is not yet ripe, are somewhat bitter or difficult or sad. But to those who have practiced the virtues to the very end, these same virtues bring the very peaceful and sweet fruit of justice. When an almond has reached the time of its maturity, when its husks have been shed and the shell opened, one finally gets to the agreeable sweetness of the nut, and what developed over a long time is picked with pleasure and joy. Just so it is no wonder that, at the end of this life, when all the effort of practicing the virtues has ceased, we shall delight solely in the pure and simple enjoyment of the virtues.

Because, in this life, the Blessed Virgin Mary flowered in the virtues more than anyone else (so that she rightly conceived by the Holy Spirit himself, immediately, at Nazareth), now on her heavenly throne, as in the house of bread,[12] she is filled to overflowing with all delights, resting upon her Beloved, whom she formed so happily in faith and delight, not so much in her flesh as in her heart.[13]

Therefore it is said, "Blessed, rather, are they who hear the word of God and keep it!" (Lk 11:28). In the meantime, while her Spouse waits to gather in his ripe myrrh along with spices, he often comes to visit the garden of nuts, to see whether the vines are flowering and bearing pomegranates (cf. Song 6:11).

—Isaac of Stella, *Sermo 52 in Assumptione*;
PL 194, 1867–68; SC 339, 222–26

---

[12] An obvious allusion to the city of Bethlehem, whose name means "house of bread" (see Jerome, *Epist. 108*, 10; PL 22, 885) and where Mary's womb brought forth the fruit conceived at Nazareth, which means "flower" (see Jerome, *Epist. 46*, 12; PL 22, 491). In this text, Isaac of Stella applies the likeness to the personal life of the Virgin: in heaven, she gathers the fruits of that flowering of virtue which she had cultivated on earth.

[13] There are clear echoes here of the patristic tradition; one thinks especially of St. Augustine.

10

PHILIP OF HARVENG
(d. 1183)

Philip of Harveng follows in the line of the Marian teaching of St. Bernard and the commentary on the Song of Songs of Rupert of Deutz. He was a Belgian monk and theologian who lived during an important period for the renewal of religious life in the West. He, too, was inspired by the Song of Songs and worked out his own original Marian doctrine of ample proportions.

We can reconstruct a very basic outline of his life, based on a few indications in his own writings. He was born at Harveng in the early years of the twelfth century to a poor family. He began his studies at an episcopal school, probably at Cambrai. He was keen on the study of classical literature, of which he acquired a deep and wide-ranging knowledge, so that references to the authors of classical antiquity are frequently met with in his works. He was among the first disciples of St. Norbert of Xanten, who in 1120 had founded the order of the Canons Regular of Prémontré, giving them the rule of St. Augustine. It may be that Philip was sent to study at Paris. In any case we know that he entered the monastery of Bonne-Espérance around 1130, and the fact that he was soon named prior might show that he was among the first monks of that monastery, together with the abbot, Odo. The actions of a monk who left Bonne-Espérance and was received by St. Bernard at Cîteaux led to serious difficulties for Philip. In 1149 he had to give up being prior and leave the monastery to take refuge in another. Once his innocence was recognized, the general chapter of the order restored him as prior of Bonne-Espérance in 1151. In 1158, he was named to succeed Odo as abbot. He voluntarily gave up that office a few months before his death, which occurred on April 11, 1183.

Philip of Harveng won a place in monastic history as a great abbot and important writer. Because of his works, the abbey of Bonne-Espérance became an important center of learning. He was a man of wide-ranging knowledge, both in the field of classical learning and in the sacred sciences. His expert knowledge of St. Augustine's thought strongly marked his exegesis, in which allegorical interpretations clearly have pride of place. Augustine's teaching also shaped his christological and anthropological ideas.

His most important work is a commentary on the Song of Songs,[1] in which he reveals his deep familiarity with Sacred Scripture and the Fathers of the Church, along with the theological precision and correctness of his ascetical doctrine. Following the example of Rupert of Deutz, Philip interprets the Song of Songs in a thoroughly Marian key.

Mary and Her Son

Influenced by the Augustinian concept of original sin and the teaching of his more recent master, St. Bernard, our author does not grant Mary the privilege of the Immaculate Conception. In fact, he goes so far as to attribute to her some small actual sins and to associate her with the common lot of all human beings, calling her a "daughter of wrath".[2]

Nevertheless, still following the bishop of Hippo, who, apart from original sin, did not hesitate to exempt the Blessed Virgin from every other sin, Philip considers her an exceptional creature. With regard to holiness, she is inferior to Christ alone. The special action of God, which made the Virgin a suitable and worthy Mother of his Son, is located by Philip, not at the moment of her conception but, rather, before the Incarnation. It was then that Mary was purified from every interior stain[3] and her soul totally freed to be united to her Son and to

---

[1] PL 203, 181–490 [Philip's commentary on the Song of Songs is remarkable in that it is composed entirely in rhyming verse. We have not attempted to reproduce this unusual feature in our English translation.—TRANS]. For the Marian thought of Philip of Harveng, see Fr. Petit, "La Doctrine mariale de Philippe de Bonne-Espérance: Note de spiritualité norbertine", AnPraem 13 (1937): 97–108; H. Riedlinger, "Maria und die Kirche in den marianischen Hohenliedkommentaren des Mittelalters", in CongrLourd 3:241–89; J. B. Valvekens, "Spiritus Sanctus et Beata Deipara-Virgo apud auctores Praemonstratenses saeculi XII, potissimum apud Philippum de Harveng", AnPraem 67 (1981): 103–13.

[2] In Cantica Canticorum 6, 14; PL 203, 459A.

[3] Ibid., 1, 17; PL 203, 227B.

become like him.[4] Thus she could conceive the incarnate Word without experiencing the influence of concupiscence.

Mary's beauty was not merely interior; it extended to her body as well. Christ himself decided to choose a beautiful mother, with pretty eyes and a rosy complexion.[5]

The mystery of the Incarnation is compared to the union of bridegroom and bride in the Song of Songs. Jesus celebrated this wonderful marriage in his Mother's womb,[6] and the terms in which this marital union is described manifest a strongly erotic realism:

> It is not only the Mother who embraces the Son so tenderly, but also the Bride who embraces the Bridegroom. Both he and she rejoice in this mutual embrace, and when he kisses her, he also rests sweetly between her breasts. . . . Rightly then does the Virgin say that her Bridegroom rests between her breasts; in other words, their tender love is strengthened by the bond of their embrace.[7]

It is easy to recognize in this text an obvious example of the use of the romantic language of the time, which expresses sentiments going far beyond the simply sensual and erotic. In the Virgin's case, it is not the eyes that see, but her mind, which, under the impulse of devotion and love, pictures a relationship of deep spiritual intimacy. Philip thinks that the tone of the Song of Songs is well suited to expressing the richness of Mary's feelings.

Assumed into the Glory of Heaven

Adopting the argument of the pseudo-Augustine,[8] Philip defends the truth of Mary's bodily assumption into heaven. He writes:

> The Mother is with her Son, not only in spirit—and of this there is not the slightest doubt—but also in body, which does not seem at all impossible to believe. For even though the canonical Scriptures do not proclaim

---

[4] Ibid., 1, 18; PL 203, 228D.

[5] Ibid., 2, 1; PL 203, 247AB.

[6] Ibid., 2, 6; PL 203, 258A.

[7] Ibid., 2, 11; PL 203, 271A.

[8] An apocryphal document that appeared at the end of the eleventh century or the beginning of the twelfth, and to which we have already referred.

it with any obvious proofs, pious faith is guided to this truth by plausible arguments.[9]

One of these arguments appears to be derived from the mystery of Mary's virginal motherhood, as a kind of corollary to it:

His Mother is above, she who furnished him with his very flesh and from her womb gave birth to the Man-God, without loss of her virginity.[10]

Mary and the Church

Philip speaks of the role Mary plays in the Church of the New Testament in relation to the moment the Church was born, when the Virgin was still on earth. She was entrusted with the task of presiding over the college of apostles:

To preside over assemblies is a sign of authority. The apostles were reminded to sit and be attentive to the Virgin who was presiding, so that she might impart orders to them and take care of them all as their Mother and so that they might listen to their Mother, as the Evangelist had stated.[11]

Mary's power over the apostles, then, is derived from her role as Mother, which is extended to all the faithful, as evidenced by the words Philip places on the lips of the Virgin herself:

When I lead you forth out of the darkness of ignorance, as if giving birth to you; when with zeal and labor I guide you to the light of truth and knowledge; when, with loving concern, I teach you the perfect rules of life, what is it I am doing if not taking the place of a mother and training you in conformity with my heart or, rather, with my conduct? Besides, the Bridegroom says to each one of you, "Behold your mother" (Jn 19:27).[12]

The reference to John 19:26–27 in the last two citations clearly shows Philip's intention to make a typological interpretation of this

---

[9] *In Cantica Canticorum*, 6, 50; PL 203, 488C.
[10] Ibid.
[11] Ibid., 2, 3; PL 203, 253B
[12] Ibid., 1, 19; Pl 203, 230C.

Gospel passage the foundation of his affirmation of Mary's spiritual motherhood.

The Virgin's Mediation in Heaven

After her entrance into heaven, the Virgin continues her mission within the Church, which consists in acting as a Mediatrix between men and her divine Son. She performs this role in virtue of her superiority over all creatures, both earthly and heavenly; however, this is a superiority of grace, not nature.[13] In the glory of heaven, Mary is inferior only to her Son. Philip teaches this in decidedly anthropomorphic terms:

> Therefore the Bride is rightly called Mediatrix of us all; the Mother is fittingly called Empress, because, asking favors of her Bridegroom, giving orders to her Son, she turns his anger into grace and his wrath into the most tender love.[14]

Philip describes Mary using the metaphor of the "neck", since she occupies an intermediate place between the head and the body. She joins two realities that had been separated and maintains their union, acting as a powerful and effective Mediatrix:

> A good neck, a good go-between; in sum, a good Mediatrix who reunites those whom Eve, the harmful separatrix, divided. She invites her Son to be generous and invites us to be obedient. She works to ensure that we will never fail to offer our submission to him and to ensure that he will never fail to confer his benefits upon us.[15]

The present mediation of the Virgin can be compared with the mediation she exercised in the mystery of the Incarnation. Then, through her, the Savior came down to us, while now, still through her, saved man can ascend to heaven. And it is precisely in the mystery of the salvation that Philip sees the Mother of the Lord at work. God chose her "that he might redeem, through her, those whom hereditary death had compelled to be damned".[16]

---

[13] Ibid., 4, 1; PL 203, 355C.
[14] Ibid., 4, 5; PL 203, 360D.
[15] Ibid., 2, 7; PL 203, 260D.
[16] Ibid., 6, 40; PL 203, 480A.

Philip's Mariology

The abbot of Bonne-Espérance speaks of Mary in other works as well. In his *Epistulae ad Johannem*,[17] taking up the arguments of the *De Trinitate* of St. Hilary of Poitiers, he takes the occasion to work out a complete doctrine of Mary's motherhood, examining the various texts Hilary cites on this theme.

But it is above all in the commentary on the Song of Songs that he shows his genius, for he was among the first theologians to discover an integrated allegory of the Virgin in this book of Scripture.[18] He presents the Song of Songs as a dramatic dialogue in which the divine Word and the Virgin Mother exchange their feelings for one another. Each of the two actors is followed by a throng singing hymns; the Word is accompanied by the first choir of angels, while the host of apostles and faithful follows after Mary.

This type of interpretation made it easy for Philip to expound both his Marian doctrine and his own feelings of devotion and love toward the Mother of the Lord.

READINGS

MOST BEAUTIFUL AMONG ALL WOMEN

That Virgin, whom the Son of God chose in advance, from all eternity, to be his Mother, in whom he took flesh at the appointed time, drawing himself together tightly, his limbs contracted, from whom he chose to be born in a new way, without breaking the enclosure of her flesh, whose Son he became without harming her chastity in any way, before his birth or after—I call her "Virgin of virgins". I consider it worthy of belief that she was more beautiful than all other women. And there is nothing wrong with such a belief.

Indeed, it is not believable that God, the Son of God, should choose a mother who was swarthy, one-eyed, conspicuously scrofulous or hunch-

---

[17] PL 203, 34–66.
[18] See N. L. Reuviaux, "La Dévotion à Notre Dame dans l'Ordre de Prémontré", in *Maria* 2:718.

backed, instead of having a white face, rosy-colored,[19] with pretty eyes and a beautiful, completely formed body, so that she who was chosen over all other women for such a dignified role should be, not only free from the infection of every vice, but also more beautiful and perfect in her physical appearance than anyone else.

Nevertheless, when she is called most beautiful among all women, this does not apply so much to the pleasing features of her face and the beauty of her body as to her perfect morals and her marvelous holiness. As the angel witnessed, she was full of grace. This is never said about any other woman, for she was the only woman who merited to become the Mother of the only Christ.

Observing her spiritual beauty, the angel said, "Blessed are you among women" (Lk 1:28).[20] And among all women she is so, in comparison to the rest; she is blessed, compared to those upon whom a harsh curse was inflicted by Eve's fault and who are conformed by wretched law to Eve, the first sinner, and subjected to sins, deformed in their maternal likeness. Among these others, wretched and deformed,[21] a fuller beauty has been granted to this Virgin, who has overcome the ancient curse and the hereditary law. As the Spirit overshadowed her, she put away from herself the passion of wickedness and the stain of sin and set herself up higher than all other women by the merits of her innocence and her inner beauty.

She rejoiced in her physical virginity, but that she might become even more beautiful, she was made with child in a totally new and unexpected manner, and in a birth beyond words the Virgin brought forth a Child like no other, such as no other woman ever bore, before or since. What is so grand and lofty as the wonderful and eminent beauty of this Virgin? Her beauty not only puts her ahead of other women but makes her by far the most outstanding and beautiful of them all!

—Philip of Harveng, *In Cantica Canticorum* 2, 1; PL 203, 247AD

---

[19] In those days the known world was limited, and the standards of feminine beauty, understandably, reflected European models.

[20] Philip of Harveng here actually misquotes Lk 1:28, which gives the angel's words as "Hail, full of grace, the Lord is with you." "Blessed are you among women" is from Lk 1:42 (Elizabeth's words).—ED.

[21] We may observe that this rather pessimistic view of women is not unrelated to the author's practice of monastic asceticism, which presented women as something to be renounced.

THE VIRGIN'S LOVE FOR THE MOST WRETCHED

The Virgin has a certain affectionate feeling of deeper goodwill toward those whom she sees to be in need of the patronage of someone stronger than themselves; that is, those redeemed by her Son whom she considers to have the desire to make progress, who have endeavored to do so, but who are so oppressed by the weight [of their sins] that they cannot make progress. The Virgin loves to let the milk from her tender breast fall onto such as these and to move the weak toward stronger things with loving goodwill. The holy Mother is sure that it would not please her Son, the Redeemer, if those whom he did not wish to hold guilty of the original debt should perish.

But because that breast and her benevolent affection are considered insufficient unless a stronger effectiveness be added to the affection, the Virgin obtains from the Son an efficacious power, so that she leads the weak effectively to the progress she desired. With this power, she helps and takes care of the one toward whom she shows mercy with affectionate solicitude.

She leans down to show compassion to the wretched, as it were, with one breast, while with the other she gives the needy the help he needs. And thus, from these two breasts, that is, from her affection and effectiveness, the Virgin pours out nourishing milk for us, and with her concerned hand she shelters us from the whirlwind and the rain. And, whenever the lion roars, she repulses and checks him with even more powerful threats. With her medicinal milk, she heals whatever the poisonous serpent has injected with his venom.

—Philip of Harveng, *In Cantica Canticorum* 4, 14; PL 203, 376

11

ALAIN DE LILLE
(d. ca. 1203)

This famous Parisian master was simply won over by the poetic attraction of the Song of Songs. He says that this brief Old Testament book refers especially and in a spiritual sense to the Church, while admitting that one can apply it in an even more particular and spiritual sense to the Blessed Virgin.[1] Another mariological strong point that may be recognized in Alain de Lille is that he took seriously the earthly reality of the body of the Mother of God, against the overly spiritualist theories of the Albigensians, who had gone so far as to attribute to Mary some kind of heavenly body.

His Life and Works

The information that has come down to us about his life is rather limited. He was born at Lille between 1114 and 1130. Apparently, he completed his studies at Paris and Chartres. He himself then became one of the famous masters of the time, at Paris and at Montpellier. In the last years of his life, he entered the Cistercian abbey of Cîteaux as a monk, and there he died around 1203.

Alain was certainly one of the more prestigious masters and authoritative practitioners of the sacred sciences in the first period of Scholasticism. He possessed a universal learning, both in profane literature as well as in the philosophical and theological disciplines. He was a great orator and also left behind some works in verse. He can be considered an important forerunner of the great Scholastic theologians of the thirteenth century. His contemporaries considered him one of the wonders of the age; not for nothing was he called Alain the Great and the Universal Doctor.

---

[1] See PL 210, 53B.

Historical correctness, however, demands a clarification. It is probable that the greatness of Alain de Lille was exaggerated by later tradition, which unwittingly attributed to him qualities and merits belonging to other masters of the same name.

Almost all of his works are published in volume 210 of the *Patrologia Latina*. For his Marian teaching, the most important work is the commentary on the Song of Songs already mentioned, *Elucidatio in Cantica Canticorum*.[2] Some of his homilies for feasts of the Virgin have also survived: on the Nativity, the Annunciation, and the Assumption. Allusions to Mary are to be found scattered throughout his other writings.[3]

The Commentary on the Song of Songs

Commenting on the verses of the Song of Songs in a poetic and evocative style, Alain tries to illustrate the events of Mary's life, beginning with the mystery of the Annunciation. He successfully combines a mariological interpretation of the text with an ecclesiological interpretation.[4]

Our commentator takes the story of the love between bridegroom and bride in the Song of Songs as a perfect paradigm for analyzing the dynamic of the relationship between God and the Virgin. It follows that his description of this relationship is clearly influenced by the rather erotic language of the Song of Songs. Alain, however, excludes any implication of a sexual character in the mystery of Mary's motherhood. God's action in bringing about the conception of Jesus protected his Mother from any reaction arising from sexual instinct. The Holy Spirit covered her like a tent or an umbrella, sheltering her from the impulse of concupiscence.[5]

---

[2] See PL 210, 51–110.

[3] For Alain's Marian teaching, the following studies may be consulted: P. Glorieux, "Alain de Lille, docteur de l'Assomption", MSR 8 (1951): 5–18; A. Garzia, "'Integritas carnis' e 'virginitas mentis'", Mar 16 (1954): 125–49; idem, "La mediazione universale in Alano de Lisle", EphMar 6 (1956): 299–321.

[4] It is impossible to understand why Hilda Graef maintains that Alain identified Mary only with the synagogue and not with the Church. Cf. her *Mary: A History of Doctrine and Devotion* (New York: Sheed and Ward, 1964), p. 257. To us it appears that he identifies Mary with both, a possibility that he certainly does not rule out.

[5] See PL 210, 65B.

Nor was this merely a protective action. The Virgin was filled with such great love that her soul felt caught up in ecstatic contemplation of the mystery of God. Alain applies to Mary the metaphor of the *cella vinaria*, used by the author of the Song of Songs, which we may translate as "wine garden":

> The phrase "cella vinaria" (Song 2:4) may be understood to signify the mental rapture, also called "ecstasy", in which the Virgin was caught up to the contemplation of heavenly realities. This phenomenon is also called apotheosis, that is, deification or theophany or divine apparition, into which the Virgin was caught up and taken far away from the love of earthly things.[6]

Bride of Christ

Following an ancient tradition begun by St. Augustine, our author thinks that Mary's motherhood was realized in her mind even before it began in her body. Moreover, he appears to distinguish different phases in this process, through which the Virgin was prepared for the great salvific event of the Incarnation. Alain says that Mary dedicated herself to holy meditation, to be properly disposed to offer herself to the Lord in view of her motherhood.[7] In her contemplation, she freed herself from every worldly care.[8] By practicing humility and obedience, she made herself even more suited to receive the advent of the Wisdom of God within her.[9] But, as was the case with Augustine, so for Alain the Virgin's faith was always the supreme condition that made possible the saving Incarnation of Christ; so much so that, if things had worked out differently, we would have looked for salvation in vain. Alain writes:

> Without the faith of the glorious Virgin, someone seeking Christ would be able to wander but unable to make any progress.[10]

As for the idea that Mary is also the Bride of her Son, it is not difficult to observe how this idea repeatedly recurs in the commentary on the

---

[6] Ibid., 66C.

[7] See ibid., 80B.

[8] See ibid., 85A.

[9] See ibid., 85B.

[10] Ibid., 91A.

Song of Songs. For Mary, the Annunciation was the day of her marriage to Christ. When the Word became flesh, he took the Virgin as his bride in a union that was not only spiritual but physical:

> He married the Virgin, not only in a union of spirits, but also in a union of natures. And so this Incarnation is called a marriage, because it was like a kind of marital union and a joy unspeakable.[11]

As Bride and Mother, Mary maintained an unshakeable faithfulness toward her Husband and Son, especially in the moment of his sorrowful Passion:

> The disciples' faith failed, but the firmness of the Virgin's faith was not diminished.[12]

For this reason, the Mother received special revelations from her Son. She was given the privilege of participating in his Passion in a unique way and, after his Resurrection, Jesus reserved special attentions for her.[13]

But Mary had the joy of observing the fruits of her suffering in a special way. Our author pictures Jesus speaking these words, to make his Mother secure in the knowledge of the value of her compassion:

> You were the first to suffer because of the bitterness of my Passion; now, rejoicing, you see how the redemption of the human race as well as my own glorification have come from it.[14]

Mary and the Church

In the Song of Songs, Alain reads the story of both Mary and the Church. Naturally, he is led to reflect on the particular likeness between the two, a likeness that presents different aspects:

> As the Church of God is the Mother of Christ in his members, by virtue of grace, just so the Virgin is Mother of Christ the Head, by virtue of his human nature. And as the Church is without spot or wrinkle, even so is the glorious Virgin. And as the Church possesses all gifts in many different individuals, so the Virgin Mary has in herself all charisms.[15]

---

[11] Ibid., 77AB.

[12] Ibid., 58B.

[13] See ibid., 69BC.

[14] Ibid., 70BC.

[15] Ibid., 60AB.

The Virgin and the Church have in common, above all, the activity of motherhood. Only Mary, however, is the Mother of Christ the Head. She can be considered the Mother of the members of the Church only because of her role as their example and educator;[16] not as a true mother, as in the case of her divine motherhood. Thus Alain rejects the doctrine of Mary's spiritual motherhood of believers, holding that their only true mother is the Church.

There is also a resemblance between Mary and the Church in the area of holiness. Both Mary and the Church are without stain of sin and without defects. Yet Alain de Lille does not believe in the mystery of the Immaculate Conception. Both possess the fullness of divine grace, in the sense that the Virgin possesses it in the singularity of her person, while the Church possesses it in the multitude of believers.

Our author also sees a relation between Mary and the synagogue, which he calls "mother of the Virgin", inasmuch as she, too, descended from the people of the Old Covenant.[17]

The Ultimate Destiny of the Blessed Virgin

Alain takes a nuanced position on Mary's bodily assumption into heaven. He personally believes that she was taken up to heaven both body and soul, but he does not want to teach this truth in a peremptory fashion, giving the following justification:

> It is reserved to the will of the Virgin, who is in harmony with the divine will, to let it be known that she has been raised up [into heaven].[18]

Thus it would not be the task of the Church to decide on this point, since not even the patriarchs, prophets, and apostles did so. Alain de Lille appears to leave the solution of this problem to a special revelation from Mary herself.

---

[16] See ibid., 54C.

[17] See ibid., 103C.

[18] Ibid., 74B.

READING

THE FOUR VIRTUES OF THE INCARNATION

So Christ came into the flesh and took flesh from me, says the Virgin, but before he entered my womb, "I did not know" (Song 6:12) that he was going to do so. I knew that he was going to be born from a virgin, but I did not know which one. And this is what she means when she says "I did not know"; namely, before the angel's arrival I did not know that he was going to be born from me. This is why I reacted to the angel's word by saying, "My soul is troubled within me" (see Lk 1:29), because I was considering in my mind what sort of greeting this might be. This is what we read in the Gospel. "And when she heard this, she was troubled by his words and considered in her mind what sort of greeting this might be" (ibid.). And this happened "because of the four-wheeled chariot of Aminadab" (Song 6:12). Note that there were four [virtues] by which Christ entered the Virgin Mary: humility, charity, mercy, and prudence.

For the greatest possible humility was seen when the Son of God came to the Virgin, so that the great pride of the first sinner might be equaled by the great humility of the Redeemer. For in our first parent such great pride was present that he rose up against his own Creator; but there was such great humility in the Son of God that he lowered himself so far as to take on our wretched flesh. The first woman wanted to be God's equal, but the glorious Virgin professed that she was God's lowly maidservant (cf. Lk 1:38).

Similarly, it was the greatest possible charity that led the Son of God to lower himself. What charity is greater than that shown when the Son of God came into the world to redeem the slave and heal the sick?

Similarly, it was the greatest possible pity and mercy that caused the Son of God to become incarnate. For what pity and mercy is greater than that shown when God emptied himself and took the form of a slave (cf. Phil 2:7), when the Creator rescued his own creation, drawing him out of the miry pit of misery (cf. Ps 39:2)?

And it was the highest prudence, when the wisdom of God became incarnate, so that man might redeem man. These four [virtues]—humility, charity, mercy, and prudence—are like a four-wheeled chariot by which the incarnate Son of God came to us. The Virgin admired these four virtues in the angel's words to her: humility, charity, mercy, and prudence, and Christ demonstrated them for us when he took flesh in her virginal womb. These four virtues are called the "chariot of Aminadab", that is, the chariot of Christ. Aminadab was the great-grandson of the patriarch Judah, who is woven into the ancestry of Christ, and his name means "volunteer of my people". And this refers to Christ, who volunteered [his life] for his people, since, though he was God, he handed himself over for his own people.

—Alain de Lille, *Elucidatio in Cantica Canticorum*; PL 210, 95D–96C

PART THREE

The Age of Scholasticism

(Thirteenth Century)

Prologue

The thirteenth century saw a continued climate of lively interest in Marian doctrine and devotion. As we have attempted to show, this was one of the most precious treasures of the preceding century. Among the more conspicuous theological components, we may single out a noticeable concern to return to biblical and patristic sources and to the most authentic monastic traditions. The goals of this movement were the rediscovery, first, of the absolutely central role of Christ the Redeemer and, second, of the role of his Mother, as indispensable requirements for the establishment of an authentically Christian existence.[1]

Artists, painters, sculptors, and architects also understood the need to distinguish the images of Jesus and Mary from those of other characters who appeared in the various artworks that enriched the marvelous Romanesque and Gothic cathedrals of the time. The objective was always to make evident the wise and providential design of God the Savior, who came down from heaven and became man in the womb of a woman. Alongside the images of the almighty Son (*Pantokrátōr*), the figure of the Blessed Virgin shines forth, both in her greatness as the Mother of God (*Theotókos*) and in her lowliness as the one who intercedes for us (*Déēsis*).[2]

A particular stimulus to the study of Marian theology and the practice of devotion toward the Mother of God came from the new mendicant orders. The Franciscans, Dominicans, Servites, and Carmelites, even while considering themselves primarily committed to the spirit of their vocation and the choice of the most radical evangelical life, did not excuse themselves from the responsibility to contribute to theological debate, especially through the works of their members best prepared for this task. We must also recognize that the scholars who made the most

---

[1] See Fr. Vandenbroucke, *Spiritualità del Medio Evo*, Storia della Spiritualità Cristiana 3/2 (Bologna, 1969), p. 102.

[2] See T. Koehler, *Maria nella storia della devozione cristiana dal sec. XIII al sec. XVII (1650)* (Verbania Pallanza: Centro Mariano Chaminade, n.d.), pp. 13–24.

valuable contribution to the advancement of theological learning in this time were predominantly religious, members of mendicant orders. In the first place, we find Franciscan and Dominican masters making an enormous contribution to bringing Scholasticism to maturity. The magnificent phenomenon known as Scholasticism took its first steps with Anselm of Canterbury and produced its finest fruits in the *summae theologicae*, those amazing cathedrals of religious knowledge. Because of the untiring labors and efforts of the mendicant friars, Marian doctrine became able to take its place within the newly devised structure and division of the theological disciplines that had been worked out according to the new scientific method of Scholasticism.

In addition, the tools for handing on theological learning were improved. To the old homiletic form was added the systematic treatise, more suited to teaching in the schools. In the treatises, exposition of Marian doctrine assumed an important place, usually within the treatise on the incarnate Word.[3]

---

[3] See L. Gambero, "Devozione mariana nei secoli XII e XIII: Componenti teologiche e aspetti devozionali", in *Loreto, crocevia religiosa tra Italia, Europa e Oriente*, ed. F. Citterio and L. Vaccaro (Brescia, 1997), pp. 7–32.

ANTHONY OF PADUA
(d. 1231)

Anthony of Padua was an extraordinarily charismatic character. On the popular level, he was best known as a great miracle worker who could obtain every sort of miraculous favor from God for those who appealed to his intercession. But he was also a famous preacher and a man of profound learning, for which he was quite rightly proclaimed a Doctor of the Church. He carried out his study and theological research with his religious and pastoral activity in mind, both within the Franciscan order and in the Church of his day. It is easy to observe how his mariological thought also reflects this pastoral concern and how it might be possible to reconstruct his Mariology by using only the contents of his sermons.

The Evangelical Doctor

Given the fame the saint acquired even before his death, the literary sources of his life were multiplied from the beginning, and the reports they give of him can be found in abundance in the so-called *legendae*.[1]

Anthony was born at Lisbon, around 1195. While still a youth he embraced the religious life of the Canons Regular of St. Augustine. At Coimbra, he received an education that guaranteed an exceptional competence in theological and biblical studies. After his priestly ordination, he began to have second thoughts about his religious vocation, to the point that he felt called to enter the Friars Minor of St. Francis. After an unsuccessful attempt to go to preach the gospel among the Saracens, on the occasion of Pentecost, 1221, he went to the Portiuncula, where the

---

[1] *Legenda Prima, Legenda Secunda, Dialogus de gestis sanctorum Fratrum Minorum, Legenda Raymundina, Legenda Florentina, Legenda Rigaldina, Legenda Benignitas, Liber miraculorum.* Cf. R. Pratesi, "Antonio di Padova", in *Enciclopedia Cattolica*, vol. 1, col. 1548.

general chapter of the Friars Minor was being held, and there he met the Poverello of Assisi. He was sent to Romagna, where, for a time, he gave himself over to the practice of penitence and the ascetical life. Later, he carried out a ministry of preaching with enormous success. In addition, he did some teaching and had other administrative responsibilities within the Franciscan order. After spending some time teaching in southern France, he was elected provincial of northern Italy in 1227. In 1230 he was released from this responsibility and again took up the ministry of preaching, but, on June 13 of the following year, he died unexpectedly near Padua. Pope Gregory IX proclaimed him a saint on May 30, 1232, and Pius XII honored him with the title Doctor of the Church in 1946.

Tradition has rightly designated him the "Evangelical Doctor", because of the zeal with which he preached the word of God. He was able to bring together the theology of the mind with the theology of the heart, by which he fascinated and won over his hearers.

His Kerygmatic Mariology

We have already mentioned that the Marian teaching of Anthony of Padua is to be found mostly in his sermons, six of which expressly deal with the Blessed Virgin and her mysteries: one on the Nativity, two on the Annunciation, two on the Purification, and one on the Assumption.[2]

Even while showing himself to be faithful to the tradition of the Fathers and Doctors of the Church, Anthony does not confine himself merely to following the same old, well-trodden path. He is capable of presenting the traditional teaching of the Church in a language that is lively and direct, sometimes illustrated by original and attractive descriptions or taking the form of eloquent images or concentrated in lapidary statements.[3]

---

[2] See A. Locatelli, *Sancti Antoni Patavini thaumaturgi incliti sermones dominicales et in solemnitatibus* (Padua, 1895). A new edition of the Latin text was published in 1979 by the Centro Studi Antoniani located at the Basilica of St. Anthony in Padua. We cite this more recent edition.

[3] There is an abundant bibliography on the Marian thought of the Evangelical Doctor. We limit ourselves to the studies most pertinent to our theme: L. Guidaldi, *Il pensiero mariano di S. Antoni di Padova* (Padua, 1938); G. Roschini, "La mariologia di S. Antonio da Padova", Mar 8 (1946): 16–67; L. Di Fonzo, "La mariologia di S. Antonio", in *S. Antonio dottore della Chiesa* (Vatican City, 1947), pp. 85–122; B. Costa, *La mariologia di*

Anthony touches on nearly all the mysteries and events of Mary's life, but his Marian teaching gravitates especially toward the foundational truth of her divine and virginal motherhood.

He also possesses a kind of prophetic vision that allows him to intuit the future course of Marian doctrine and devotion, especially with regard to truths not yet held to be binding truths of the faith, such as the Assumption and the Immaculate Conception. It is difficult to define Anthony's exact position on the privilege of the Immaculate Conception. In any case, it appears certain that he never took a position against it.[4]

St. Anthony's Marian doctrine has a wonderfully noble quality because of his extraordinary oratorical abilities, but these never led him into wordiness or exaggeration. His doctrine is expressed with passion, but also with balance and theological precision.

The Virgin Mother of God

Everything that the Evangelical Doctor preached about the Blessed Virgin appears as the fruit of a heart overflowing with love, dedication, and admiration for this extraordinary woman, whom the Lord destined for a mission unique in the history of the human race: to become the Virgin Mother of the incarnate Word. In this divine choice, he sees the ultimate cause of all the graces and gifts that made Mary an exalted creature, higher than all other created beings. Anthony exclaims:

> What grace or mercy was ever given to any angel or any man, what grace
> or mercy could ever be given as great as the grace and mercy shown to the

---

S. Antonio da Padova (Padua, 1950); R. Huber, "The Mariology of St. Anthony of Padua", in Studia Mariana 7 (Burlington, Wisc., 1952): 188–268; F. M. Bauducco, "Mariologia cherigmatica di S. Antonio di Padova", in CivCatt 4 (1952): 547–51; R. Laurentin, "La Vierge Marie chez saint Antoine de Padoue", Il Santo 22 (1982): 491–520; D. Montagna, "Tracce di pietà medievale nei 'sermones' di S. Antonio", Il Santo 22 (1982): 521–35; J. Schneider, Mariologische Gedanken in den Predigten des hl. Antonius von Padua, Bücher Franziskanischer Geistigkeit 26 (Werl [Westf.], 1984).

[4] Some scholars hold that St. Anthony was inclined to accept the doctrine of the Immaculate Conception, while others hold the exact opposite, referring to certain statements of the saint himself. For example, in the sermon In Nativate (4, 2:108), he states that the Virgin was sanctified when she had already been conceived in her mother's womb. Cf. C. M. Romeri, De Immaculata Conceptione B. M. V. apud S. Antonium Patavinum (Rome, 1939).

Blessed Virgin? For it was she whom God the Father chose to be the Mother of his own Son, equal to him and born before all ages. . . .

Truly the grace of the Blessed Virgin was greater than any other grace, for she and God the Father had the same Son, and thus this day she merited to be crowned in heaven.[5]

Often Anthony likes to repeat that the Son of God and the Son of Mary are one and the same, as if to underscore the transcendent nature of the Virgin's relationship with God himself:

Today, Blessed Mary brought to the Temple and offered [Jesus], God's Son and hers.[6]

The greatness of the Mother appears in all its sublimity precisely because of the infinite disparity of nature between her and her Son. Speaking to Christ, Anthony exalts Mary, who was introduced into such an incomparable mystery:

Truly blessed is the womb that bore you, God and Son of God, Lord of the angels, Creator of heaven and earth, Redeemer of the world! The daughter has borne the Father; the poor Virgin has borne the Son! O cherubim! O seraphim! O angels and archangels! Cast down your faces, bow your heads, and reverently adore the Temple of the Son of God, the sanctuary of the Holy Spirit.[7]

This infinite distance between the Son and the Mother was, as it were, bridged by the action of the All-powerful and his grace, in which Mary, more "quickly and more deeply than all others, was rooted in love".[8]

Mary's active participation in the saving event of the Incarnation conceals certain hidden consequences. As a result, while her mother-hood is visible in some of its manifestations, it can also appear "veiled by a cloud",[9] the cloud of the divine mystery.

One of the hidden aspects of Mary's motherhood is, undoubtedly, its virginal character. Anthony tries to give an idea of the mystery by using—as he frequently does—a comparison to flowers:

---

[5] *In Assumptione* 3; (Padua, 1979), 2:148.
[6] *In Purificatione* 9; 2:139.
[7] *Dominica 3 in Quadragesima* 3; 1:159.
[8] Ibid., 5; 1:161.
[9] *In Annuntiatione* 15; 2:125.

As lilies retain their freshness, beauty, and fragrance, even when water washes over them, so Blessed Mary, after giving birth to her Son, retained the freshness and beauty of virginity.[10]

Just as her life was never marred by the iron of concupiscence,[11] even so the effects of carnal desire were never felt in her motherhood, since it was virginal.

The Evangelical Doctor shares the conviction that Mary made a vow of virginity before the Annunciation. It was precisely because she did this that the prophecy of Genesis 3:15 was fulfilled in her:

Blessed Mary crushed his head; that is, the root of the devil's temptation, when she made her vow of virginity.[12]

Mary carried out her role as the Mother of the Son of God, not only in giving him human birth, but also in nurturing him, preparing him for the difficult mission to come: "Christ endured his Passion in the body that was nourished by the Virgin's milk." [13]

Mediatrix of Salvation and Grace

One phrase clearly summarizes Anthony's thought on the mission the Virgin carries out as our Mediatrix:

You have given us salvation through the hands of your Daughter and Mother, the glorious Virgin Mary.[14]

While this categorical statement does not seem to admit of restrictions, he adds others that further clarify his thought. The Virgin's mediating function began in the mystery of the Incarnation:

Today the Sun of Justice, the Son of God, enters into the cloud, that is, into the glorious Virgin. The Virgin has become like a rainbow, a sign of the covenant, of reconciliation and peace, shining among the clouds of glory, that is, between God and sinners.[15]

---

[10] Ibid., 16; 2:126. Cf. In Nativitate 12; 2:121.

[11] In Purificatione 2; 2:128.

[12] Ibid., 4; 2:131.

[13] Dominica 3 in Quadragesima 6; 1:162.

[14] In Purificatione 7; 2:136.

[15] In Annuntiatione 6; 2:113. Later on, we read, "After the sun entered the Virgin, peace and reconciliation were accomplished" (ibid., 2:114).

Obviously, Mary's reconciliation recalls the fact that human beings had become sinners and thus the enemies of God, since reconciliation is made between two persons, one of whom is the offended party and the other the offender. The saint repeats:

> The Blessed Virgin Mary, our Mediatrix, reestablished peace between God and the sinner.[16]

Our preacher passes from this brief statement to an urgent invitation addressed to those who feel guilt:

> Then fly to her, O sinner, for she is a stronghold where you may take refuge![17]

He addresses our Mediatrix in a beautiful prayer of invocation, hope, and confidence:

> And so we beseech you, our Lady, our hope, that you, the Star of the Sea, may shine on us when we are tossed by the storm of this sea and guide us to a safe harbor and protect our going out by your sheltering presence, that we may safely come forth from prison and happily reach the goal of inexpressible joy. May he grant this, whom you bore in your blessed womb and nursed at your holy breasts.[18]

A Woman Filled with Gifts and Virtues

St. Anthony places in Jesus' mouth an exclamation of wonder and delight in his Mother's beauty:

> How beautiful in spirit, how comely in body, is my Mother, my Spouse.[19]

The theme of the Virgin's physical attractiveness recurs several times in the homilies of the saint of Padua. But his insistence on this serves primarily to emphasize the spiritual beauty of this exceptional creature who, while she was part of the Church militant, possessed all the virtues.[20] The gifts she received from the Lord are only manifestations of her fullness of grace, and they surpass, in quantity and quality, those of

---

[16] Ibid., 11; 2:120.

[17] *Dominica 3 in Quadragesima* 6; 1:161.

[18] Ibid., 7; 1:163.

[19] Ibid., 4; 1:160.

[20] See *In Purificatione* 6; 2:135.

any other creature. Aligning himself with St. Bernard's thinking, he particularly praises Mary's humility:

> The soul of no other saint has gathered together such riches of virtues as has holy Mary. For she, because of her outstanding humility, merited to conceive and give birth to the untouched Flower of virginity, the Son of God.[21]

In addition to humility, he praises the Mother of the Lord for her poverty and virginity,[22] her obedience,[23] her spirit of contemplation, her justice, and her strong spirit.[24] Speaking of contemplation, Anthony compares the Virgin to Mary the sister of Lazarus (cf. Lk 10:42), stating that when she made sure that the young Jesus had all the care and assistance he needed, she was behaving like Martha, and when she pondered in her heart all that had happened and been said about her divine Son (cf. Lk 2:19), she surpassed Mary of Bethany in the exercise of contemplation.[25]

And so, the preaching of Anthony of Padua was designed to invite the faithful to praise this great woman, to contemplate her life, and to imitate her virtues.

READING

THE VIRGIN AND THE ALLEGORY OF THE BEE

Our Lady, Blessed Mary, gave birth to the Son of God without corruption, because the Holy Spirit came upon her, and the power of the Most High overshadowed her (cf. Lk 1:35). She was the good bee (cf. Sir 11:3). She was small, because of her humility, and round, because she contemplated heavenly glory, which is without beginning or end. She was made dense by charity, for one who carried charity in her womb for nine months could not lack charity. She was compact because of her poverty and cleaner than all others because of her virginity.[26]

---

[21] *In ramis palmarum* 3; 1:191.

[22] See *In Assumptione* 3; 2:144ff.

[23] See *In ramis palmarum* 3; 1:191.

[24] See *In Nativitate* 2; 2:106.

[25] See *In Assumptione* 4; 2:149.

[26] St. Anthony is appealing to the writings of Aristotle, who says that the best kind of bee is small, round, dense, and compact. He says also that the bee is the cleanest of

For this reason the fetid smell of sensual pleasure—if I may so express myself—weighs her down, while the sweet fragrance of virginity or chastity delights her. And so, whoever wishes to please the Blessed Virgin should flee sensual pleasure and concentrate on chastity. Mary does not run away from any animal; that is, she will not run away from any sinner.[27] Instead, she accepts all who fly to her for refuge, and so she is called "Mother of Mercy". She is mercy for the miserable and hope for the hopeless.

In the Song of Songs, the bridegroom says, "I am the flower of the field and a lily of the valleys" (Song 2:1). Having refused all others, Blessed Mary chose this flower and clung to him and received from him what she needed.

And the name "Nazareth", the place where she conceived, is rendered "flower", for this place above all others she chose for herself. For "the flower sprung from Jesse's stem" (Is 11:1) loves the flowering country. He was Blessed Mary's food, her Son, the honey of angels, the sweetness of all the saints. Her life was sustained by him whom she fed. The Son, to whom she gave milk to drink, gave her life.

This good bee prepared a home; that is, she prepared her spirit by humility and her flesh by virginity, preparing a home for the King of angels to inhabit. And notice that the bee begins to build from the top down; this means that Blessed Mary began to build, not from the bottom up (that is, in the sight of men), but from the top down (that is, in the sight of the Divine Majesty). And little by little, that is, step by step and in an orderly fashion, she began to come down where men might see her. Thus she, who was already chosen in God's sight, became wonderful in the sight of men.

Therefore let us say, "the bee is small among flying creatures" (Sir 11:3). Even though many virtues shone forth from Blessed Mary in an outstanding way, her humility shone forth even more brightly. Thus, as if she had forgotten all her other virtues, she brings humility to the fore, saying, "He hath regarded the humility of his handmaid" (Lk 1:48, Douay-Rheims). The "flying creatures" are her merits, which fly all the

---

all animals. Cf. *De hist. an.* V, 22, 553b, 22–23; IX, 40, 624b, 20–24; IX, 40, 626a, 24–28.—TRANS.

[27] Aristotle says that the bee flees from no other animal; see *De hist. an.* IX, 40, 626a, 13–15.—TRANS.

way up to the highest heaven. Thus the last book of parables says of her, "Many daughters have gathered together riches"—that is, virtues—"but you have surpassed them all" (Prov 31:29), because she flew higher than all the others. Even though she was rich with so many treasures of virtues and raised up by so many privileges because of her merits, nevertheless she was short, that is, humble, our bee, who today in the Temple has offered to God the Father a honeycomb; that is, the incarnate Word, who is God and man.

—St. Anthony of Padua, *In festo Purificationis* 9–10, 3:109–11

2

BONAVENTURE
(d. 1274)

Philosopher, theologian, mystic—Bonaventure was among the greatest representatives of the Franciscan school in the first decades of the order's life. At the same time, he was one of the masters of Scholasticism who took up the theme of Mary with a rigorously scientific methodology, working out a doctrine that brings together solid theology and an agreeable spiritual harmony. His Marian theology is built on decidedly christocentric foundations, in such a way that the absolute primacy of the Son is never endangered by undue exaltation of the Mother.

The Seraphic Doctor

Bonaventure was born at Bagnoreggio, near Viterbo, in 1221. While still quite young, he was seized by an irresistible feeling of admiration and devotion toward St. Francis of Assisi, a factor that influenced the future choices of his life. Around 1243, while he was living in Paris as a student, he decided to take the Franciscan habit. During his theological studies, he was a disciple of such outstanding teachers as Alexander of Hales and Jean de la Rochelle. In 1248, still in Paris, he himself was called to teach, first Sacred Scripture and then theology, commenting on the *Sentences* of Peter Lombard. During those years, he was caught up in the controversy of the opposition to the mendicant orders begun by William of Saint-Amour, who not only denied the brothers' right to teach at the university but also called into question their very existence as religious orders. In 1257, Pope Alexander IV intervened, imposing a solution to the conflict, and Bonaventure was then admitted among the doctors of the university. In the meantime, however, he had been nominated Minister General of the Friars Minor, so that he had to give up his university chair. For seventeen years, he governed the order with great wisdom and balance; he calmed dissensions and internal disagreements; he published the constitutions prepared by the general chapter of Narbonne in 1260; he came to the defense of studies within the order, which some considered contrary to the spirit in which it had been founded. Living, as a rule, at Paris, he had occasion to denounce, in explicit statements, the dangers of Averroism, which was putting down roots in the university. In 1273, Pope Gregory X named Bonaventure a cardinal and made him bishop of Albano, with the special responsibility of preparing the Council of Lyons, which was opened May 7, 1274. But by then Bonaventure's health was threatened by the strain of travel and work. He died July 14 at Lyons. Because of his modesty, goodness, and amiability, he has passed into history under the title *Doctor Seraphicus*.

The critical edition of Bonaventure's works, in ten folio volumes, was brought to completion by the Franciscans of the Collegio San Bonaventura of Quaracchi, between 1882 and 1902.

His Marian Doctrine [1]

Passages occupied with the mystery of Mary are to be found almost everywhere in the works of the Seraphic Doctor: in the commentaries on the books of the *Sentences* and on the Gospels of Luke and John, in the conferences on the gifts of the Holy Spirit and the Hexameron, in the *Breviloquium*, the *Soliloquium*, the *Lignum vitae*, and the *Vitis mysterica*.

But his inspired Marian teaching comes forth in greatest measure from his sermons, especially the twenty-four sermons dedicated to the Virgin Mary. The text of these, however, exists only in abbreviated form, in notes taken down by his hearers.

---

[1] Here we recall only some of the many studies of St. Bonaventure's Marian doctrine: G. Roschini, "La dottrina di S. Bonaventura sulla mediazione universale di Maria", Mar 2 (1940): 59–80; E. Chiettini, *Mariologia Sancti Bonaventurae* (Sibenici-Rome, 1941); L. Di Fonzo, *Doctrina Sancti Bonaventurae de universali mediatione B. M. V.* (Rome, 1938); T. Koehler, "Le Vocabulaire de la 'misericordia' dans la dévotion mariale du Moyen-Age latin, de saint Bonaventure à Gerson", in CongrRom 4:313–30; G. Kirwin, "The Sermons of Saint Bonaventure on Mary and Their Relationship to the Cult of Mary", in CongrRom 4:447–65; S. Vergés, "Exégesis de Bonaventura sobre la mediación de María en relación con su culto. Teología bíblica de símbolos mariológicos", in CongrRom 4:467–94; L. Staud, "Die zeitliche Geburt Christi in der Jungfrau Maria: De nativitate in utero nach den Schriften des hl. Bonaventura", in *Bonaventura: Studien*, ed. I. Vanderheyden (Werl, 1976), pp. 68–78.

While, in expounding his thought, Bonaventure habitually uses the Scholastic and didactic style made up of citations, divisions, and subdivisions, nevertheless he does not hide his attractive personal approach as a philosopher and theologian. In him, the teacher is joined to the zealous and devout servant, who appeals to the hearers of his words to have a sincere devotion and authentic love for the Mother of God. He also puts them on their guard against exaggerated tendencies that might lead them into attitudes contrary to the faith or correct Christian conduct. He writes, for example:

> No one can be too devoted to Mary. But his devotion should be such that he believes nothing about her that is contrary to the truth of Sacred Scripture and the Christian faith. This truth must precede all our devotion, whether it is directed toward God or toward his Mother.[2]

Moreover, our Doctor is convinced that the Virgin has no need to be praised and venerated beyond proper limits:

> It is not necessary to invent new honors to honor the Virgin, for she who is so full of truth has no need of our falsehood.[3]

We can easily recognize the thought of St. Bernard in this severe admonition. Bonaventure's Marian doctrine was hardly immune from Bernard's influence; indeed, the teaching of the great Cistercian abbot constituted the primary reference point of all Marian theology during the final centuries of the Middle Ages. This state of affairs helps us understand how Bonaventure could have rejected the Immaculate Conception, which he considered prejudicial to the uniqueness of the privilege of Christ; nor did he see how this truth could be reconciled with the dogma of the universal redemption accomplished by the incarnate Word.[4] But the rejection of this truth, not yet solemnly proclaimed by the Church's Magisterium, did not prevent Bonaventure from recognizing in Mary every kind of perfection and virtue. He calls her the Temple of God, adorned with divine wisdom, consecrated by grace, and filled

---

[2] *In 3 Sententiarum*, d. 3, p. 1, a. 1, q. 1; *Doctoris Seraphici S. Bonaventurae . . . Opera omnia*, 10 vols. (Quaracchi, 1882–1902), 3:64. (Hereafter cited as Quaracchi.)

[3] Ibid., d. 3, p. 1, a. 1, q. 2; Quaracchi, 3:68.

[4] See ibid., d. 3, p. 1, a. 1, q. 1; Quaracchi, 3:62. Bonaventure closely follows the same argument used by Thomas Aquinas.

with the presence of God. In sum, the Virgin possesses all the perfections that the saints have, in complete fullness.

In his treatment of other Marian themes, Bonaventure appears more original and bold. The questions he faces with greatest interest and care are Mary's divine motherhood and her association with her Son, from which all her other privileges derive, among which the most obvious are her perpetual virginity, her compassion at the foot of the Cross of Jesus, which Bonaventure defines as the biblical foundation of her spiritual motherhood, her assumption into heaven, and her universal mediation in heaven.

In encouraging the devotion of the faithful toward the Virgin Mary, Bonaventure appeals precisely to the unique maternal role she plays in helping and guiding her children on the way of salvation. He makes an interesting reference to the relationship between the Virgin and the Eucharist: just as the body of Christ in the Incarnation was given to us by means of Mary, so too our eucharistic offering and Communion must be given through her hands.

Mary and the Incarnation

The personal bond established between the Virgin Mary and the Son of God in the mystery of the Incarnation is the ultimate foundation of all her greatness:

> The Creator of all things rests in the tabernacle of the virginal womb, because here he has prepared his bridal chamber in order to become our brother; here he sets up a royal throne to become our prince; here he puts on priestly vestments to become our high priest. Because of this marital union, she is the Mother of God; because of the royal throne, she is the Queen of heaven; because of the priestly vestments, she is the advocate of the human race.[5]

Bonaventure asks himself whether the great event of the Incarnation should be considered a pure grace of God or whether the human creature could have had some part in meriting it. First he brings up the personal case of the ancient fathers and takes into account that their holiness was not essentially able to merit such a grace. In the following

---

[5] *Sermo 4 de Annuntiatione* 1; Quaracchi, 6:672.

question, he applies the same line of reasoning to Mary and affirms that she merited to conceive the incarnate Word only by *merito congrui,*[6]

> because, on account of her great purity, humility, and kindness, she was fit to become the Mother of God.[7]

After the Annunciation, Mary also merited *merito digni* to become the Mother of the Lord because of her dignity, which remains, nevertheless, always a grace received from God. In any case she was never able to merit *merito condigni*, because the conception of the Son of God is an event that goes beyond all merit.[8]

Mary truly cooperated with the Holy Spirit in the conception of the incarnate Word, because she furnished a physical element that not only had all the characteristics of matter, namely, passivity and receptivity, but also because she had the sufficiency and capacity to give birth to off-spring. This he sees confirmed in the Scripture, which sometimes speaks of Christ as born of the Virgin and sometimes as made by the Virgin.[9]

Mary's Mediation

Bonaventure's sure and profound vision of the mystery of salvation allows him to develop a doctrine on Mary's mediation and spiritual motherhood in a manner that is theologically sound and inspiring on the devotional level.

Going back to the traditional Eve-Mary parallel, our doctor clearly defines Mary's function in the mystery of salvation, a function that makes the woman a protagonist in the mystery, as had been the case with the first sin. For the reparation had to correspond to the Fall:

> As the Fall happened in both sexes, that is, it began in the woman and was then completed in the man, so would it be in the reparation. The woman, by believing and conceiving, would begin to conquer the devil in secret, and later her Son would conquer him openly, in a duel, that is, on the tree of the Cross.[10]

---

[6] That is, it was not owed to her in justice.—TRANS.

[7] *In 3 Sententiarum*, d. 4, a. 2, q. 1–2; Quaracchi, 3:105–7.

[8] Ibid.

[9] Ibid., d. 4, a. 3, q. 1; Quaracchi, 3:112.

[10] Ibid., d. 12, a. 3; Quaracchi, 3:272.

Mary began her Son's victory over sin in the mystery of the Incarnation, when she became the Mother of God:

> After the Fall of man in sin, divine wisdom foresaw a way to come to his
> aid in the incarnation of the Word, through which man would be made
> capable of receiving grace. This happened in the Virgin's womb. So the
> angel greeted her: "Hail, full of grace, the Lord is with you!" And the
> apostle Paul exhorts those who want to obtain grace that they should
> approach the throne of grace; in other words, the glorious Virgin. "Let us
> then with confidence draw near"—he says—"to the throne of grace"
> (Heb 4:16). So, then, there appeared to us first the Father of mercies, then
> the Mother of mercies, and then the Son, light of mercies. In this way is
> revealed the origin of the grace that is within us, given us by the incarnate
> Word. Some do not know this origin; what wretches they are! For they
> cannot receive grace.[11]

In addition to the role played by the Virgin in the Incarnation, the
special protection God gave her against sin enables her to function as a
true Mediatrix. However much she may have been subjected to original
sin by nature, she was exempt from it in her soul, and this puts her
between us and her divine Son. Thus she is the Mediatrix between us
and Christ, as he is the Mediator between us and God.[12]

One who wishes to be sanctified must follow the Virgin. It is she who
takes us from the condition of slavery to sin to paradise:

> Eve expels us from paradise and sells us [into the slavery of sin], but Mary
> brings us back and buys our freedom.[13]

Mary plays this role in a passive way, not an active one. Bonaventure
explains this through an allegorical interpretation of Proverbs 31:10:
"Who can find a perfect woman? Her value is beyond pearls":

> Mary, the strong and faithful woman, paid this price, since when Christ
> suffered on the Cross to pay this price to redeem us, the blessed Virgin
> was present, accepting God's will and consenting to it.[14]

He goes on to explain that Christ is the only Redeemer, since he
alone was able to restore to God the honor that had been taken away;

---

[11] *De donis Spiritus Sancti*, collectio 6, 5; Quaracchi, 5:488.

[12] See *In 3 Sententiarum*, d. 3, p. 1, a. 1, q. 2; Quaracchi, 3:68. This is the only passage
in which Bonaventure uses the term "mediatrix".

[13] *De donis Spiritus Sancti*, collectio 6, 14; Quaracchi, 5:486.

[14] Ibid., collectio 6, 15; Quaracchi, 5:486.

Mary makes her contribution by consenting to the sacrifice of Christ as the price of our redemption.[15]

In heaven, Mary continues to carry out her function as Mediatrix, to the point that all the graces that come to us pass through Mary. Our Doctor uses St. Bernard's famous metaphor of the aqueduct. Mary has an important part to play in our sanctification:

> Those who are rooted in the Virgin Mother with love and devotion are sanctified by her, because she asks her Son to give it to them.[16]

Mary's Spiritual Motherhood

In addition to the Eve–Mary parallel, Bonaventure speaks of the parallel between Eve and the Church. Eve came forth from the side of Adam, and the Church comes forth from the side of the Redeemer dying on the Cross. This second parallel, which has a neatly patristic stamp, is suggested to him by a reflection that leads him to affirm the Virgin's motherhood of men:

> As Abel and his descendants were formed from Adam and Eve, so from Christ and his Church the whole Christian people was formed. And as Eve is the mother of Abel and of us all, so the Christian people has the Virgin for a mother.[17]

Mary's spiritual motherhood begins on Calvary and appears as the result of her full acceptance of the plan of salvation willed by God for humanity. At the foot of the Cross, she combines loving compassion for her firstborn with a feeling of great mercy for all her other sinful children, for whom she offers the fruit of her womb as the price of their ransom.[18] Therefore the infinite mercy of God for sinful man becomes, for Mary, the criterion and paradigm of her own attitude and conduct in our regard.[19]

Mercy and piety, then, are the usual ways in which Mary expresses her maternal love for us:

---

[15] See ibid.

[16] *Sermo de Purificatione* 2; Quaracchi, 9:646.

[17] *De donis Spiritus Sancti*, collectio 6, 14 and 20; Quaracchi, 5:486–487.

[18] See ibid., collectio 6, 20; Quaracchi, 5:486.

[19] See *Sermo in Pentecostem* 8, 1; Quaracchi, 9:350.

What a merciful Mother we have! Then let us make ourselves like unto our Mother; let us imitate her piety. She was so merciful toward souls that she considered temporal loss and physical suffering to be as nothing.[20]

Devotion to Mary

Considering all that she has done on behalf of the human race, the Virgin deserves the fervent veneration of the Christian people. Taking his inspiration from the conduct of the saints, Bonaventure recommends devotion to the Virgin Mary. He himself was greatly devoted to her; nevertheless, he lays down well-defined criteria with a view to containing Marian devotion within correct limits.

In general, it is necessary to make sure that the honor due to the Mother does not detract from the glory of the Son, which must always dominate.[21] Thus one cannot pay to Mary an honor due to Christ alone, claiming that any honor rendered to Mary is converted into honor for the Son. In such a case, this could directly constitute a dishonor. It is good, then, to honor the Mother, but it is much more necessary to honor the Son.[22]

Bonaventure adopts the well-known distinction between the worship of *latria*, owed only to God, that of *dulia*, given to the saints, and what is called *hyperdulia*, that is, the veneration owed to the Mother of the Lord, which is greater than simple *dulia*. Indeed, whatever honor is given to the saints must be attributed to Mary in full.[23]

READING

"STANDING BY THE CROSS OF JESUS" (JN 19:25)

Here we note the tiny number of those who showed compassion, for, out of all the persons dear to him, three women were present, among whom was also the Mother of the Lord, toward whom the Lord himself

---

[20] *De donis Spiritus Sancti*, collectio 6, 20; Quaracchi, 5:487.
[21] See *In 3 Sententiarum*, d. 3, p. 1, q. 2; Quaracchi, 3:68.
[22] See ibid.
[23] See *Sermo 2 in Assumptione* II; Quaracchi, 9:692.

would show compassion. Four circumstances present themselves: the compassion of the women toward the Lord, the Lord's concern for his Mother, the entrustment that follows upon this concern, and, finally, the acceptance of this entrustment.

The compassion of the women is seen in the statement: "Standing by the cross of Jesus". They stood by him physically, then, because they were drawn to him by the feeling of compassion. By contrast, others distanced themselves because of their lack of compassion, so that the psalm says, "All those who were close to me stand far away" (Ps 38:12). But the women remained nearby because they loved him more, as did his Mother, who surpassed them all in compassion, so that we read in the second chapter of Luke, "A sword will pierce through your own soul" (Lk 2:35). Then there was present "his mother's sister, Mary of Cleophas", James' mother. It should be noted that Anna, according to what was said, had three husbands: Joachim, Cleophas, and Salome; and from these three husbands she had three Marys: namely, the Mother of the Lord, who was the daughter of Joachim; the mother of James, daughter of Cleophas; and the mother of Simon and Jude, daughter of Salome.[24] There was also "Mary Magdalene", so called because she was from Magdala. These three women stood by the Cross of Jesus in an attitude of great compassion.

"Jesus, seeing his mother. . . ." These words indicate the second circumstance; namely, the Lord's compassion toward his Mother, clearly seen in his act of looking at her and looking at him to whom he would entrust her. Therefore the text says, "Jesus, seeing his Mother. . . ." He sees her in the manner of one who has concern, as we read in 1 Timothy 5:8, "If any one does not provide for his relatives, and especially for his own family. . . ." Moreover John Chrysostom states: "In this moment, the Lord showed great love toward his Mother and commended her to the care of the disciple, in order to teach us that we must have the greatest consideration, until the last breath, for those who have given birth to us."[25] And it is written in Exodus 20:12, "Honor your father and your mother." What he commanded he also practiced.

---

[24] Bonaventure is taking the story of Anna's three husbands and the resulting three Marys from the *Golden Legend* by Jacobus de Voragine, who is in turn drawing on the apochryphal Protoevangelium Iacobi.

[25] *In Joannem*, homily 85, 2; PG 59, 462.

"He saw there also the disciple whom he loved"; and therefore he could entrust Mary to him as to a relative. John was standing there, but he did not distance himself; therefore, he was among those about whom it was said in Luke 22:28, "You are those who have continued with me in my trials."

"He said to his Mother. . . ." Here is mentioned the third circumstance, namely, the diligent commendation that echoes in the words, "Woman, behold your son!" It is as if he had said, "Trust him as if he were your own son."

"Then he said to the disciple, Behold, your mother!" It is as if he had said, "Care for her as if she were your own mother."

"And from that hour the disciple took her to his own home [*in sua*]." Here we observe the reception of the commendation; that is, he took the Mother into his home to honor her, watch over her, and take care of her, as a son does for his mother.

But Augustine reads the expression in the accusative plural, *in sua*, and asks: Why ever does it say *in sua* if he does not possess anything of his own? He answers: *In sua* means among his obligations, his duties, and his goods, not into his property, for he had none.

—St Bonaventure, *In Joannem 19, 37–39*,
Opere di S. Bonaventura, vol. 7, pt. 2
(Rome: Città Nuova, 1991), pp. 312–14

3

CONRAD OF SAXONY
(d. 1279)

Conrad of Saxony is the author of a celebrated treatise titled *Speculum seu opusculum salutationis Beatae Mariae Virginis*. The first publishers of the treatise wrongly attributed it to St. Bonaventure, under whose name it became widely known.

Our author was born Conrad Holzinger to a noble family of Braunschweig (Brunswick), in Saxony, in the first years of the thirteenth century. He entered the order of St. Francis and became a most able theologian, preacher, and author of ascetical works. After having been a lector in the conventual *studium* of Hildesheim, he served as provincial minister of Saxony from 1247 to 1262, and again from 1272 until his death.

The *Speculum*[1] takes the form of an extended commentary on the Angelic Greeting, or *Angelus*, and is divided into eighteen readings. Conrad also composed some sermons, some fifteen of which treat Marian themes, especially the mystery of the Annunciation. He is faithful to the tradition of the Church and is fond of quoting or frequently referring to authors who lived in the century before him, such as Bede,

---

[1] The critical edition of the *Speculum* and the Marian sermons has been published by Pedro de Alcántara Martínez, O.F.M.: Conradus de Saxonia, O.F.M., *Speculum seu salutatio Beatae Mariae Virginis ac sermones*, Bibliotheca Franciscana Ascetica Medii Aevi 11 (Grottaferrata, Rome: Ad Claras Aquas, 1975). For Conrad's Marian thought, see L. Di Fonzo, *La regalità di Maria in una celebre opera mariana di Fra Corrado di Sassonia*, in *Luce Serafica* 19 (1943): 69–71; S. Girotto, *Corrado di Sassonia, predicatore e mariologo del sec. XIII*, Biblioteca di Studi Francescani (Florence, 1952); idem, *Corrado di Sassonia e l'Assunzione della Vergine in cielo*, excerpt from *Studi Francescani*, S. 3, 23 (1951): 1–20; idem, *Il cantico dell'Ave: Invocazioni alla Vergine SS. tratte dall'opusculo "Speculum B. M. V."* di Corrado di Sassonia O.F.M. (1279) (Roncade, 1957); P. de Alcántara Martínez, *El culto a María según Conrado de Saxonia*, in CongRom, 4:583–603.

Ambrose Autpert, Anselm, Peter Damian, the pseudo-Jerome and the pseudo-Augustine of the treatises on the Assumption, and Bernard. He recognizes various titles and roles of the Virgin. He calls her Help, Mediatrix, Advocate of human beings before God, higher in dignity and power than all angelic and earthly beings, Associate of the Redeemer in the work of salvation, Mistress of heaven and earth, and universal Mother of the faithful. But he is content especially to extol the greatness, the dignity, and the holiness of the Mother of God.

Mary's Blessed Birth

Conrad shared the common opinion of his time and did not think that the Virgin was conceived without original sin. Instead, he held that she was freed from original sin before her birth and explains this by appealing to a Scripture verse:

> "Take away the dross from the silver and a most pure vessel will come forth" (Prov 25:4). The dross was taken away from the silver when Mary was purified of original sin in her mother's womb, from which she came forth, certainly, as a most pure vessel.[2]

Even if the same fate befell other famous men, such as the prophet Jeremiah and John the Forerunner, nevertheless the case of Mary remained exceptional and presented a noteworthy difference:

> Whoever came forth from the womb sanctified was like a pure vessel, however much the inclination to mortal or venial sin remained in him, as some say was the case with Jeremiah. Whoever came forth from a womb so sanctified would be an even purer vessel, for in him the inclination to mortal sin was extinguished, as was the case with blessed John the Baptizer, of whom the Church sings: "You could not stain your life, not even with a small desire."[3] Now when the Blessed Virgin was born, she was the most pure vessel of all, because she came forth from the womb with such a measure of holiness that, as is believed, no inclination to sin, either mortal or venial, remained in her.[4]

---

[2] *Speculum* 1, 1; Quaracchi, p. 374.

[3] Liturgical hymn for the feast of the Baptist, attributed to Peter the Deacon; PG 95, 1597B. Cf. Chevalier, *Repertorium hymnologicum*, no. 1214 [1892], 1:74.

[4] *Speculum* 1, 11, 1; Quaracchi, pp. 374–76.

The Blessed Virgin's birth, therefore, is seen to be completely privileged, and one could say that it appeared as a sign, foretelling what her whole life would be like: a life never tainted to the slightest degree by the shadow of sin. But this condition is only the negative aspect of her holiness.

Mary's Spiritual Beauty

The positive aspect of Mary's holiness is seen in a unique way in the mystery of her virginity. Taking his inspiration from the Scripture, as always, Conrad explains this with the help of metaphors:

> "Who is this that looks forth like the rising dawn, fair as the moon, bright as the sun?" (Song 6:10). Rightly is Mary compared to these three resplendent realities; namely, to the dawn, the moon, and the sun, because of the three motives of excellence found in her. Her luminous virginity was excellent, both in her flesh and in her mind. Moreover, in her virginity there was an excellent and luminous fruitfulness: in that fruitfulness was located an excellent and luminous uniqueness.[5]

Our author concludes that, while it is true that all holiness is a reflection of the light of God, as the moon reflects the light of the sun, Mary's spiritual perfection has to be beyond compare, because the divine Son himself was conceived and dwelt within her.

Queen of Earth and Heaven

Conrad sees a prophecy of the Blessed Virgin in the biblical figure of the Queen of Sheba (cf. 2 Chron 9:1; Mt 12:42; Lk 11:31). Appealing to the etymology of the term "Sheba", which he translates as "a cry", he remarks that the world is full of cries and groaning. Thus to say that Mary is the Queen of Sheba is equivalent to saying that she is the Queen of the world.

But the Mother of the Lord is also the Queen of heaven, where cries also resound, though not accompanied by groaning. To the contrary, in heaven there are cries of joy, directed to the glorification of God and the

---

[5] Ibid., 1, 11, 2; Quaracchi, p. 376.

heavenly Queen. To her are addressed the words of the Psalm: "At your right hand stands the queen in gold of Ophir" (Ps 45:9). Citing a text of St. Bernard, our author recalls that the Blessed Virgin in heaven is also a point of reference for us on earth:

> They can confidently follow this queen in her kingdom if they will have followed her faithfully in this world.[6]

To follow in the train of this Queen in eternal life is a reward that presupposes a commitment to her in this present life. Conrad shows that devotion to Mary has practical implications: we need to follow her, to imitate her virtues and example.

Mary's Intercession

Conrad interprets Mary's intervention with her Son during the wedding at Cana (see Jn 2:2–5) as a sure sign of the great mercy she feels in her heart with regard to all the needs of the faithful. It is this deep merciful love that moves her to address her prayers to Christ on our behalf. Conrad analyzes this Mother's heart and sums up her actions on our behalf:

> In her direct relations with us, she shows her mercy in four ways: by consoling us in our troubles, by helping us in our necessities, by freeing us from eternal damnation, and by rewarding us for our service with the reward of the beatific vision after this life.[7]

Our author sees a confirmation of this truth in the fact that Mary became the tabernacle of Christ, that is, the Mother of the Head of the Mystical Body. In this role, she cannot refrain from guaranteeing her protection and help to Christians, who are the members of this Body and profess themselves to be her devoted servants. Rightly, then, the faithful turn to her with the words of the *Salve Regina*: "Turn, then, thine eyes of mercy toward us, and after this our exile, show unto us the blessed fruit of thy womb, Jesus."

In a precise summary, Conrad sums up the reasons why Mary's prayers to her Son and Lord meet with success:

---

[6] Ibid., I, II, 3; Quaracchi, p. 381.

[7] *Sermo de Evangelio*; Quaracchi, p. 563.

Her intercession with God is efficacious for three reasons: because in the sight of God Mary is beautiful, sweet, and worthy. She is beautiful because of her luminous virginity, sweet because of her great humility, and worthy because of her maternal authority.[8]

These reasons perfectly combine the gifts Mary received from above, included in her role as Mother of God and her personal merits, as expressed in her vow of virginity and the practice of her wonderful humility.

When contemplating the mysterious role of the Mother of God, to which Mary was called by a providential design, we can do nothing but wonder and give thanks. When, however, we consider her life and conduct, we are invited to cultivate an authentic devotion toward her by imitating her virtues:

> So let us imitate the chastity of the Blessed Virgin as much as we are able; let us follow her humility; let us be ready to do the will of the heavenly Father. Then our faces will be presentable before God, and the most sweet Mother herself will beg for us, from her sweet Son and our Lord, the wine of eternal joy.[9]

READINGS

MARY'S WONDERFUL BEAUTY

She is so beautiful in God's eyes, because of the splendor of her shining virginity, that she easily obtains from God every assent she desires, according to the words of the book of Esther, "Esther was very beautiful, and found favor in the eyes of all. And the king loved her more than all his wives, and she found grace and favor in his sight more than all other women" (Esther 2:15, 17).

Esther means "hidden", and this refers to Blessed Mary and the virgin birth [of Jesus], which is hidden from sensible and rational experience. Moreover, because of the inexpressible beauty of her chastity, she finds favor in the sight of all and easily attracts the love of the King of heaven himself.

—Conrad of Saxony, *Sermo de Evangelio*; ed. Quaracchi, p. 566

---

[8] Ibid., pp. 565–66.
[9] Ibid., p. 568.

THE HUMBLE SWEETNESS OF THE MOTHER OF GOD

She is also very sweet to God because of her great humility, so sweet that no bitterness caused by our sins could provoke God to such an extent that she could not soften his wrath. Therefore Anselm states: "We sinners stand before a terrible judge, whose hands brandish the sword of his wrath over our heads; and who will turn it away? No one is so suited to oppose his hand to the Lord's sword on our behalf as are you, O most beloved Lady, thanks to whom we have received mercy from the hand of our God for the first time on earth." [10]

And this is why she is called and truly is "a land flowing with milk and honey",[11] because she makes all things sweet with the abundance of her sweetness: man is made sweet by devotion, the angel by praise, and God is made sweet by being propitiated.

—Conrad of Saxony, *Sermo de Evangelio*; ed. Quaracchi, p. 567

THE EXALTED DIGNITY OF THE MOTHER OF GOD

Because of her maternal authority, her dignity in God's sight is so great that it is impossible to think that God does not hear her petitions, as is said in the first book of Kings: "Make your request, my mother, for I will not refuse you" (1 Kings 2:20). In the same way Bernard says, "How could the same majesty that took its origin from the flesh of your flesh oppose itself to your power?" For you go into the presence of that golden altar of human reconciliation, not only to pray, but also to command, not as a handmaid, but as a queen." [12]

—Conrad of Saxony, *Sermo de Evangelio*; ed. Quaracchi, p. 568

---

[10] The text is by Egbert of Schönau. See PL 95, 1515A.

[11] See Richard of St. Lawrence, *De laudibus B. M. V.*, lib. 8, c. 1, no. 2; published among the works of Albert the Great, ed. Borgnet, vol. 36 (Paris, 1898), p. 401B.

[12] The text is by Nicholas of Clairvaux, *Sermo 1 in Nativitate B. M. V.*; PL 144, 740D.

4

ALBERT THE GREAT
(d. 1280)

Historical-critical research has deprived Albert of the authorship of two important mariological works wrongly attributed to him.[1] Yet, among the Doctors of the medieval Church, he remains among those who paid the greatest attention to the mystery of the Mother of the Lord. Tradition, reinforced by scattered witnesses in his writings and by reports, documents, and records of his time, unanimously recognizes his marked interest in Marian doctrine and especially his strong devotion to Mary. In the biography written by Peter of Prussia, we read that Albert "wrote of Mary so abundantly that there is no book written by him in which his Beloved is forgotten".[2]

A Great Son of St. Dominic

Albert was born around the end of the twelfth century in Lauingen, a village on the Danube, to a military family. While still very young, he dedicated himself to his studies with unusual seriousness, quickly mani-

---

[1] In particular we are referring to the treatise *De laudibus B. M. V.*, in twelve books, held to be Albert's work until 1625, when J. Bogard restored it to its true author, the canon Richard of St. Lawrence, of Rouen (*Domini Richardi a Sancto Laurentio, qui ante quadrigentos annos floruit, de Laudibus B. M. V. libri XII, mira pietate ac eruditione referti* (Douay, 1625). Richard of St. Lawrence, a follower of the Cistercian school of spirituality, may be considered a first-rank witness to the theological vitality of the thirteenth century. The other important work erroneously attributed to Albert is the famous *Mariale super "Missus est"*. It was not until 1950 that the attribution of this work to Albert the Great was proved to be incorrect. Cf. B. Korosac, *Mariologia sancti Alberti Magni eiusque coaequalium* (Rome, 1954), pp. 3ff.

[2] We take the citation from G. Roschini, *Maria SS. nella storia della salvezza*, vol. 1 (Isola del Liri, 1969), p. 442. The work of Peter of Prussia is the earliest known biography of Albert, even though it was written in 1486, two centuries after Albert's death.

festing a marked attraction to the natural sciences. To complete his education, he was sent to the university of Padua, where he came to know the Friars Preachers and felt a vocation to the religious life. After he entered the Dominican order, his superiors sent him to Germany to teach the sacred sciences as a lector. He subsequently lived in various Dominican houses. In 1245, we find him as master of theology at the University of Paris. It was there that he began to compose his great scientific encyclopedia, to which he devoted practically all his attention during the remainder of his life.

In 1248, he was called to be director of the general studium of his order at Cologne, where Thomas Aquinas was one of his students. In 1254, he was elected superior of the huge province of Germany. In 1260, Pope Alexander IV named him bishop of Regensburg, from which responsibility he asked to be released in 1263. In 1274, he took part in the Council of Lyons.

Albert generously devoted his extraordinary abilities and energy to study, teaching, and writing his works; in addition, he was an untiring pastoral worker, a prudent organizer of religious life, and an enlightened spiritual guide. He successfully discharged the many missions with which both popes and his own superiors entrusted him. He died at Cologne on November 15, 1280.

Albert stands out as a great teacher, able to reconcile an intense intellectual and scientific activity with care for the spiritual and ascetical life. His life was a wonderful example of the practice of Christian virtue, especially in his piety, humility, zeal, and love for his vocation as a son of St. Dominic. He lived these virtues to such a degree that the veneration that sprang up around his extraordinary personality did not remain limited to his order but extended to later Christian generations. In 1931, he was proclaimed a saint and Doctor of the Church; ten years later, Pius XII named him patron of natural scientists.

His Marian Doctrine

The theological, philosophical, and scientific activity of Albert the Great embraces all fields of knowledge, so that his collected works present a truly impressive appearance. The first edition of his works was prepared by the Dominican Pierre Jammy, who published it at Lyons in 1651, in twenty-one folio volumes. A reprint in thirty-eight volumes was edited at Paris between 1890 and 1899 by Auguste Borgnet. Since 1951, the critical edition of the Albertus Magnus Institut at Cologne has been underway, and many volumes of this edition have already appeared.

We necessarily limit ourselves to recalling those works in which Albert expounds his Marian doctrine at length. These are the commentaries on Isaiah, Jeremiah, the four Gospels, the pseudo-Dionysius, and the four books of the *Sentences* of Peter Lombard, the *Summa* on creation, as well as the *Disputed Questions* and the treatises *On the Good, On the Sacrifice of the Mass, On the Sacrament of the Eucharist, On the Nature of the Good,* and *On the Incarnation.*[3]

In his writings, Albert demonstrates a scrupulous fidelity to the Scriptures as well as a deep attachment to tradition, from the Greek and Latin Fathers of the Church down to the great Doctors closest to him in time, such as St. Anselm, St. Bernard, and Peter Lombard. His doctrinal statements are consistently characterized by theological rigor, and they faithfully respect the teaching of the Church's Magisterium. As the founder of Christian Aristotelianism, he is fond of frequent recourse to the authority of the Philosopher, even when he is expounding his own Marian doctrine.

Albert wrote a great deal about the Mother of the Lord. The work in which he treated this theme most fully is his commentary on the Gospel of Luke. He was able to assign his Marian doctrine a well-defined place within Christology. Nevertheless, the comparison between Mary and

---

[3] We have a series of studies on the Marian thought of Albert the Great carried out by Albert Fries: "Die Gedanken des hl. Albertus Magnus über die Gottesmutter", in *Thomistische Studien*, vol. 7 (Freiburg, Switz., 1958); "Vom Denken Alberts des Grossen über die Gottesmutter", *Freiburger Zeitschrift für Philosophie und Theologie* 5 (1958): 129–55; "Des Albertus Magnus Gedanken über Maria-Kirche", in CongrLourd 3:319–74; *Was Albertus Magnus von Maria sagt* (Cologne, 1962) (hereafter cited as Cologne); "Marienkult bei Albertus Magnus", in CongrRom 4:605–39; "Zur Verwertung und Erklärung der Schrift in der 'Mariologie' Alberts des Grossen", in *Mariologische Studien*, vol. 2 (Essen, 1963), pp. 53–79. Among other studies we may mention: H. Barré, "Marie et l'Église de Vén. Bède à saint Albert le Grand", EtMar 9 (1951): 59–143; R. J. Buschmiller, *The Maternity of Mary in the Mariology of St. Albert the Great* (Carthagena, Ohio, 1957); B. Korosak, "Randbemerkungen zur Mariologie des hl. Albert des Grossen", *Freiburger Zeitschrift für Philosophie und Theologie* 5 (1958): 327–33; R. Masson, "Les Réflexions théologiques de saint Albert le Grand sur la sainte Vierge", Mar 23 (1961): 106–13; L. Ciappi, "La maternità divina e la corredenzione di Maria SS. secondo Sant'Alberto Magno e la costituzione dogmatica 'Lumen Gentium'", in *Scripta de Maria* 4 (1981): 523–49.

Christ, which is often found in his writings, always ends up in explicit statements about the immeasurable difference between the Son and the Mother. Here we will limit ourselves to recalling certain mariological themes on which Albert clearly intended to take a definite position.

Mary's Immaculate Conception and Holiness

It is well known that, in the centuries preceding the life of St. Albert, the doctrine of the Immaculate Conception had already begun to attract the attention of theologians. The faith and piety of the people of God felt more and more obligated to accept it.

Albert, however, was resolved to accept the authority of St. Bernard and the Parisian masters on this point, and so he denied that the Virgin was conceived without original sin.[4] His reason was not new: Without original sin, one could not see how Mary could have been redeemed in the same manner as the other members of the Mystical Body of Christ.

Albert admits, however, that Mary was the subject of a special intervention in which God sanctified her from her mother's womb,[5] granting her a condition of holiness far superior to that of the prophet Jeremiah and St. John the Baptist and superior to the sanctification that happens through the effects of the sacraments. Not only was the inclination to mortal sin taken away from her, but also the inclination to venial sin, so that her purity makes her the creature closest to her divine Son.[6] This purifying and sanctifying intervention of God would have happened immediately after the ensoulment of the fetus,[7] freeing her soul from concupiscence:

> With regard to immunity from the inclination to sin [fomes] and from attraction to sensual pleasure: the inclination to sin was completely extinguished within her.[8]

Another exceptional sanctifying divine intervention happened in the mystery of the Incarnation, when the Holy Spirit came down upon

---

[4] See In 3 Sententiarum, dis. 3, a. 4, solutio; in Opera Omnia of Albert the Great, ed. August Borgnet (Paris, 1898), 28:47.

[5] See ibid., a. 5; Borgnet, 28:48.

[6] See ibid., a. 6; Borgnet, 28:49.

[7] See ibid., a. 5; Borgnet, 28:48.

[8] De bono; Cologne, 28:171–72.

Mary and the Word of God dwelt within her. For this reason the Virgin's holiness or, rather, her fullness of grace, exceeds that of all the saints, while remaining inferior to that of Christ, who possesses the fullness of the divine nature. Moreover, thanks to the presence in her of all the gifts of the Holy Spirit, Mary led an interior life that was perfectly ordered toward God.

Mother and Spouse of Christ

Because of her exalted virtues, Mary, in a certain way, merited the gift of the divine motherhood. She merited this gift, however, not in justice, but in fittingness.[9]

In his writings, Albert expresses the greatest admiration for the Virgin because of this wonderful gift. He poses the rhetorical question: "Of which Jesus was Mary the mother? " and answers it thus:

[She was the Mother] of him who makes his temporal birth from his Mother resemble his eternal birth from his Father; [the Mother] of him who transforms and renews human birth with new qualities beyond number.[10]

In superlative terms, Albert praises the dignity and purity of the Mother of God, who represents a unique case among all the mothers of this earth:

Behold, "the Mother of Jesus", Mother immaculate, Mother untouched, Mother who never experienced the pains of motherhood, Mother uncorrupt, Mother not deprived of the virtue of virginal chastity. She is spotless, a fitting Mother for the spotless Lamb.[11]

The eternal Word became incarnate in Mary even before the Annunciation to dispose her to receive the angel's words in faith and give her consent in a condition of total freedom:

The purpose of the Annunciation, considered from the angel's point of view, was to notify the Virgin that she had been chosen to become the

---

[9] Our author uses the expression *per modum congruitatis* (*De incarnatione*, tr. 2, a. 5; Cologne, 26:176–77).

[10] *In Matthaeum 1,18*; Cologne 21.1:27.

[11] Ibid., Cologne, 21.1:26.

Mother of God. Considered, instead, from the Virgin's point of view, the goal was to bring her to believe the angel's words and give her consent to what was announced to her.[12]

Mary not only became the Mother of God; she also entered into a spousal relationship with him:

> He came forth like a bridegroom from the bridal chamber of [Mary's] womb (cf. Ps 18:6). When he was born from Mary, he did not violate her as a mother; rather, he loved her as a bride, consecrating her as a bride without spot or wrinkle.[13]

The Virginity of the Mother of God

Albert the Great wrote a great deal on this theme. He does not doubt that Mary was a virgin before, during, and after giving birth:

> The Blessed Virgin was a virgin in conceiving and in giving birth. . . . Nor was she ever deflowered afterward.[14]

Her virginity did not prejudice the validity of her marriage to Joseph, in which, though she did not experience a man's bed, she contracted an honorable marriage, at the same time preserving her soul pure from every impulse of concupiscence.[15] For this reason, too, the marriage was even more holy:

> For this reason, the marriage of the Blessed Virgin and Joseph was a true marriage. Moreover, it was holier than other marriages since, unlike them, it was immune from the concupiscence of carnal intercourse.[16]

Following a tradition that originated with the great fourth-century Fathers of the Church, Albert thinks that Mary made a vow of virginity even before receiving the angel's announcement and that Joseph did the same.[17]

---

[12] Ibid.

[13] *In Lucam 1,35*; ed. Borgnet, 22:103–4.

[14] *De bono*; Cologne, 28:170.

[15] See *In Matthaeum 1,18*; Cologne, 21.1:27.

[16] Ibid., Cologne, 21.1:25.

[17] See ibid., Cologne, 21.1:28.

Mary Assumed into Heaven

In agreement with the pseudo-Augustine, Albert the Great accepts as a pious belief the truth of Mary's bodily assumption into heaven. He did not get very much involved in this theological territory, restricting himself to some reflections on the event.

The question is raised: To where was the Virgin's glorious body moved? The answer is based on a distinction that Albert introduces into the concept of heaven. There is one heaven called the empyrean, where the angelic choirs dwell and into which the saints also gain entrance. The very humanity of Christ dwells in this heaven, in which, however, it occupies a place higher than all the angels and saints.[18]

The body of the Virgin was assumed into this heaven, and placed between her Son and the saints:

> The part that is already risen is the part that has attained the stole [of immortality] of the soul, as is understood from what has been said above; or rather, the stole of the body and the soul, if there are some who already find themselves in the homeland together with the Lord; and this I believe to be absolutely true for the Blessed Virgin and for others who have risen with the Lord (cf. Mt 27:52–53).[19]

Then there is another heaven, the trinitarian heaven; this incorporeal and uncreated heaven remains the exclusive dwelling place of God.[20]

Mary's Place in the Economy of Salvation

The mystery of the redemption is an event that concerns the human race, considered both as a whole and as individual persons. Albert defines that, in strict justice, only Christ the Redeemer could pay the general debt that all humanity contracted in Adam. The saints, for their part, are able to offer only a particular collaboration on behalf of individual persons, because of their merits that are considered acceptable by God (*ex congruo*). The Blessed Virgin's contribution is placed on this level.[21]

---

[18] See *De resurrectione*, tr. 2, q. 9, a. 5; Cologne 26:288.

[19] *In 4 Sententiarum*, dis. 13, a. 14, ad quaest. 2; ed. Borgnet, 29:360. Cf. also *De resurrectione*, tr. 2, q. 5; Cologne, 26:263.

[20] See *De resurrectione*, tr. 2, q. 9, a. 3; Cologne, 26:286.

[21] See *In 3 Sententiarum*, dis. 19, a. 1; ed. Borgnet, 28:337.

Nevertheless, her cooperation in salvation extends to the whole process of human redemption. Albert the Great defends Mary's cooperation based on the principle, already stated by the Fathers, of her association in the life and work of Christ (*principium consortii*), as Mother of the Redeemer. For, in the mystery of the Incarnation, the fullness of divinity dwelled in her bodily, and she became, as it were, the source and conduit of grace for us.

The Virgin's cooperation continues even after her exaltation to eternal glory, because she intercedes from heaven to help us. The term "Mediatrix" and other equivalent terms recur frequently in Albert's Marian writings. He describes Mary's role concisely and clearly:

> Through the Mother we have access to the Son, and through the Son to the Father. With such guides to lead us, let us have no fear at all of being refused reconciliation.[22]

When she intervenes with her Son, Mary excludes no one from her prayer of intercession. Our Doctor refers to the famous story of the conversion of Theophilus, from which it is plainly seen how the Mother of the Lord does not leave anyone behind:

> She is the hope of forgiveness for those who are sorry for their sins and expiate them in this world. And in the underworld, they cite the example of the miracle of Theophilus, whom Mary reformed by the grace of forgiveness. But those above, innocent in grace, have in Mary the channel of that grace, by which they are kept from sin.[23]

We see, however, how Albert particularly underscores the mercy of the Mother of God toward sinners:

> Moved by pity and mercy, she speaks persuasively to her Son, interceding for sinners, and, by the support of her merits, she restores the repentant to the level of grace they had lost.[24]

But our Doctor does not share the opinion that to Christ belong only judgment and condemnation, while the exercise of mercy and interceding on our behalf falls to Mary. Jesus himself is a God of love and mercy. And so, Albert also rejects the image of a Blessed Virgin in heaven who

---

[22] *De natura boni*; Cologne, 25.1:59.

[23] *In Lucam 1,48*; ed. Borgnet, 22:130.

[24] *De natura boni*; Cologne, 25.1:51.

has regard only for us. She is, above all, absorbed in the contemplation of God, and thus she reconciles in herself the attitude of Martha and that of Mary (cf. Lk 10:41–42). Albert takes well-defined positions against certain intemperate statements that were beginning to insinuate themselves into the Marian doctrine of his time.[25]

Mother of Men

As the Mother of the incarnate Word, Mary is also the Mother of all men, since all men are called to faith. And so the role that she plays on our behalf is maternal by nature, and, in the final analysis, it is revealed by actions that aim to make the image of her divine Son grow within us:

> For the Virgin Mother even now nurses, with her sweetness, the Christ formed in the hearts of many. And if she did not, then he who was but recently formed there would perish.[26]

To her, Mother of all the faithful, the faithful owe their virtues and their merits, which were obtained by her intercession. Albert, however, does not call Mary "Mother of the Church". Instead, she is the Church's model and type:

> And so, as Ambrose says, she is the model [exemplum] of holy Church, just as Joseph is the model of the prelates of the Church.[27]

Mary, by her act of giving birth, is an image of the Church who gives her children birth unto the Christian life:

> For the Mother, who conceives and bears in her chaste womb, is a figure of the Church, while her Son is a figure of those who have been born again.[28]

Mary is also an image of the Church as Virgin and Bride. Citing Origen, our author writes:

> And so she is married (cf. Mt 1:18), so that she might stand for the Church, who is Virgin and Bride.[29]

---

[25] On Albert the Great's teaching about Mary's mediation, see M. M. Desmarrais, *Albert le Grand, docteur de la médiation mariale* (Paris, 1935).

[26] *In Lucam 11,27*; ed. Borgnet, 23:127.

[27] *In Lucam 2,5*; ed. Borgnet, 22:197.

[28] *Postilla super Isaiam 11,1*; Cologne, 19:163.

[29] *In Matthaeum 1,18*; Cologne, 21.1:25.

Devotion to Mary

The principal justification for the veneration of Mary consists in her divine motherhood. Because her Son is God, she is the Mother of God and, therefore, the highest of creatures after her Son, the only one who can equal her.

Albert, however, does not hold that anything said or done to honor Mary necessarily redounds to the glory of her Son. Devotion to Mary must be expressed within defined limits. The kind of veneration appropriate to the Blessed Virgin is *hyperdulia*, which must never be transformed into the worship of *latria*, owed to God alone. He writes:

> The Blessed Virgin must be honored with the veneration of hyperdulia. However much the honor paid to the Mother goes to the honor of the King, nevertheless, because he had a separate generation in his divinity, she has no right to divine honors, since her Son did not receive his own divinity from her.[30]

And yet, devotion to the Virgin cannot be reduced to praise and invocation alone, even though these are important expressions of piety. In addition, the faithful need to imitate her life and her virtues, especially her great faith.

READINGS

BLESSED ARE YOU BECAUSE YOU BELIEVED!

Notice that [Elizabeth] adds a mention of blessedness (cf. Lk 1:45). If being blessed is an act in conformity with perfect virtue of spirit, then Mary was most blessed, for she was full of virtues and grace. She was so prudent and had such great faith and trust that she merited to conceive [the Lord], and by her faith she became the foundation and pillar of the whole Church.

For to believe, as Augustine says, is to think with assent and to cling to the object of faith with complete devotion. In giving her assent, she said, "Let it be done to me according to your word", but in thinking, she

---

[30] *In 3 Sententiarum*, dis. 9, a. 9; ed. Borgnet, 28:132.

asked how it would happen. And with her devotion, she sought the object of her faith, when in prayer she drew the Word to herself, saying in spirit the words of the Song of Songs, "My Beloved is mine and I am his" (Song 2:16), and again, "I cling to my Beloved" (Song 8:5).

As blessed Dionysius says, faith is the light that introduces the truth into believers and the truth dwelling in them. Therefore, Mary clung completely to the first truth of the Wisdom of God, who is her Son, as it says in 1 Corinthians 1:24, "Christ [is] the power of God and the wisdom of God." And so [Elizabeth said to Mary] "blessed are you who believed", because she, in her contemplation, thought of the truth with wonder. Full of faith and truth, she gave her assent, and with this love for the truth, she sought the truth most devotedly in prayer.

Through the Son she conceived, she found the truth; through knowledge, she came to dwell in the truth; and by the Son's taking flesh, the truth came to dwell in her. Genesis 28:16 says, "Surely the LORD is in this place." Because God has made this place an unfathomable mystery.

While the truth dwells in the hearts of all the faithful, in the Blessed Virgin the truth also dwelled in her womb. So let us give no sleep to our eyes, to our eyelids let us give no slumber, until we find a place for the Lord, a tabernacle for the God of Jacob (cf. Ps 131:4–5).

—St. Albert the Great, *In Lucam 1, 45*; ed. Borgnet, 22:121–22

THE VIRGIN'S INTERVENTION AT CANA

"They have no wine" (Jn 2:3). She does not say, "Give them some wine", because she wants to show respect for her Son, placing her hope in her Son's freedom and mercy. And so she mentions only the lack [of wine]. Chrysostom asked, for what reason did she presume that her Son would have been able to do this, considering that he had worked no miracle during his infancy?[31] But the problem does not exist, because she knew that her Son was God by nature and able to do all that he willed. Moreover, she had previously known the miracle of the star, the prophecy of Simeon, the adoration of the Magi, the words of the shepherds, the joy of the angels, the witness of John [the Baptist], the voice of the Father, and the figure of the dove.

---

[31] See *In Joannem*, hom. 21, 1; PG 59, 129.

In all these events, his divinity had begun to manifest itself; and so she knew that the hour of his manifestation through signs had now begun, so that she asked for a sign in a case where it was so needful and would be so useful. For this reason the prudent Mother of Jesus, who "kept all these things in her heart" (Lk 2:51), said to him, "They have no wine" (Jn 2:3).

—St Albert the Great, *In Joannem* 2, 3; ed. Borgnet, 24:91-92

5

THOMAS AQUINAS
(d. 1274)

A perusal of Aquinas' works might give the impression that the Angelic Doctor did not pay much attention to Marian doctrine. Compared to the immense mountain of his writings, those pages in which he considers the Blessed Virgin are relatively few. And yet, it has been recognized that some fundamental directions for later mariological developments and the scientific organization of Mariology were suggested by his towering contribution to theology, along with the ingenious way its various components are organized, and his methods of research.

Marian Doctor

Thomas was born at Roccasecca, to the family of the counts of Aquino, around 1224. When still a small boy, he was sent to the Benedictine monastery of Monte Cassino to be educated and introduced to the monastic life. Because Thomas was the youngest son, his family was planning an ecclesiastical career for him. But he did not embrace the Benedictine life. In 1239, he took the Dominican habit and enrolled in the general *studium* of the order in Naples. In 1245, his superiors sent him to Paris, where his teacher was St. Albert the Great, whom he followed to Cologne in 1248. He himself became a master of theology in Paris from 1252 to 1259, after which he returned to Italy to teach, first at Anagni, then at Orvieto, and finally at Rome. We find him again in Paris from 1269 to 1272, teaching theology. In 1272, he returned to Naples to teach. In 1274, while traveling to France to take part in the Council of Lyons at the behest of Pope Gregory X, he fell gravely ill and died on March 7 in the abbey of Fossanova.

His biographers have emphasized his exceptional devotion to Mary, which he practiced while still in infancy. After entering the order of

Friars Preachers, he breathed in the atmosphere of Marian piety that characterized the order from its beginning; nor can the personal influence of his master, Albert the Great, be undervalued. His first biographer, William of Tocco, passed on this significant piece of information:

> The Virgin named him her doctor and enriched him with that most exceptional learning and purity which set him apart from others.[1]

His Marian Doctrine [2]

Most of Aquinas' Marian texts belong to works tied to his teaching activity, such as the *Summa Theologiae*, the *Summa contra Gentiles*, his commentary on the *Sententiae* of Peter Lombard, and his various commentaries on Sacred Scripture. Among his writings we also find a commentary on the *Ave Maria* and some Marian content in his sermons.

Thomas' doctrine regarding the Mother of God is thoroughly incorporated into his Christology and developed on strictly theological foundations. He considers the plan of God as a whole. After the estrangement from God caused by sin, the plan envisions our return to him through the Incarnation of his Son. Mary plays an essential role in this mystery of salvation. Thomas derives this soteriological vision from the Scriptures, reinforcing his theses with the authority of Church councils and the

---

[1] Cited in C. Roschini, *Maria santissima nella storia della salvezza*, vol. 1 (Isola del Liri, 1969), pp. 440–41.

[2] We confine ourselves to some basic bibliographic references: F. Margott, *Maria nella dottrina di San Tommaso d'Aquino* (Piacenza, 1888); G. Roschini, "La mariologia di San Tommaso", *Studi Mariani* 2 (Rome, 1950); M. Cuervo, *Santo Tomás en mariología* (Villava-Pamplona, 1968); F. Smith, "Mary in the Perspective of St. Thomas' Teaching on the Gifts of the Holy Spirit", in CongrRom 4:509–15; F. Jelly, "St. Thomas's Theological Interpretation of the 'Theotokos' and Vatican II's Hierarchy of Truths of Catholic Doctrine", in CongrRom 4:517–28; W. Cole, "Thomas on Mary and Woman: A Study in Contrasts", in CongrRom 4:529–81; J. L. Illanes Maestre, "La vida de María en cuanto objeto del saber mariológico (Aproximación al tema en Tomás de Aquino)", ScriptaMar 6 (1983): 153–67; D. Bertetto, "Maria SS. nella Summa Theologiae", *Sacra Doctrina* 36 (1991): 505–33; P. Giustiniani, "Le prediche sull'Ave Maria di San Tommaso d'Aquino", *XVI Centenario del Concilio di Capua (392–1992)* (Capua 1993), pp. 459–98; H. M. Manteau-Bonamy, "La Liberté du Fiat de Marie selon les oeuvres de Saint Thomas d'Aquin", *Mater Fidei et Fidelium*, Marian Library Studies 17–23 (1985–1991), pp. 289–96; D. Ols, "La Bienheureuse Vierge Marie selon Saint Thomas", in *Littera, sensus, sententia* (Milan, 1991), pp. 435–53.

Fathers, both Latin and Eastern. He refers especially to Ambrose, Jerome, Augustine, Leo the Great, Anselm, Bernard, Hugh of Saint-Victor, John Chrysostom, Cyril of Alexandria, and John Damascene. Thomas also had the great insight to allow himself to be inspired by the great masters of his own time, such as Peter Lombard, Alexander of Hales, Albert the Great, and Bonaventure.

A New Mariological Perspective

In the third part of the *Summa Theologiae*, Thomas begins with the centrality of the incarnate Word in the mystery of salvation, placing the Virgin Mother within the perspective of the Son whom she conceived by the working of the Holy Spirit. When we consider the Incarnation in this perspective, we see the Son of God, not ascending but, rather, lowering himself:

> In the mystery of the Incarnation there was not an ascent, as if there some preexisting reality [Christ's body] was raised to the dignity of union [with the Word of God]. This was the opinion of the heretic Photinus.[3] Instead, the Incarnation is considered to be a descent, in the sense that the perfect Word of God took on the imperfection of our nature, in accordance with the Gospel saying: "I have come down from heaven" (Jn 6:38, 51).[4]

Aquinas defines the main reason why Christ's conception must be called supernatural and miraculous in an absolute sense: its active principle is the Holy Spirit. At the same time, from another angle it can be considered natural; that is, according to the material that was conceived, since his Mother conceived a normal human body.[5]

Nevertheless, Mary did not conceive a human creature who was subsequently assumed by the Word; rather, she conceived Jesus' body, which, from the first instant, was the body of the incarnate Word. This explains why she is truly the Mother of God. Therefore, she entered into a real and personal relation with the Son of God. This relation involved,

---

[3] Fourth-century heretic. He became bishop of Sirmium; but he was deposed and exiled in 351. We do not have an exact knowledge of his errors because none of his writings has survived. Probably he professed a form of Sabellianism.

[4] III, q. 33, a. 3 ad 3.

[5] Ibid., a. 4, corpus.

not merely her physical element, but her whole person. The personal relation of the Mother of God to her Son surpasses all the relations of creatures with their Creator.

It follows that the divine motherhood, in the Thomistic view, represents the *raison d'être* of all the other privileges of Mary. It is the basic explanation of why it is fitting that these privileges have been conceded her by the Lord in such generous measure.

The Sanctification of the Virgin

In keeping with the theology of his time, Thomas appears to reject the Marian privilege of the Immaculate Conception. Some scholars hold that it is difficult to clarify Aquinas' position on this point with certainty, because he would not have expressed himself in these exact terms.[6] In any case, we can say that his thought is clearly presented, at least in the *Summa Theologiae*: Mary could not have been immune from original sin without taking something away from the dogma of the redemption. Aquinas treats the argument in the six articles of question 27 of the third part. Posing the question whether the Blessed Virgin was sanctified before her body received a soul, he responds in the negative, for two reasons:

> The sanctification of the Blessed Virgin cannot be understood to have happened before ensoulment, for two reasons. In the first place, because the sanctification of which we speak consists in purification from original sin, for sanctity is "total purity", as Dionysius says. But guilt can be purified only by grace, and only a rational creature can be the subject of grace. Therefore the Blessed Virgin was not sanctified before the infusion of a rational soul.
>
> In the second place, because only a rational creature is subject to guilt, the offspring conceived is not susceptible to any guilt before the infusion of a rational soul. And so, if the Blessed Virgin had been sanctified in any way before ensoulment, she would never have incurred the stain of original sin.
>
> In this case, she would have had no need of the redemption and salvation that come from Christ, of whom the Gospel says: "He will save

---

[6] See J. A. Robilliard and P. M. de Contenson, "Bulletin d'histoire des doctrines médiévales", RSPhTH 39 (1955): 464–65.

his people from their sins" (Mt 1:21). But it is not fitting that Christ not be "the Savior of all men" (1 Tim 4:10), as St. Paul says.

And so, the only possibility left is that the sanctification of the Blessed Virgin happened after her ensoulment.[7]

This reasoning is founded on the conviction that some interval of time intervenes between conception and the infusion of the soul, during which the fetus conceived cannot be the subject either of grace or of guilt.

However, in the previous article, the Angelic Doctor had accepted the opinion that Mary was sanctified in her mother's womb before her birth, even though Scripture says nothing about it. This kind of biblical lacuna does not constitute an insuperable obstacle. A similar case arises with regard to the truth of the Assumption into heaven, which Augustine (actually, the pseudo–Augustine) upholds and defends even in the absence of explicit scriptural witnesses. Therefore, Thomas concludes:

> We may reasonably argue that she was sanctified in her mother's womb. For it is reasonable to believe that she, who gave birth to "the only-begotten Son of the Father, full of grace and truth" (Jn 1:14), received greater privileges of grace than all others. This is why the angel said to her, "Hail, full of grace" (Lk 1:28).[8]

The privilege of sanctification was also conceded to others, such as Jeremiah and John the Baptist. All the more reason it is fitting that it should be granted to the Mother of the Lord.[9]

Sanctification brings, not only liberation from guilt, but also the gift of grace, which God gives to each, according to the end for which he was chosen. He granted Mary the fullness of grace, as the consequence of her being chosen to be the Mother of God:

> The Blessed Virgin Mary obtained such a fullness of grace that she was made very close to the Author of grace, so that she contained within herself the One who is full of every grace, and, giving birth to him, she in some way made grace reach everyone.[10]

---

[7] III, q. 27, a. 2, corpus.

[8] Ibid., a. 1, corpus.

[9] See ibid.

[10] Ibid., a. 5 ad primum.

Mary and Salvation

Thomas never speaks of Mary exercising a role as Mediatrix in heaven. However, the text just cited opens up the theme of her participation in the mystery of human salvation, although the words of the Angelic Doctor seem to urge an attitude of prudent caution about the matter.

Above all, he envisions the mediation of grace on Mary's part solely in relation to her motherly participation in the mystery of the Incarnation, in view of which she received the fullness of grace. He reasons in this way:

> The closer something gets to a principle, the more it participates in that principle's effects. . . . Now, Christ is the principle of grace, authoritatively in his divinity and instrumentally in his humanity. . . . But the Blessed Virgin was the closest to Christ with regard to humanity, because he took his human nature from her. And so, she had to receive from Christ a fullness of grace, greater than that of all others.[11]

This fullness, which Mary received in the divine Person of the Word made flesh in her womb, is not meant for her alone. Through her, it is distributed to all men who accept it in order to be saved. Thomas explains this at length in his commentary on the *Ave Maria*. The Virgin's fullness of grace can be considered from three points of view:

1. in relation to her soul, to which it was granted in perfect measure, in order to help her do good and conquer evil;

2. in relation to her body, which was rendered worthy to conceive the Son of God by grace;

3. in relation to other human creatures. For every man who possesses grace is able to have an influence on the salvation of some of his fellowmen. Christ and Mary, however, possess such a fullness of grace that it is sufficient for the salvation of all men of this world.[12]

At this point we can understand the expression "in some way" (*quodammodo*) used in the text cited above.[13] Aquinas uses it to mean that he does

---

[11] Ibid., corpus.

[12] See *Expositio super salutatione angelica scilicet Ave Maria*, in Opuscula omnia, vol. 4, ed, P. Mandonnet (Paris, 1927), pp. 456–60.

[13] See III, q. 27, a. 1, corpus.

not intend to attribute to Mary a mediation in the strict and direct sense; rather, he is speaking a kind of indirect mediation, which is expressed in and through her role as Mother of God.

Further, always in relation to the mystery of the Incarnation, the Angelic Doctor considers Mary a representative of all humanity:

> In the Annunciation, the Virgin was being asked to give her consent in the name of the whole human race.[14]

In Mary's *fiat*, spoken in response to the message of the angel Gabriel, is included the consent of every human being who decides to accept the plan of salvation that God has prepared for him in Christ, the Redeemer.

READINGS

THE MARRIAGE BETWEEN MARY AND JOSEPH WAS A TRUE MARRIAGE

Matrimony or marriage is said to be "true" when it attains to its perfection. But the perfection of a thing is twofold: first perfection and second perfection. The first perfection of a thing consists in its very form, from which it receives its species, while the second perfection of a thing consists in the operation of the thing, through which a thing somehow attains its end. Now the form of matrimony consists in a certain indivisible joining of souls, through which one spouse is bound to keep faith with the other indivisibly. The end of matrimony, however, is the birth and upbringing of offspring, the first of which is attained by conjugal intercourse, and the second of which is attained by the other actions of husband and wife, by which they assist one another to rear their offspring.

So it must be said, as to the first perfection, that the marriage of the Virgin [Mother] of God and Joseph was absolutely a true marriage, because both consented to the conjugal bond, but not expressly to a physical bond, except on this condition: that it be pleasing to God. For this reason the angel calls Mary Joseph's wife, saying to Joseph, "Do not fear to take Mary [as] your wife" (Mt 1:20). And when Augustine comments on these words in his book *De nuptiis et concupiscentia*, he says,

---

[14] III, q. 30, a. 1, corpus.

"She is called 'wife' because of her first pledge to marry him, whom he had not known nor was ever to know by intercourse." [15]

But as to the second perfection, which is attained by the act of marriage, if this be referred to physical intercourse, through which offspring are begotten, then this marriage was not consummated. For this reason Ambrose says in his commentary on Luke, "Let it not surprise you that Scripture frequently calls Mary 'wife' (see Lk 1:26–27). For this word does not signify a loss of her virginity, but, rather, it witnesses to the fact that she was married and declares that a wedding was celebrated." [16] And yet, this marriage had its second perfection, with regard to the upbringing of offspring. Which is why Augustine says in his book *De nuptiis et concupiscentia*, "Every good of marriage was fulfilled in the parents of Christ: offspring, mutual faith, and sacrament. We know that there was offspring: the Lord Jesus himself. We know that they kept faith with each other, because there was no adultery; we know there was a sacrament, because there was no divorce. The only thing missing was marital intercourse." [17]

—St. Thomas Aquinas, *Summa Theologiae*, III, q. 29, a. 2, corpus

THE BODY OF CHRIST WAS FORMED FROM
THE MOST PURE BLOOD OF MARY

In the conception of Christ, it was in accord with the condition of nature that he was born of a woman, but it was above the condition of nature that he was born of a virgin. The natural condition is such that in the generation of a living creature the female supplies the matter, but it falls to the male to supply the active principle in generation, as the Philosopher demonstrates in his book.[18]

But a woman who conceives with the participation of a man is not a virgin. And so it belongs to the supernatural mode of the generation of Christ that the active principle in his generation was the supernatural divine power of God; but it belongs to the natural mode of his generation

---

[15] 11, 12; PL 44, 420.

[16] 2, 1, 5; PL 15, 1555.

[17] 11, 13; PL 44, 421.

[18] See Aristotle, *De generatione animalium*, lib. 1, cc. 2 and 20; lib. 2, c. 4; lib. 4, c. 1.

that the matter from which his body was conceived was in conformity with the matter that other women contribute to the conception of off-spring.

Now this matter, according to the Philosopher, is the blood of the woman, and not just any kind of blood, but blood subjected to a certain fuller concentration by the generative capacity of the mother, so that it becomes suitable matter for conception. And so it was from this sort of matter that the body of Christ was conceived.

—St. Thomas Aquinas, *Summa Theologiae*, III, q. 31, a. 5, corpus

MARY IS EXEMPT FROM THE CURSES OF SIN

Three curses were given to men because of sin. The first was given to a woman, namely, that she would conceive in corruption, carry her children with heaviness, and give birth in pain. But the Blessed Virgin was immune from this curse, because she conceived without corruption, carried her child in solace, and gave birth to the Savior in joy, as Isaiah says, "It shall blossom abundantly, and rejoice with joy and singing" (Is 35:2).

The second curse was given to man, namely, that he would earn his bread in the sweat of his brow. The Blessed Virgin was immune from this; because, as the Apostle says, "Virgins are released from the cares of this world and free to live for God alone" (cf. 1 Cor 7:34).

The third curse was common to both men and women, namely, that they would return to dust. And the Blessed Virgin was immune from this, because she was assumed into heaven with her body. For we believe that, after her death, she was raised and carried up into heaven. As the Psalm says, "Go up, O Lord, to your rest; you and the ark of your holiness" (Ps 131:8).

And so, she was immune from every curse and, thus, "blessed among women" because she alone took away the curse and bore a blessing and opened the gate of heaven. Thus the name "Mary", which is rendered "Star of the Sea", suits her. Because just as sailors on the ocean are guided to a harbor by a star, so Christians are guided to glory by Mary.

—St. Thomas Aquinas, *Expositio super salutationem angelicam*

6

JOHN DUNS SCOTUS
(d. 1308)

The famous Franciscan philosopher and theologian John Duns Scotus has passed into history under the title "Doctor of the Immaculate Conception", and deservedly so. For, by opposing the teaching of the majority of the theologians of his time, he opened the way to a positive understanding of this Marian privilege. Five and a half centuries later, Mary's Immaculate Conception was solemnly defined as a revealed truth and dogma of the faith by the extraordinary Magisterium of the Church.

Outline of His Life and Times

It is certain that our author was born in Scotland around 1265. After completing his initial studies, he entered the Franciscan order at a very young age, about the year 1280. He received priestly ordination in 1291, and, in 1303, after gaining his bachelor's in theology, he obtained a teaching post in Paris, as commentator on the books of Peter Lombard's *Sententiae*. Very soon, however, he was obliged to leave the city. This happened because, in June 1303, he had refused to subscribe to an appeal to the Council that had arisen against Pope Boniface VIII at the initiative of Philip the Fair, King of France, a proud adversary of the pontiff. The following year, Scotus returned to Paris to work toward a doctorate, which he obtained in 1305.[1] He subsequently taught at Oxford, Canterbury, again at Paris, and finally at Cologne, where he died in 1308.

Although Duns Scotus died at a rather young age, he left behind an impressive reputation for knowledge and holiness. He was named *Doctor subtilis* and recognized as the greatest representative of the Franciscan

---

[1] See H. S. Denifle, *Chartularium Universitatis Parisiensis*, vol. 2 (Paris, 1891), p. 117.

theological school, which took up the Scotist system as its own doctrinal foundation.

The first critical edition of Duns Scotus' writings appeared in 1639 in Lyons, edited by the Irish Franciscan theologian and historian Luke Wadding, and was reprinted in twenty-six volumes between 1891 and 1895 in Paris by Louis Vivès. Not all of the works published in this edition, however, are authentic. Some are definitely spurious, while others are the notes of students who followed the master's lectures, to which he subsequently gave his approval. Given this situation, the work of the Scotist Commission is highly commendable. The Commission was established at the Pontifical Atheneum Antonianum in Rome and has been publishing a new critical edition of Scotus' works since 1950. To date, volumes 1–7 and 16–19 have been published as the *Editio Vaticana*.

Scotus' Marian Doctrine [2]

Marian doctrine occupies a place of great importance in the theological system of John Duns Scotus. He expounds it especially in his commen-

---

[2] Studies of the Marian doctrine of John Duns Scotus are extremely numerous. We cite those that appear most helpful, namely, those that are up-to-date and most suited for deepening our knowledge of this great Franciscan's teaching on the Mother of God: C. Balić, *Joannis Duns Scoti, doctoris mariani, theologiae marianae elementa* (Sibenik, 1933); idem, *De debito peccati originalis in B.V.M. Investigationes de doctrina quam tenuit Joannes Duns Scotus* (Rome, 1941); idem, *Ioannes Duns Scotus, Doctor Immaculatae Conceptionis*, vol. 1, *Textus auctoris*, Bibliotheca Immaculatae Conceptionis 5 (Rome, 1954); idem, "Il reale contributo di Giovanni Scoto nella questione dell'Immacolata Concezione", *Antonianum* 29 (1954): 457–96; idem, "Ioannes Duns Scotus et historia Immaculatae Conceptionis", *Antonianum* 30 (1955): 386–440, 486–88; idem, "De regula mariologica Joannis Duns Scoti", *Euntes Docete* 9 (1954): 110–33; B. Innocenti, "Il concetto teologico di maternità divina in Giovanni Duns Scoto", *Studi Francescani* 3 (1931): 404–30; I. Uribesago, "La coredención mariana a la luz de la cristología de Escoto", EstMar 9 (1944): 219–37; G. Roschini, "Duns Scoto e l'Immacolata", in Mar 17 (1955): 183–258; idem, "Questioni su Duns Scoto e l'Immacolata", EphMar 7 (1957): 372–407; L. Babbini, *Ancora su Duns Scoto, dottore dell'Immacolata: Valutazione delle tre repliche del rev. Padre G. Roschini* (Genoa, 1958); J. F. Bonnefoy, *Le Vén. Jean Duns Scot, docteur de l'Immaculée Conception: Son milieu, sa doctrine, son influence* (Rome, 1960); G. Roschini, *Duns Scoto e l'Immacolata secondo il Padre J. Fr. Bonnefoy* (Rome, 1961); K. Koser, "Die Immaculatalehre des Joannes Duns Scotus", *Franziskanishe Studien* 36 (1954): 337–84; R. Rosini, "Il volto dell'Immacolata nel pensiero di Giovanni Duns Scoto", in CongrRom 5:1–29; R. Zavalloni and

tary on the *Sententiae* of Peter Lombard, in particular the *In 3 Sententiarum*, d. 3, q. 1[3] and d. 4.[4] He lays particular stress on three mariological principles: Mary's divine motherhood, her perpetual virginity, and her freedom from original sin.

Mary's Motherhood

Basing his exposition on the authority of St. John Damascene, our author explains that Mary is the true Mother of God. For she did not give birth to a mere human being whose nature was later joined to divinity, as Nestorius claimed, but to a human nature that, from the first instant of its existence, had been assumed by the Word of God so as to form one single being in which the Person of the Word supplies the personhood that belongs to a human nature. For this reason it is said that the Person of the incarnate Son of God subsists in two natures; and Scotus demonstrates this by the fact that the Word immediately assumed a complete human nature, for which his Divine Person supplies the absence of human personhood.[5] He receives his original existence from the divine nature of the Word, while he receives a second existence, that is to say, his existence as man, from his human nature, which is secondary.[6]

In the mystery of the Incarnation, the Virgin truly cooperated in the conception of the incarnate Word. She furnished the Word with a human nature, thus fulfilling the role he had granted her, becoming a mother in the fullest possible sense of the word. Scotus strongly emphasizes the role played by the Mother of the Lord in the Incarnation, which guarantees a fully human dimension to the bodily conception of the Son of God. In addition, Scotus' thesis introduces a genuinely new element in comparison to the scientific theories of his time, which, being anchored in the teaching of Aristotle,[7] assigned the woman a purely passive role in procreation. These theories held that only the man had an active

---

E. Mariani, eds., *La dottrina mariologica di Giovanni Duns Scoto*, Spicilegium Pontifici Atenaei Antoniani 28 (Rome, 1987) (the second part contains the Marian texts of Duns Scotus, ed. E. Mariani).

[3] Ed. Vivès, 14:159–76.

[4] Ibid., 14:180–203.

[5] See *In 3 Sententiarum*, d. 2, q. 2, n. 5; ed. Vivès, 14:131.

[6] Ibid., d. 6, q. 3, n. 2; ed. Vivès, 14:326.

[7] See *De animalium generatione* 1, 21.

role, while the woman was limited to offering the matter needed for the formation of her offspring's body. Scotus, by contrast, followed a thesis already formulated by Galen, according to which both parents have an active role in the generative process. Scotus' explanation takes as its point of departure a purely natural point of view:

> Every active cause that has the power to bring about any effect, if not preceded by something else totally causing that effect in the very instant it is produced, can act on behalf of its own production. If this was the case with all other mothers, then it was the case with Mary; namely, as a non-principal active cause. The Holy Spirit gave her, at the same time, the potential to receive and to bear, not however that he gave her that fruitfulness in a miraculous way, by which she cooperated; no, she had it naturally, because she was not sterile, and because of this capacity she could have cooperated naturally to bring forth a son, should a natural father have begotten one by her.[8]

But Scotus points out that the woman's generative capacity is not the principal and independent cause of conception; by nature, it is subordinate to the man's generative capacity, and therefore it cannot function without having been activated by the involvement of a man. In the generation of the incarnate Word, the action of the principal natural cause (a man) was replaced by the mysterious and miraculous action of the Holy Spirit, who activated the Blessed Virgin's capacity for fruitfulness, which she possessed by nature, acting in her case as the principal cause and conferring an unmistakably supernatural character.

On the other hand, the action of the Holy Spirit did not in any way diminish Mary's role in the generation of the Son. Duns Scotus points out that Mary was able to cooperate fully by means of her own personal causal action, since the intervention of the Holy Spirit, who acted with the causality proper to divine omnipotence, could not pose any obstacle to the exercise of her maternal function. The Holy Spirit only supplied, to an outstanding degree, the causality of a human father.[9]

---

[8] *In 3 Sententiarum*, d. 4, q. unica, n. 10; ed. Vivès, 14:194. Scotus adds, "Only that mother had the obediential potency to be the Mother of the Word. For she was the Mother of the Word by the fact that the Word subsisted in that [human] nature which he had united to himself" (ibid.).

[9] See ibid., nn. 8–10; ed. Vivès, 14:192–94.

Nevertheless, since there was no involvement of a human father in the generation of the incarnate Word, it seems obvious that Mary's active role acquired an exceptionally important quality, being the unique instance of its kind. Consequently, Mary, as a unique mother, acquired a maternal, and thus a uniquely personal, relation to her Son, who, by virtue of his divine nature, was already subject to an eternal and uncreated relation to his heavenly Father. Given the absolutely central position of the incarnate Word in the economy of salvation, it is clear that Mary's divine motherhood acquires a fundamental importance and represents a function that is considered fundamental with respect to all the other prerogatives and functions of the Virgin Mother.

Mary's Virginity

Scotus' treatment of Mary's perpetual virginity is somewhat inconsistent. His analysis of this theme considers its three components: before, during, and after the birth of Christ. Accepting an opinion already shared by some Fathers of the Church and later theologians, he says that the Virgin took a vow of virginity in absolute terms, not reserving the option to renounce the vow, in case she should come to know that God had arranged things differently:

> In every vow, however absolute, it seems that this condition is included: if God pleases. Because no one should offer anything to God whether God wills it or no, and no one acts rightly when he intends to offer something to God in this way. Therefore a vow remains absolute, even with this condition understood.[10]

The absolute character of Mary's vow is seen to be asserted by the Virgin's words to Gabriel: "How can this be since I do not know man?" (Lk 1:34). Scotus explains:

> If she had simply not known man, without intending never to know one, there would be no problem because, if she had subsequently known a man, provided she was not sterile, she would have conceived. And so it was a question about the more-than-marvelous way [she would conceive], because she had most firmly decided, or vowed, that she would never be known by man, and to make this understood the angel

---

[10] *In 4 Sententiarum*, d. 30, q. 2; ed. Vivès, 19:278.

explained when he answered her: "The Holy Spirit will come upon you" (Lk 1:35).[11]

Scotus thinks that the Blessed Virgin, without having been aware of it beforehand, made a vow that fully coincided with certain details of God's plan for the Incarnation of his Son.

The Virgin Is Preserved from Original Sin

The third main point of Scotus' Mariology concerns the mystery of the Immaculate Conception, which the Scottish theologian defended with conviction. As we have said, this is the most interesting and original chapter of his Marian doctrine, its proudest hour. We will focus our attention primarily on this theme, which best allows us to evaluate the historical and theological importance of Duns Scotus' Marian doctrine. In terms of strict historical order, he was not the first author to teach the mystery of the Immaculate Conception. We have already mentioned Eadmer, and we could add Robert Grosseteste and William of Ware, as authors who had already declared in favor of this truth of the faith. These are all ecclesiastical figures from in or around England, as was Duns Scotus himself, and this confirms that a certain mentality existed in that region of Christendom that tended to accept the Immaculate Conception. This may also be deduced from the fact that England was the first country in the West in which the celebration of the liturgical feast of Mary's Conception was introduced. First observed around the middle of the eleventh century, then suppressed after the Norman conquest of 1066, it was restored around 1127.[12] But it was Scotus who fully developed the doctrine of Mary's preservation from original sin and bolstered it with vigorous probative argumentation, thus outlining a true theological proof of the doctrine.

It must be recognized that this sort of theological proof lacks a consistent proof based on Scripture and that appeal to the tradition of the Fathers of the Church appears rather weak. Yet, Scotus let himself be

---

[11] Ibid.

[12] See A. W. Burridge, "L'Immaculée Conception dans la théologie mariale de l'Angleterre du Moyen-Âge", *Revue d'Histoire Ecclésiastique* 32 (1936): 570–97; A. M. Cecchin, "L'Immacolata nella liturgia occidentale anteriore al secolo XIII", Mar 5 (1943): 58–114.

led by his intuition as a believer, thus managing to outline a doctrine that contains all the fundamental elements of the dogma. He formulates a second principle, according to which it is legitimate to attribute to the Blessed Virgin what seems to be more excellent, as long as this is not opposed to the witness of Scripture and to the teaching authority of the Church,[13] and he applies this principle to the mystery of the Immaculate Conception.

Using his considerable logical ability, Scotus was able to overrule the objections traditionally raised against the Virgin's immunity from original sin. In essence, these objections may be reduced to two: the unavoidable transmission of original guilt to all the descendants of Adam and the universal scope of the redemption wrought by Christ, because of which no human being can obtain salvation without having been redeemed by the incarnate Word.

Duns Scotus was able to demonstrate how the truth of these two conditions does not necessarily create any obstacle to the Marian privilege of the Immaculate Conception. He admits that, if only the law of nature had been at work in Mary, she too would have had to contract original guilt. In her case, however, there was an exceptional preservative intervention on God's part, based on the foreseen merits Christ the Redeemer acquired by his redemptive work. In this connection, Scotus writes:

> As a consequence of common generation, Mary would have had to contract original sin had she not been preserved by the grace of the Mediator.[14]

These words clearly show our author's reasoning. Mary's exceptional condition was caused, not by the introduction of a change into human nature, but by an external supernatural intervention. Further, her exemption from original sin does not in any way mean that the redemption was useless. Instead, her privilege shows how redemption was wrought in the Blessed Virgin in a unique way. Instead of being liberated from a

---

[13] See *In III Sententiarum*, d. 3, q. 1, n. 5; ed. Vivès, 14:165. Scotus employs a variant of the famous axiom: *Potuit, decuit, ergo fecit*, which, often erroneously attributed to Scotus, was already present, in substance, in earlier theological tradition; the precise form is the work of the Scotists. See R. Rossini, *Mariologia del beato Giovanni Duns Scoto* (Castelpetroso, 1994), p. 80, n. 16.

[14] Balić, *Joannes Duns Scotus, Doctor Immaculatae Conceptionis*, 1:16.

sin she had contracted, she was preserved from contracting it, by virtue of the foreseen merits of Christ the Redeemer. In her case, then, there was a preservative redemption. It would be wrong to say that the Mother of the Lord had no need of redemption; to the contrary, it must be recognized that a different form of redemption was applied in her case. Scotus writes:

> Just as others needed Christ, so that through his merits they might receive the forgiveness of sin already contracted, so she needed the Mediator to preserve her from sin.[15]

Purification and liberation from sin are not the only means to redemption; it can also be accomplished by preventing sin from being transmitted to a person. Thus the universality of redemption is not called into question, because Christ is the Mediator and Redeemer of all human beings, including his Mother. In her case, Christ is Mediator and Redeemer in a more perfect and outstanding way. Duns Scotus demonstrates this by articulating, at this point, his theory of the most perfect Mediator:

> The most perfect Mediator merits the removal of every punishment from the one whom he reconciles, but the original fault is a greater punishment than even the loss of the vision of God . . . because, of all punishments that might befall the intellectual nature, sin is the greatest. Therefore, if Christ reconciled in the most perfect way possible, he merited to remove that most heavy punishment from [at least] someone—and this could only be his Mother.[16]

To his great credit, John Duns Scotus gave the dogma of Mary's exemption from the sin of Adam such a defined form as to make it an integral part of the mystery of redemption. Mary's preservative redemption is viewed as a necessity, postulated on the basis of the most perfect nature of Christ's mediative and redemptive work for the salvation of the human race.

---

[15] Ibid.
[16] *In 3 Sententiarum*, d. 3, q. 1, n. 6; ed. Vivès, 14:161.

READING

THE IMMACULATE CONCEPTION AND THE MEDIATION OF CHRIST

[Mary] did not contract original sin because of the excellence of her Son, inasmuch as he is Redeemer, Reconciler, and Mediator. For the most perfect mediator would perform the most perfect act of mediation on behalf of any person for whom he mediated. But Christ is the most perfect Mediator. Therefore, Christ showed the most perfect possible degree of mediating with respect to any creature or person whose Mediator he was. But for no other person did he exhibit a more excellent degree of mediation than he did for Mary. . . . But this would not have happened if he had not merited that she should be preserved from original sin.

I prove this with three arguments. First, in reference to God, to whom Christ reconciles others; second, in reference to evil, from which he liberates others; third, in reference to the debt of the person whom he reconciles to God.

First. No one placates another in the highest or most perfect way for an offense that someone might commit except by preventing him from being offended. For, if he placates someone who has already been offended, so that the offended party remits [punishment], he does not placate perfectly. . . . Therefore, Christ does not perfectly placate the Trinity for the guilt to be contracted by the sons of Adam if he does not prevent the Trinity from being offended by at least someone, so that consequently the soul of some one descendant of Adam would not have this guilt.

Second. The most perfect Mediator merits the removal of all punishment from the one whom he reconciles. But the original fault is a greater punishment than even the loss of the vision of God . . . because, of all punishments that might befall the intellectual nature, sin is the greatest. Therefore, if Christ reconciled in the most perfect way possible, he merited to remove that most heavy punishment from [at least] someone—and this could only be his Mother.

Further, it seems that Christ restored and reconciled us from original sin more directly than from actual sin, because the necessity of the Incarnation, Passion, and so forth, is commonly attributed to original sin, but it is commonly supposed that he was a perfect Mediator with respect to [at least] one person; for example, Mary, given that he preserved her from all actual sin. Therefore, he acted similarly on her behalf and preserved her from original sin. . . .

Third. A person who has been reconciled is not indebted in the greatest possible way to his mediator unless he has received the greatest possible good from him. But that innocence, which is the preservation from contracting or needing to contract guilt, can be had by means of a mediator. Therefore, no person would be indebted in the highest possible way to Christ as his Mediator if Christ had not preserved someone from original sin.

—John Duns Scotus, *In 3 Sententiarum*, d. 3, q. 1;
ed. Mariani, pp. 181–84

PART FOUR

Toward New Expressions
of Marian Faith and Devotion

(Fourteenth and Fifteenth Centuries)

Prologue

The historical period that embraces the two centuries prior to the Renaissance presents us with a Church marked by many contradictions. A certain malaise in the area of doctrinal study was combined with laxness and abuse in the practice of the Christian life. On the other hand, the Church did not lack for religious individuals and groups who called for serious reforms to bring Christendom back to a more evangelical way of life. These calls for reform were expressed by some remarkable individuals, who have also left us writings of great theological and ascetical value.

In the first decades of the fourteenth century, the *Divina Commedia* of Dante Alighieri offered a magnificent poetic synthesis of the whole of medieval theology. In it, the great poet was able to consider the Mother of the Lord in original terms, bringing to the fore, not only those aspects already familiar to the faith and piety of the Christian people, but also the main mariological questions being discussed and developed by theologians.[1] During these two centuries, other famous poetic voices, such as those of Francesco Petrarch, Giovanni Boccaccio, Lorenzo the Magnificent, Angelo Poliziano, and Girolamo Savonarola, show the widespread interest in the Virgin Mary among writers and artists. Should we go beyond the world of the Italian language, the discussion would become even longer.

In the popular understanding, Mary was the one who preserved and liberated men from evil; she guided them toward salvation; she was the object of blessed contemplation by the elect in the glory of God. Holding these beliefs, the faithful considered her to be someone close to them, and they were moved to a Marian devotion that stressed the more human aspects of the relationship between Christ and Mary. When they contemplated her, they pictured her as a Mother, smiling as her Holy Child embraces her; she nurses, guards, and protects him. In the same way, they thought of the mystery of the Passion, to emphasize the presence of the sorrowful Mother alongside her suffering and crucified

---

[1] See the excellent article of T. Koehler, "Storia della Mariologia", in NDM, p. 1395.

Son: a Mother who cannot bear the overwhelming sorrow that has befallen her and that, according to some writers and painters, makes her unable to cope with human weakness.

These devotional tendencies are deeply rooted in various expressions of Marian piety. Theologians and preachers made this new religious and psychological climate their starting point for inviting believers to a relationship with the Virgin. In so doing, they seemed to make certain external practices the privileged means to achieve a deeper faith and a more intense love for Mary. They called upon her heavenly protection, especially when faced by the strikingly frequent evils and calamities that characterized this historical period. During this time, the recitation of the Rosary and the Little Office of the Blessed Virgin became very widespread.

The religious orders, both those of ancient foundation and those more recent, could not remain detached from this phenomenon, of course. Their members tried every means to renew and intensify their devotion to the Mother of God. The orders continued to guarantee that the Church would have men able to work as zealous leaders, experienced guides, and authoritative teachers in giving renewed direction to the Marian piety of the Christian people.

An important chapter in this history of doctrine and devotion was written by mystics. They had a very influential role in the evolution of Christian spirituality through accounts of the apparitions and extraordinary revelations with which they were favored. Their influence was not limited to popular devotion; their writings were also positively received within the world of theology proper. The case of St. Brigid is typical, demonstrating the authoritative way in which mystical literature positively shaped the Marian theology of the time. The mystics gave it a spiritual inspiration more obvious than that found in the treatises of Scholasticism, which were organized according to a more rigid and scientific plan.

One of the doctrines that aroused the greatest interest in this historical period was the spiritual motherhood of the Blessed Virgin. It was preached and promoted with special fervor by St. Bernardine of Siena and St. Antoninus of Florence. At that time, theologians generally attempted to establish Mary's role as spiritual Mother on its two most obvious foundations: the Incarnation, and Christ's words to his Mother on Calvary (see Jn 19:25–27).

I

RAYMUND LULL
(d. 1316)

The final years of this extraordinary man's life reached into the fourteenth century, when Scholasticism was already beginning to decline and the world of learning was looking for new ideas, new modes of expression, and a new equilibrium. Lull's personality was rich and complex; his interests ranged from philosophy to theology to mysticism, from literature to poetry. His own literary output was prodigious. History has rightly granted him the title "The Illuminated Doctor" because of the depth and clarity of his reflections as well as his inventive genius. In his Latin and Catalan writings, he paid special attention to the Mother of the Lord, to whom he was lovingly devoted.

He was born at Palma, Majorca, to a noble family, so that at the age of fourteen he was called to be a page at the court of James I of Aragon, the sovereign who had freed the island of Majorca from Arab domination in 1228. He was married in 1256 and had two children. It is said that when he was around thirty, he was favored with a vision of Jesus, after which he conceived a strong desire to become a missionary and convert the Muslims. So he dedicated years of his life to studying Arabic and deepening his knowledge of Christian theology. Then, from 1287 on, he undertook numerous voyages in search of permits and assistance in realizing his plan to convert the Muslim world. In 1316, during one of his voyages to Barbary, Raymund's life ended in martyrdom. Soon afterward, he was venerated as a Blessed both on his native island and throughout Catalonia.

Among his many works, those of the greatest interest for their Marian content are his *Disputatio* on certain questions of Peter Lombard's book of *Sentences*, the seven sermons collected in the *Liber de Ave Maria*, and two short poems, the "Plant de Nostra Dona Santa Maria" and the "Horas de Nostra Dona Santa Maria". The first of these is in thirty-two strophes, and the second is divided according to the seven canonical hours.[1] These works will allow us to discover the prominent place of the Blessed Virgin in the theology and spirituality of Raymund Lull.[2]

Lull and the Immaculate Conception

Following the favorable attitude of some Franciscan theologians to this truth, the position taken by Lull on the question toward the end of the thirteenth century took on great significance, because it paved the way for the doctrine of Duns Scotus, even if it probably had no direct influence on him. Raymund treats the question in several of his works and was the first author to use the expression "Immaculate Conception" to designate the Virgin's exemption from original sin. Moreover, he appears to have been the first to teach this doctrine publicly at the University of Paris—not a very favorable environment at that time—and to have set the immaculist movement in motion.

To explain this Marian privilege, he resorts to three arguments of a typically christological nature:

1. The Son of God could not become incarnate in a mother who was stained by sin in any way. He writes:

> God and sin cannot be united in the one and the same subject. . . . Thus the Blessed Virgin did not contract original sin; rather she was sanctified

---

[1] Lull's works have been published in various editions. Today we use the critical edition, published in the series CCM, vols. 32–39 and 75–80.

[2] Lull's Marian doctrine has been the object of numerous studies, which have brought to light his remarkable qualities. Cf. M. Caldentey, "'Nuestra Señora Santa María' fué madre por causa del pecado? o el primado universal de Jesucristo y María, según el Doctor Iluminado", EstMar 8 (1949): 363–81; M. Guix, "La Inmaculada y la Corona de Aragón en la baja Edad Media (Siglos XIII–XV)", in *Miscelanea Comillas* 22 (1954): 193–326 (Lull: 199–212); Andrés de Palma de Mallorca, "La Inmaculada en la Escuela Lulista", *Estudios Franciscanos* 55 (1954): 171–94; Maduell Alvaro de Barcelona, "Llull i el doctorat de la Inmaculada", *Estudios Lulianos* 5 (1961): 61–97; 6 (1962): 5–49, 22–255; 8 (1964): 5–16; idem, *Llull i el doctorat de la Inmaculada*, Maioricensis Schola Lulistica (Palma de Mallorca, 1964); M. Ruffini, "Osservazioni sulla rima finale del 'Plant de Nostra Dona Santa María'", in *Estudios Lulianos* 10 (1966): 129–40; 11 (1967): 21–30; J. M. Cascante Davila, *El culto a María en los escritos del B. Ramón Llull*, in CongrRom 5:65–103; L. Scheffczyk, "Das 'Ave Maria' des Abtes Blanquerna bei Raimundus Lullus als Beispiel einer apostolischen Marienverehrung", in CongrRom 5:105–26.

in the instant in which the seed from which she was formed was detached from her parents.[3]

2. There had to be a certain likeness between the Son's generation without sin and the generation of his Mother:

It was also fitting that the Blessed Virgin should have been conceived without sin, so that her conception and that of her Son might have a like nature, so that between the two there might be the greatest possible likeness and harmony, and so that there might be greater love between the Son and his Mother.[4]

3. The second creation, that is, the redemption, which began with Christ and Mary, had to happen under the sign of the most total purity, as was the case with the first creation:

Just as Adam and Eve remained in innocence until the original sin, so at the beginning of the new creation, when the Blessed Virgin Mary and her Son came into existence, it was fitting that the Man and the Woman should be found in a state of innocence *simpliciter*, in an absolute way, without interruption, from the beginning until the end. Should the opposite have been the case, the new creation could not have begun. It is clear, however, that it did have a beginning, and therefore the Blessed Virgin was conceived without original sin.[5]

The third proof is the most consistent, because it is based on Mary's cooperation with her Son, the Redeemer, in the work of human salvation.

Mary's Divine Motherhood and Her Humility

In his book on the *Ave Maria*, Raymund introduces some considerations that combine the dogmatic dimension with the demands of devotion in a most suitable way. He sees the Incarnation as the ultimate end of creation itself, and this truth becomes the starting point for his celebration of the exalted dignity of the Mother of God. And yet he does not forget that the Blessed Virgin was called to this mission because of her

---

[3] *Disputatio Eremitae et Raimundi super aliquibus questionibus Sententiarum Magistri Lombardi*, q. 96, 1; *Opera Omnia*, vol. 4 (Mainz, 1737), pp. 83–84.

[4] Ibid., q. 96, 3; *Opera Omnia*, 4:84.

[5] Ibid., q. 96, 4; *Opera Omnia*, 4:84.

great humility. Her example, and the example of Jesus, is authoritative for us:

> [Mary} conceived the Son of God with humility. And, without humility, he could not have become incarnate. Therefore, if you want to be saved, it is necessary that you greet our Lady, Holy Mary, with humility.[6]

Fullness of Grace

Commenting on the title "full of grace", Lull specifies the meaning it has in the case of the Blessed Virgin, namely, a grace that includes all the gifts granted to other creatures:

> The grace [given to Mary] was equal to the fullness of the capacity to recall, to understand, and to love possessed by all the heavenly angels and all the blessed men in glory. And it will also be the fullness of their whole capacity to imagine and perceive after the final day of the judgment.[7]

Our author wants to bring out Mary's superiority with respect to all other creatures, while showing that she is inferior only to her divine Son. The Lord was so generous with the Virgin because she would later have to act as the distributor of all graces.

Trinity and Incarnation

When the angel assured Mary that the Lord was with her, he meant that the whole Trinity was involved in the mystery of the Incarnation:

> Because God exists as a Trinity of Persons, God the Father was with our Lady when she conceived the Incarnation of God his Son when the angel greeted her. And the Holy Spirit took part in that Incarnation, for he breathed himself into our Lady the Virgin, that she might conceive the Son while remaining a Virgin. And the Son, when he took flesh, took it in the holy conception of our Lady.[8]

The choice of Mary by the One and Triune God was explained by the fact that she led a holy life, in virginity, justice, prudence, and in all

---

[6] *Liber de Ave Maria, sermo* 1, 2; CCM 76, 86.

[7] Ibid., *sermo* 2, 1; CCM 76, 87.

[8] Ibid., *sermo* 3, 1; CCM 76, 90.

the other virtues. Raymund defines the role played by the individual Persons in bringing about this event. He attributes an empowering and sanctifying action to the Holy Spirit:

> The Spirit came upon our Lady in order to raise her up in goodness, higher than nature, in order that the Son of God might take from our Lady a better nature, higher than nature.[9]

In the Lucan phrase "the power of the Most High", we should see a reference to the Person of the Father. It is the Father who, in his infinite activity, generates the Son from all eternity. In the Incarnation, he acts together with the other two Persons:

> The power of the Most High is God himself, who is superior to all creatures. And lest his power appear inactive, useless, unhealthy, and devoid of nature, it is found in a Trinity of Divine Persons, so that God the Father, by his power, gives birth to God the Son, who is power. . . .
>
> And the three Persons are one God, one power, essence, substance, and nature. And the power, which is God the Son, covered our Lady with his shadow, inasmuch as he took his human nature from her.[10]

In the overshadowing of the Blessed Virgin, all three of the Divine Persons are at work because, since this is an action *ad extra*, their activity is inseparable. Lull is aware that distinguishing the Persons of the Trinity when speaking of God working *ad extra* is a way of speaking that has a purely symbolic value.

The metaphor of the shadow suggests an eminently practical application to our author. Overshadowed by the Holy Spirit, the Virgin became a sheltering, protective shadow for sinners:

> [Our Lady] covers sinners with her virtuous shadow when they virtuously hope in her. And the same thing may be said of the other virtues.[11]

From this text we may clearly see our author's tendency to find ideas with a practical application to living the Christian life within theological meditation.

---

[9] Ibid., *sermo* 6, 1; CCM 76, 98.

[10] Ibid., *sermo* 7, 1; CCM 76, 100.

[11] Ibid., *sermo* 7, 2; CCM 76, 102.

READING

THE FRUIT OF MARY'S WOMB

The blessed fruit of our Lady's womb is Jesus Christ, who is true God and true man. He is God the Son, and he is man, the Son of our Lady. The man, her Son, is the blessed fruit because he is God the Son; for it is true that the goodness of the Son who is God and the goodness of the Son who is man are joined together and united in one person, who is Jesus Christ. And the goodness of the man, [Mary's] Son, is an instrument of the Son, who is God. With this instrument, he shows his goodness to all creatures, who are good. And so, if the natural goodness of the Son of man comes from the womb of our Lady, who then is able to conceive of, or describe in words or writing, the great blessing that came to be and was given from the womb of our Lady, seeing that without him, no woman's womb would even exist? For it is true that every creature was created for this: that God the Son might become man, the Son of our Lady.

Jesus Christ is the fruit of life for all those who have been clothed with justice. And justice is the instrument and virtue with which the Son of God, who is life, gives eternal life to all those who serve with justice Jesus Christ, the Son of our Lady. Therefore, it is fitting that the fruit of our Lady's womb is blessed, because of his great justice.

The blessed fruit of our Lady blesses all those men and women who bless our Lady with prudence, reverence, and honor. For it is true that prudence is the virtue by which man is blessed for choosing a greater good before a lesser good and for fleeing a greater evil before a lesser evil.

The blessed fruit of our Lady's womb, who is Jesus Christ, blessed with eternal life all those men and women who show respect and honor to our Lady with fortitude of spirit. For it is true that fortitude of spirit is the virtue by which one acquires patience, boldness, abstinence, humility, and the remaining virtues.

The blessed fruit of our Lady blesses all those who love temperance, so that they serve our Lady with temperance. For it is true that temperance is the virtue that gives health and begets abstinence, and conquers gluttony.

The blessed fruit of our Lady blesses all those who desire to believe in the fourteen articles of the Creed, which are believed by all Christians who recognize our Lady's sovereignty. And rightly so, since faith is the light that enlightens the understanding to deepen its knowledge of the blessed fruit of our Lady and of his divine attributes, namely, his divine goodness, greatness, and so on.

The blessed fruit of our Lady blesses all sinners who hope in our Lady. For it is true that hope is the virtue by which one waits for our Lord Jesus Christ, the Son of our Lady, to grant his gift: mercy, grace, and forgiveness.

The blessed fruit of our Lady blesses all those men and women who love charity, so that they show reverence and honor to our Lady with charity. For it is true that charity is the virtue and the instrument by which a man loves God above all things and loves his neighbor as himself.

The blessed fruit of our Lady blesses all those who have the wisdom to serve and venerate our Lady. For it is true that wisdom is the instrument and power given to human understanding that puts foolishness to flight and makes human understanding to understand aright whenever it understands.

—Raymund Lull, *Liber de Ave Maria, sermo* 5, 1; CCM 76, 95–96

2

UBERTINO OF CASALE
(d. after 1325)

The life and works of Ubertino are identified with the so-called spiritual Franciscans. He was among the most involved members of this movement as well as one of its outstanding leaders. His writings show how the Christian spirituality of his time promoted a lively interest in the life of Christ and of his Mother, drawing from these sources the inspiration and example for a practical definition of Christian existence. According to our author, the presence of Mary alongside Jesus and her association with his mysteries show that there is no alternative to union with Mary for a Christian who wants to be transformed in Christ.

An Eventful Life

Ubertino was born at Casale Monferrato in 1259. He entered the order of St. Francis in 1273. In 1285, he was sent to the convent of Santa Croce, in Florence, for purposes of study. Later, after a time at Rome, he went to Greccio, where Blessed John of Parma introduced him to apocalyptic literature. From 1289 to 1298, he lived in Paris, studying Sacred Scripture and lecturing. While in Paris, Ubertino suffered a crisis of depression, from which he quickly recovered. Returning to Umbria, he made the acquaintance of Blessed Angela of Foligno and helped her to recover a life of intense spiritual fervor.

Because of his reformist religious ideas and his criticisms of ecclesiastical institutions, he was denounced to Pope Benedict XI. He was also unjustly accused of immorality and sent off to the convent of La Verna in 1304. There, in 1305, he finished writing his most important and well-known work: the *Arbor vitae crucifixae Jesu*, in five books. This work was enormously influential on the religious literature of his time and in the decades that followed. Suffice it to recall that St. Bernardine of Siena reproduced in his writings, almost word for word, fully forty-seven of the 103 chapters of the *Arbor vitae*, especially those in which Ubertino writes about the Blessed Virgin.[1]

The date of Ubertino's death is not known, but it must have happened after 1325. The last years of his life saw him very much involved in defending his reformist ideas, and, as a result, he was accused of heresy.

Mary in the Life of Jesus

In his *Arbor vitae*, Ubertino reflects on the most important episodes of the life of Jesus: his birth, circumcision, presentation in the Temple, flight to Egypt, finding in the Temple, Passion, and Resurrection. To doctrinal, spiritual, ascetical, and mystical considerations, he adds digressions of a controversial character, inspired by the teaching of Joachim of Fiore. Again and again, he returns to his central thesis: that the Church has become carnal and unfaithful to her Lord. In the end, however, she will return to him, the tree of life, and recover her proper condition as a spiritual Church.

Taking the allegory of the tree of life as his starting point, he explains how the roots, trunk, branches, and fruits of this tree symbolize the mysteries of the life of the Savior, among which his Passion and the compassion of his Mother have pride of place.

Mary in the Mysteries of Jesus' Infancy

Contemplating the mystery of the Incarnation of the Son of God and his birth at Bethlehem, Ubertino (a true Franciscan!) is in ecstasy as he considers the spectacle of the poverty of the Child and of his Mother. He exhorts his soul to go out to meet the Virgin Mother, who, even though she was carrying the Savior of the world in her womb, was

---

[1] The *Arbor vitae crucifixae Jesu* was published in a one-volume edition in 1485 in Venice. This edition was reprinted in facsimile in Turin in 1961 (La Bottega di Erasmo, ed. C. T. Davies). For the Marian content of this work, see M. Zugaj, "Assumptio B. M. V. in "Arbor vitae crucifixae Jesu" (a. 1305) fratris Ubertini de Casali O. Min.", *Miscellanea Francescana* 46 (1946): 124–56; G. M. Colosanti, "I SS. Cuori di Gesù e di Maria nell'Arbor vitae di Ubertino da Casale", in *Miscellanea Francescana* 59 (1959): 30–69; idem, "Maria SS. nella vita di Cristo secondo l'Arbor vitae di Ubertino da Casale", Mar 24 (1962): 349–80.

refused any decent hospitality at Bethlehem. It is the responsibility of the faithful and generous soul to open to Mary the dwelling place of his heart:

> O my soul, let yourself be entirely seized by compassion as you meet the Virgin Mother carrying the Savior in her womb, seeing her wandering and not receiving any assistance. Try to introduce her with kindness into the dwelling place of your heart. For she will not shrink from turning to you, who for your sake willed to turn to such great indigence. Because of your bestial defects, a stall full of grain will not be lacking within you, but you will be able to remove it, thanks to the great kindness of the newborn King and to the Virgin Mother's advocating on your behalf.[2]

Mary's divine motherhood, which begins in the mystery of the Annunciation, puts her into a privileged relationship with each of the Persons of the Trinity and makes her a kind of holy Temple of God:

> Today [the Annunciation] is the most important solemnity of the Mother of God, [the day] on which she became the bride of God the Father, the Mother and Associate [*socia*] of God the Son, the marvelous treasure chest of the Holy Spirit, the shrine and most beautiful Temple of the whole Trinity, the Queen and Mistress of the angels.[3]

The term "associate" (*socia*) appears to indicate Mary's role as a collaborator with Christ and as mediatrix, a term Ubertino uses to describe the extraordinary role that the Virgin played and continues to play in the history of salvation. Hugging her Firstborn to her bosom, she embraces all those who will later become his brothers:

> The generation to come and the devotion of the faithful children whom she already carried and was generating within her . . . were not hidden from her. She nursed and fed them together with the little Jesus, Firstborn of these children, with loving affection, as a mother does.[4]

Mary became the true Mother of all the faithful, to whom she had given birth along with Jesus:

> [She became] the Mother of all the elect and thus the whole treasury of the gifts of the Most Blessed Trinity, so that not even a drop of it or even

---

[2] Ibid., lib. I, c. 11; reprint (Torino, 1961), pp. 52–53.

[3] Ibid., c. 9; p. 45, col. 2.

[4] Ibid., c. 11; p. 76, col. 1.

the smallest grace is granted without first passing through Mary's management [*dispensatio*].[5]

At other times Ubertino repeats that Christ the Lord entrusted the distribution of grace to his Mother:

The most gracious Son has placed everything in the hands of his Mother, as the dispenser of all graces.[6]

Convinced of this consoling truth, he rejoices in the thought that the Mother of God herself is also his own Mother:

I rejoice to see you enclosed, imprisoned in the womb of my Mother, but I desire to see you come forth in the delightful birth of your nativity.[7]

Consequently, he begs Jesus to help him develop a deep filial relationship with Mary:

Look upon me as your brother and introduce me into the bridal chamber of my Mother, your parent, that I may convert in her loving heart. O sweet Emmanuel, let me eat the sweet butter and fat of the Most Holy Virgin, made great with child by the Holy Spirit.[8]

Even more consoling and reassuring is the certainty that God has offered to us sinners a Redeemer and a Mother who are full of goodness and mercy:

O what pleasant solace I find in the sight of the King! To see the most pleasant Mother, the advocate for forgiveness; to see the Judge made a little infant, becoming speechless in delivering his sentence; to see the most generous Child remitting all debts; to see him giving to the converting sinner, smiling at him, embracing him, kissing him, and drawing him to his own Mother's breasts, if only he will have converted completely and become like this little child.[9]

In speaking of the mystery of the circumcision, Ubertino emphasizes the first shedding of the Redeemer's blood, in which he already recognizes a highly salvific value. To the pain of Jesus is joined the pain of his Mother:

---

[5] Ibid., c. 9; p. 45, col. 2.

[6] Ibid., lib. 3, c. 6; p. 169, col. 1.

[7] Ibid., lib. 1, c. 11; p. 53, col. 1.

[8] Ibid., p. 75, col. 2.

[9] Ibid., p. 58, col. 1.

How much pain do you think the Mother felt, when she saw [these things happen] to the Son of God, her tender Babe, when, with great suffering in her heart and outpouring of tears, she tried to comfort her little one and console him as he hurt and cried and hold him to her breasts and hold him lovingly in her holy arms, how she was pierced through, as much by his love as by his pain! [10]

However, Ubertino views the circumcision, not only as a mystery of pain, but also as a mystery of joy and hope, because it foreshadows the shedding of blood on Calvary and the salvation of humanity. [11]

At the Presentation in the Temple, Mary officially offers her Son to the human race:

[When the Magi came], the Church did not thereby come into possession [of mercy], but today, from the common Mother, the glorious Virgin, in a common place (because the Temple is common to all persons) Simeon received a gift, and the Church came into possession of what she had been lacking; namely, mercy. [12]

Ubertino places this offering against the background of the Virgin's cooperation in the redemptive work of her Son:

With the fullest and most perfect charity, I give my most beloved Son Jesus to form, instruct, redeem, remake, and glorify those who wish to share in his redemption and favor. And I give them myself to be their advocate, mother, protector, and supporter, their absolver and defender from all enemies. [13]

In contrast to Calvary, where Mary will be present in discreet silence, in the Temple she is more active, in that she is the one who offers Jesus to the eternal Father, impelled by obedience to divine law and by love for humanity. In making this offering, she imitates the love of the Father, who handed over his own Son to a redemptive death (see Jn 3:16). [14] Simeon's prophecy of the sword that would pierce the Mother's heart (see Lk 2:35) does not make Mary shrink from offering her Son. This

---

[10] Ibid., lib. 2, c. 1; p. 80, col. 2.

[11] See ibid., p. 58, col. 1.

[12] See ibid., c. 5; p. 104, col. 2.

[13] Ibid., p. 104, cols. 1–2.

[14] See ibid., p. 102, col. 2 to p. 103, col. 2.

offering will prove to be full of consequences, because it will make her the Mother of all those believers who will receive the gift of salvation from her Son.[15]

The flight into Egypt offers Ubertino the opportunity to recall the state of poverty, disadvantage, and suffering in which the Holy Family found itself in that situation. Mary's heart was particularly struck by everything her Son had to bear during their flight and exile, which, according to our author, lasted seven long years.[16]

For Mary, losing Christ in the Temple was more a trial than a suffering. Jesus was removed from Mary's custody for a few days in order to arouse in her heart a quest for God, who sometimes hides himself out of love. Our author admits that this trial was superfluous in the Virgin's case, but she underwent it to be an example to us. Thus he writes:

> Although the most holy Virgin did not need to be tested by such [trials], since from the moment God was conceived she was filled with the indwelling of the Holy Spirit, nevertheless, the boy Jesus acted toward her thus, so that the life of both the Mother and the Son would serve as an aid and example for us.[17]

Mary in the Paschal Mystery

It is on Calvary that the human mind shows itself incapable of understanding the mystery of the sorrow uniting the Mother to her divine Son:

> O, that my poor soul might feel, with you, how great was the sorrow of the compassion that Jesus' heart felt for his beloved Mother! Consider, as hard as you can, how great was the measure of the sufferings within the Virgin's heart. For, in the Virgin's heart, not only was there no reason that might lessen the power of this sorrow, but there was only reason that would increase its power.[18]

This sorrow finds external expression in tears, sighs, and physical collapse. In the Virgin's case, however, all this must be taken, not as a

---

[15] See ibid., p. 104, col. 1.
[16] See ibid., c. 6; p. 120, col. 2.
[17] Ibid., c. 7; p. 126, cols. 1–2.
[18] Ibid., lib. 4, c. 15; p. 321, col. 2.

sign of weakness but, rather, as the effect of the inexpressible love she felt for her Son.[19] While the Passion of Christ caused sorrow in his Mother, the anguish she felt in her heart increased the suffering within him:

> And this, O good Jesus, is what increased your sorrow: that you were crucified in such a deadly fashion, not only in your own person, but in another, that is, in your Mother's heart.[20]

According to Ubertino, the Virgin participated in the mystery of Christ's suffering on Calvary because Jesus explicitly willed to support his Mother's burning desire to be united to him.[21]

Finally, in Jesus' words, "Woman, behold your son" (Jn 19:26), our author perceives a cause of further suffering in Mary's heart, because he holds that in that moment a disproportionate and disturbing substitution took place: a disciple took the place of the divine Son in her life:

> When he said, "Woman, behold your son", while pointing to John, it was as if he had said, "In place of your beloved Jesus, miraculously conceived in you by the working of divinity, whom you possessed on earth as your Son and the Son of God the Father, accept now the son of Zebedee, a man who is common and small, compared to me, because your beloved Jesus whom you conceived is now bodily brought to an end before your eyes, slain by the humiliating torture of a fearsome death.[22]

Further, the Virgin received all men as her sons in the person of the apostle John, and this, too, was a reason for sorrow because she also became the Mother of those who had crucified her Firstborn.[23]

In any case, Ubertino is among the first authors to interpret John 19:26–27 as an explicit proclamation of Mary's spiritual motherhood with regard to men:

> In saying ["behold your mother"], he made John stand for all the elect and established them as the legitimate children of Mary's maternal charity. For they are represented in John, who has grace. And all the elect are adopted by grace, whence these elect, too, if they want to have a share in

---

[19] See ibid., c. 25; p. 337, cols. 1–2.

[20] Ibid., c. 15, p. 321, col. 2.

[21] See ibid., p. 324, col. 2.

[22] Ibid., c. 21, p. 331, col. 1.

[23] See ibid., c. 15, p. 321, col. 1.

this grace, must strive to experience spiritually the sorrows of Mary's maternal heart, like John, who felt the sorrows of Jesus' crucifixion and his Mother's compassion more deeply than anyone else.[24]

In describing the appearance of the risen Christ to his Mother, Ubertino imagines a dialogue between the two, from which emerges the Virgin's total awareness of the extension of her spiritual motherhood to the followers of her Son:

> As you were dying on the Cross in pain, you entrusted John to me. Because you include all men in John, this means that my affection embraces all the elect.[25]

Having been associated with the Passion of Jesus in a unique way, the Blessed Virgin had to be the first creature to participate, in an outstanding way, in the glory of his Resurrection. Ubertino deduces this from the Apostle's words, "If you have been sharers in his sufferings, you will also be sharers in his resurrection" (2 Cor 1:7).[26] He is convinced that, even if Mary was not the first to see the risen Christ, certainly she was the first to have been informed of her Son's Resurrection, through a special intuition coming from her unshakeable faith. That is why she did not go to the tomb, for she already knew that it was empty.[27]

The Arbor vitae, Witness to a Spirituality

The Marian doctrine of this Franciscan, whose personality was restless and combative but whose thinking was profound and amiable, contains some points that are unquestionably new, as we have underscored above. His stress on the events of the life of Christ and of the Virgin shows how the spirituality of his time was oriented toward the search for a greater familiarity and intimacy with the Savior and his Mother. The events of their lives challenge Ubertino to go beyond a simple description to make a penetrating psychological analysis of their feelings. He does this in a lively style, with dramatic emotionalism and with a loving sense of engagement.

---

[24] Ibid., c. 14, p. 320, col. 2.

[25] Ibid., c. 29, p. 351, col. 1.

[26] See ibid., p. 350, col. 2.

[27] See ibid., p. 351, col. 2 through p. 352, col. 1.

The *Arbor vitae* reveals how complex were the spiritual movements that had sprung up in the Latin Church since the beginning of the 1300s, with their excesses and their strong craving for a radical gospel life-style and for mysticism. Ubertino's own brand of spirituality, along with other similar phenomena, witnesses to how fourteenth-century devotion was searching for an attitude and a language marked by greater familiarity in the dialogical relationship with Christ and His blessed Mother. To this end, it looks to the mystery of the Incarnation as to the primordial source of the Christian life. In it, the presence of Mary is that of a most loving mother, attentive to the needs of her children. She intercedes for them; she listens to them; she guides and protects them. Thus, life in Christ cannot be considered apart from Mary's maternal activity.[28]

READINGS

JESUS TEACHES US TO LOVE HIS MOTHER

Love is experienced in two ways: first, the most sweet and transforming feelings experienced in the presence of the beloved. Jesus showed this kind of love to his Mother in his past deeds of affection, giving sweet looks and embraces, both spiritual and physical, to his holy Mother. The second kind of feeling is bitter, afflicting, troubling. This kind of love increases merit. It is experienced when the beloved mysteriously departs or is lost, so that the soul, totally dependent on the beloved, cannot rest, always jealously anxious lest the beloved should depart because of some offense and always unsure of herself, unless she be restored by the attention of the beloved. In which case she abandons herself completely to him, forsaking herself. From which it follows that the soul wanders about, seeking her beloved and asking help from every creature in order to find the one her soul loves (cf. Song 3:3).

The Mother herself shows what great sorrow she felt, caused by the highest virtue, when she says, "We have been looking for you in sorrow" (Lk 2:48). She includes St. Joseph and, like a humble person, puts him ahead of herself, saying "Your father and I" (ibid.). Although the most

---

[28] See T. Koehler, *Maria nella storia della devozione cristiana dal sec. III al sec. XVII (1650)* (Verbania Pallanza: Centro Mariano Chaminade, n.d.), p. 59.

holy Virgin did not need to be tested by such [trials], since from the moment God was conceived she was filled with the presence of the indwelling Holy Spirit, nevertheless, the boy Jesus acted toward her thus, so that the life of both the Mother and the Son would serve as an aid and example for us. She showed us how much the soul progresses in such a sorrowful experience, because of the absence of the beloved and the soul's anxious search for him.

—Ubertino of Casale, Arbor vitae I. 2, c. 7, f. 62rv

MARY'S MISSION AFTER THE RESURRECTION OF HER SON

And when, enlightened by the Holy Spirit, she sensed that the hour of the Resurrection had arrived—that is, that her Son's life was arriving— so that he might take her body into his own glory, she spoke devoutly, saying, "Beloved Son, what have you come to do? Do you want me to be swallowed up in glory with you, that I might restore the treasure that I alone guard? But if, as long as I shall live, you want to preserve me from your suffering in passible flesh and if, with your medicine, you want to heal the wounds of your body, in which I live alone, I give my assent. But in truth, O beloved Son, you wanted to deprive me of your suffering in this passible flesh. And now, why do you want to deprive me of this conformity [with you]? Oh, seeing that I, uprooted from myself, was crucified and died along with you, did I not deserve from you the favor of being totally immersed in your sufferings? Therefore, Oh, take me with you into glory or, as I have repeated so often, leave me to share the pangs of your sufferings.

Her most kind Son answered her with respect, in a consoling tone: My sweetest Mother, this little flock of your children cannot be deprived of your presence. For they would decline in number were they not strengthened by the support of your faith. If they were deprived at the same time of me, their Shepherd and Father, and you, their Mother and Teacher, it would be too much for them to bear. Through them, I must still obtain for myself a people, who will be born from your womb of charity. Therefore, O sweetest Mother, bear it with patience when I leave you with them for a time and raise my body to the glory of Majesty.

His devoted Mother answered him: This is what I was pondering attentively: that, as you were dying on your most holy Cross, in the midst of your sufferings, you entrusted John to me (cf. Jn 19:25–27). Because you include all men in John, this means that my affection embraces all the elect. Then how will I be able to cover the multitude of sinners in your sight if you take from me the cloak of your flesh? How will I wash their disfigured faces if you take from me the bath of your blood? How will I nail them to the cross of your wounds if the mark of those wounds is seen no more? How will I bury them in your death if you take away the experience of your death? Take these things into account, O my beloved Son, and leave me, along with your sufferings, the instruments of your Passion: the nails, the thorns, the Cross, the spear, for without them I cannot live in my passible flesh. You know, O dearest Son, that I never defied your will to the slightest degree, and so, if you hear and grant my desire, I will return to you the substance of the flesh that I conceived in my virginity.

Then sweetest Jesus, all aflame with love for his Mother, hearing her lament so sorrowfully and lovingly, said to her: Dearest Mother, I see that you are pleased by my total glorification. I leave you the treasure of my love and my bitter suffering, and I impress upon your mind the instruments of my Passion.

—Ubertino of Casale, *Arbor vitae,* 4, c. 29, f. 175r

3

BRIDGET OF SWEDEN
(d. 1373)

The fourteenth century saw the flowering of intense mystical experiences, such as those lived by and illustrated in the writings of the Dominicans Meister Eckhart, Henry Suso, Johannes Tauler, and the Flemish author Jan van Ruysbroeck. The mysticism of these famous authors dealt mainly with lofty doctrinal speculation and forms of contemplation. In the second half of the same century, Bridget of Sweden, by contrast, was able to bring her ascetical and mystical way of life to the attention of Christianity, but in much more practical terms. She did this for Marian doctrine and devotion as well. She presented a model that could be understood by a large number of the faithful, one that could attract them to undertake an itinerary of the Christian life in which the Blessed Virgin could occupy a prominent place and play a real and important role on their behalf.

Her Life and Writings

Bridget was born around 1303, in Uppland, a region located to the north of Stockholm, to a family related to the royal family of Sweden. She was married at about fourteen years of age and had nine children. In 1341, she and her husband made a pilgrimage to the shrine of St. James at Compostela. Upon their return, her husband entered a Cistercian monastery, where he died shortly thereafter. Bridget withdrew to a daughterhouse of the Cistercian monastery of Alvastra. There she began to receive supernatural revelations. In 1346, she laid the foundations of the order of the Most Holy Savior, which was composed of two branches, one male and one female. She went to Rome for the Jubilee of 1350 and, from there, went on pilgrimage to different Italian shrines, facing all the difficulties and inconveniences of such an undertaking with courage and tenacity. Her last pilgrimage was to the Holy Land, but she returned to Rome in very precarious health and died there July 23, 1373.

The book of *Revelationes* is her most widely known work. To this book, written in a simple and clear style, Bridget entrusted her Marian thought, the fruit of the extraordinary revelations with which she had been graced. A sort of supplement to this work appeared under the title *Revelationes extravagantes*. In her *Sermo angelicus de Virginis excellentia*, Bridget collects twenty-one pieces on Mary's life. We will translate the texts from the edition of Durante for the revelations (*Revelationes sanctae Brigittae, olim a Cardinale Turrecremata recognitae, nunc a Consalvo Duranto illustrate* [Rome, 1606]) and of Eklund for the *Sermo angelicus* (*Sermo angelicus de Virginis excellentia*, in vol. 2, *Opera minora*, ed. S. Eklund [Uppsala, 1972]).[1]

A Follower of the Franciscan School

Bridget, who was a third-order Franciscan, felt bound to follow the Marian teaching of John Duns Scotus, especially on the theme of the Virgin's preservation from original sin and on her role in the divine economy of salvation.

With regard to the truth of the Immaculate Conception, she attests that she received a revelation from the mouth of the Virgin herself, who spoke to her in a way suited to explaining how the event happened. Just as someone who wishes to fast will nevertheless decide to eat, if given a reason to obey a command to eat, so it was out of obedience that marital relations took place between Mary's parents, leading to Mary's conception:

> The truth is that I was conceived without original sin and not in sin, because just like my Son, I too never sinned, and so there was no marital union more honorable [*honestius*] than the union from which I came forth.[2]

---

[1] For more on St. Bridget's Marian doctrine, see *La Madre di Dio e degli uomini descritta nei libri delle sue rivelazioni*, florilegio ed. Raffaele Ballerini (Rome, 1895); H. Redpath, *God's Ambassadress* (Milwaukee, 1947); B. Thierry d'Argenlieu, "Marie, reine du Nord", in *Maria* 4:404–14.

[2] *Revelationes*, lib. 6, c. 49; ed. Durante, p. 547.

With these words, the Blessed Virgin seems to intend to explain how there was no possibility of original sin being handed on in her conception, which was free from the spirit of carnal passion or concupiscence.

Such a special divine intervention in the very first instant of the Virgin's earthly existence could have no other explanation than an incomparable preferential love for her on God's part. Comparing this love with the love God showed toward Abraham, Bridget addresses the Virgin in these words:

> But almighty God himself loved you, O most sweet Virgin Mary, with great love, before anything was created, because he foreknew from all eternity that, when you were born, it would be the greatest joy for him.[3]

Mary and Redemption

Bridget repeatedly emphasizes the role Mary played in the work of our salvation, as the associate of Christ the Redeemer. The words she avows to have heard from the mouth of the Mother of God are strong and explicit:

> For this reason I boldly say that his worry was my sorrow, because his heart was my heart. Just as Adam and Eve sold the world for one apple, so my Son and I redeemed the world, as it were, with one heart. Therefore, my daughter, imagine how I felt in the instant of my Son's death, and you will not find it burdensome to abandon the world.[4]

The Mother's words are confirmed by the words of her Son, who seems to give an unequivocal confirmation of Mary's participation in the objective redemption of the human race:

> Therefore I can well affirm that my Mother and I saved man, as it were, with a single heart, I by suffering in my heart and flesh, and she with the suffering and love of her heart.[5]

Mary's participation in redemption happens, not on a physical plane, but only on the spiritual and moral plane. Nevertheless, this takes nothing

---

[3] *Sermo angelicus*, lib. 3, c. 3; ed. Eklund, p. 84.

[4] *Revelationes*, lib. 1, c. 35; ed. Durante, p. 56.

[5] *Revelationes extravagantes*, ed. C. Durante (Rome, 1606), c. 3, p. 804.

away from its real character, and so Bridget does not hesitate to call the Mother of the Savior "hope of our salvation".[6]

St. Bridget received lengthy and detailed revelations about the sufferings Mary endured throughout her earthly life. They were always caused by her Son and by her supreme love for him, so intimate was the bond uniting their hearts and lives:

> Consider, daughter, the Passion of my Son, whose members were like my own members to me and like my own heart. For he was inside me, just as other children are commonly inside their mothers' wombs. But his conception was caused by the burning charity of divine love, while others are conceived out of fleshly desire. Which is why John his cousin rightly says: "The Word was made flesh." For it was charity that brought him into the world, so that he dwelt in me. But both the word and charity caused him to be in me. Indeed, he was like my own heart to me. Therefore, when he was being born from me, I felt as if half of my heart was being born and going forth from me. And when he was suffering, I felt as if my own heart were suffering. For if half of my heart were outside my body, and half remained inside, and if the part on the outside were pierced, the inside part would feel pain equally.[7]

The Virgin revealed to Bridget how her union with her Son is so close that one could say that the pain of his Passion and his heart are identical with her pain and her heart.[8]

The Six Sorrows of the Mother of God

Bridget summarizes in six points the causes of the sufferings Mary endured during her earthly life: (1) the sorrow deriving from her advance knowledge of her Son's Passion; (2) the sorrow of hearing, caused by the insults, false accusations, and snares laid for Jesus; (3) the sorrow of sight, when she saw her Son bound, scourged, and hung upon the Cross; (4) the sorrow of touch, when she touched her Son after he had been taken down from the Cross, reduced to a disfigured corpse; (5) the suffering of desire, that is, of her strong desire to rejoin her Son in heaven after his Ascension; (6) the sorrow caused by the trials and

---

[6] *Sermo angelicus*, lib. 3, c. 6; ed. Eklund, p. 93.

[7] *Revelationes*, lib. 1, c. 35; ed. Durante, p. 56.

[8] Ibid.

tribulations encountered by the primitive Church. Nevertheless, the Virgin herself confided to Bridget that her sorrow, although continuous, was always lightened by consolation, up to the moment of her bodily Assumption into heaven.[9]

Mediatrix of Grace

Mary's participation in the redemptive Passion of her Son, being so very close and strong, clearly indicates that she has a well-defined role in the distribution of grace. Although she does not give Mary the title "Mediatrix", Bridget does not hesitate to repeat that all graces come to us through Mary. This happens because Mary's intercession is powerful, since she is Queen of heaven, Mother of the elect, and Mother of Mercy.[10]

Mary's mediation extends to the whole world, without distinction among human creatures. She herself explained this reality to Bridget using the figure of the rainbow:

> I am she who hovers over the world in unceasing prayer, like the rainbow that stands above the clouds, which seems to bend down and touch the earth with its two ends. And I consider myself to be like a rainbow, because I bend down to the inhabitants of the world, touching the good ones and the bad ones with my prayer. I bend down to the good ones, to make them firm in keeping the precepts of holy Church. And I bend down to the bad ones, lest they persevere in their wickedness and become even worse.[11]

READINGS

THE BEAUTY OF MARY'S SON

I am the Queen of heaven, and my Son loves you with all his heart. So I advise you to love nothing except him. For he is so desirable that if you have him, you will not be able to desire anything else. He is so beautiful

---

[9] Ibid., lib. 6, c. 57; ed. Durante, p. 562.

[10] See, for example, *Revelationes*, lib. 1, c. 50; ed. Durante, p. 82.

[11] Ibid., lib. 3, c. 10; ed. Durante, p. 183.

that the beauty of the elements of this world, or the beauty of light, is like shadow in comparison to him. Whence when I was nursing my Son, he was endowed with such great beauty that whoever looked upon him was consoled and relieved of any sorrow he may have had in his heart. And so, even many Jews said one to another, "Let us go to see Mary's Son, that we may be consoled." And even though they did not know that he was the Son of God, nevertheless they received great consolation upon seeing him. Also, his body was so pure that no louse or other worm ever lit upon it. Because the worms showed reverence for their Maker. Nor was any tangle or dirt ever found in his hair, nor was it combed.

> —Bridget of Sweden, *Revelationes*, lib. 6, c. 1;
> ed. Durante, pp. 473–74

THE VIRGIN PRAISES HER HUSBAND, JOSEPH

When Joseph, to whom I was betrothed, understood that I was pregnant, he was amazed. And considering himself unworthy to live with me, he was full of anxiety and did not know what to do. Then the angel said to him in a dream, "Do not leave the Virgin betrothed to you, because what you have heard her say is quite true. She did conceive by the power of God's Spirit and will bear a Son, the Savior of the world. Therefore serve her faithfully, and be the guardian of her virginity and a witness to it."

From that day onward Joseph served me as his wife, and I humbled myself to perform the least tasks. After this I was continually in prayer, wishing to see and be seen but rarely and very rarely going out, except to observe important feasts by attending the vigils and lessons that our priests used to read.

> —Bridget of Sweden, *Revelationes,* lib. 6, c. 59;
> ed. Durante, pp. 566–67

4

4

JEAN GERSON
(d. 1429)

Jean Gerson was a prominent figure in the Church at the end of the fourteenth century and in the first decades of the fifteenth. Although he felt that God had given him a strong inclination to the contemplative life, he did not hesitate to get involved in the events of his time, when convinced of his duty to help solve problems related to the good of Christendom. He acquired a distinguished reputation as a theologian, humanist, apostle, and preacher, a reputation later centuries have confirmed.

A Difficult and Committed Life

Jean Gerson was born in 1363 in Barby, a village in the county of Rethel, in the diocese of Reims. In 1377 he went to Paris to study at the College of Navarre, where he received the degree *magister artium* in 1382. Soon after, he began to study theology, obtaining a doctorate, probably in 1394. During these years, he had already begun to alternate teaching with his studies, and he continued to do so until 1395, when he was named chancellor of Notre-Dame and the University of Paris. He was also appointed court preacher.

At that time, the Church was going through a difficult period of internal strife, which gave rise to confusion and difficulties in the consciences of believers. At the same time that legitimate supreme pontiffs were being elected, illegitimate popes were elected by uncooperative and rebellious factions, so that two successions of anti-popes occurred: the anti-popes of the Avignon obedience and those of the Pisan obedience.[1] In this

---

[1] In 1378, the deplorable schism broke out that suddenly introduced a grievous division into the Christian West. At the beginning of the fifteenth century, three men simultaneously claimed legitimate authority over Christendom: the anti-popes

shameful climate of ongoing schism, the Council of Constance was held (1413–1418). In 1417, the Council elected Martin V as pope. Gerson made a valuable contribution to the Council proceedings, even though his approach, which was somewhat too open to the thesis of conciliarism, might leave him open to criticism. In a discourse pronounced in the presence of the Council fathers, he expressed himself warmly and with conviction. His aim was to arouse in the Council fathers an awareness of their grave responsibility and of the presence of the Holy Spirit, always mysteriously at work in the life of the Church and, consequently, in the conciliar assembly. Then, referring to the apostles gathered in the upper room in Jerusalem, he recalled that Mary was present there as well (cf. Acts 1:14). Just as Mary continues to offer her assistance as Mediatrix and intercessor in the Lord's presence, so she offers her aid and illumination as the work of the Council proceeds. Gerson says:

> You are present with your spiritual influence over us and your watching over us, turning your eyes of mercy toward us. To you do we sigh, mourning and weeping in this valley of tears, begging the coming of the Holy Spirit among us and upon us through you, O most merciful Virgin.[2]

A victim of the political intrigues of his time, Gerson had to leave Paris in 1418 and live as an exile in Austria. He returned to France the following year, taking up residence in Lyons, where he died in 1429.

He was a prolific author, leaving behind an impressive pile of works, not only in the field of dogmatic theology, but in moral, spiritual, and mystical theology as well. The first edition of his writings was edited by E. Du Pin, in five volumes, and published at Antwerp in 1706. Today there is a critical edition: *Œuvres complètes*, edited by P. Glorieux in eleven volumes (Tournai, 1960–).

Jean Gerson develops his Marian doctrine especially in his treatise *De susceptione humanitatis Christi*, dedicated to the theology of the incarnate Word, in another large, twelve-part work that bears the title *Collectorium super Magnificat* and, of course, in his sermons for the feasts of the Virgin.

Benedict XIII at Avignon and John XXIII at Pisa, and the legitimate pontiff of Rome, Gregory XII. As for Jean Gerson, we know that he quickly committed himself to reestablishing unity and peace in the Church, especially after he was named chancellor of the University of Paris in 1395.

[2] Jean Gerson, *Opera Omnia . . .*, ed. L. Ellies du Pin, 2nd ed. (Hagae Comitum: P. de Hondt, 1728), 3:1234C.

His Mariology appears very balanced. His four criteria for interpreting the Virgin's role in the economy of salvation are still authoritative today.

Gerson does not limit himself to doctrine; he also sets out to teach an authentic and deep devotion to Mary. Sometimes he addresses the Virgin directly, in prayerful tones, or he depicts her speaking. Always he is moved by the fervor of his own personal Marian devotion,[3] which he presents as a deep and solid dimension of his interior life.

Theological Prudence and Abundant Thought

In his treatise *De susceptione*, our author gives a series of twenty-four truths that he considers a summary of the complete doctrinal teaching of the Church;[4] fifteen of these have Marian content. These appear as normative principles for theological discourse about the Blessed Virgin and are intended to offer a safeguard against possible exaggerations or abuses. In this way, Gerson proposes to anchor Marian theology in the statements of Scripture, in the teaching of the faith and Catholic tradition, and in the wisdom of Christ, which he repeatedly emphasizes. On the other hand, he is concerned to restrict the use of the argument from fittingness to certain facts of revelation.

His way of proceeding, however, does not present us with a reductionist reflection on Mary. Rather, he simply wants to ensure a valid point of departure, from which he may proceed to much more positive considerations, more favorable to further development. The themes proposed in his Marian writings combine a particular consideration of Mary's place in the mystery of salvation and her role on behalf of human creatures. For these, she is a motherly sign of God's mercy and a light giving direction to their lives:

> Light spreads out because of its natural generosity, so that it is rightly called "illuminatrix". This, then, is the meaning of my own name,

---

[3] For the Marian doctrine of Jean Gerson, see J. Bover, "Universalis B. M. V. mediatio in scriptis Joannis Gerson", Greg 9 (1928): 242–68; L. Mourin, "Jean Gerson, prédicateur français pour les fêtes de l'Annonciation et de la Purification", RBPhH 27 (1949): 363–98; A. Combes, "La Doctrine mariale du chancelier Jean Gerson", in Maria 2:863–82; M. Lieberman, *Gersoniana: A Latin Sermon on the Immaculate Conception Ascribed to Jean Gerson* (New York, 1951); P. Glorieux, "Note sur le 'Carmen super Magnificat' de Gerson", RTAM 25 (1958): 143–50.

[4] Ed. du Pin, 2:450A–457A.

"Mary". Thus, as Mary, I am called etymologically "Star of the Sea", because my role is to illuminate.[5]

Supporter of the Immaculate Conception

On the one hand, it is understandable that Gerson supported the doctrine of Mary's exemption from original sin, since the theology faculty of the University of Paris had already required its professors to accept and teach this Marian privilege. But we should add that Gerson was personally attached to this truth, which he propounded as a probable and pious opinion. He demonstrated the truth of the Immaculate Conception by repeating an argument that had been formulated by Duns Scotus. Gerson reasoned:

> If Christ was the most perfect Redeemer of all men, suffering death for all, it was fitting that he should redeem his Mother in the most perfect manner. But this could not have been done in a more fitting way than by preserving her from falling, instead of rescuing her in case she did fall.[6]

In this case, Gerson considered it legitimate to apply the principle of fittingness, while rejecting it in other cases, where it was clearly abused. For this reason he refused to accept, on the grounds of fittingness, a whole series of assertions made by authors who claimed to be more zealous in giving honor to the Mother of God. They held, for example, that the Virgin had been granted the use of reason from the moment of her conception or that she never needed to sleep and that in every moment of her life she had always been absorbed in thoughts of God or that she was always intently contemplating God, even while sleeping, or that Christ revealed the entire course of her life to her in advance. Gerson did not consider these strange ideas to be justified by the desire to honor and exalt the Mother of God.

Even more, he refused to grant a value of absolute necessity to the principle of fittingness, and did not admit its application to facts separated from the data of revelation. Certainly, it is legitimate to hold that Christ granted his Mother such graces and privileges as befit her, but this does not mean that he granted her everything that would have been

---

[5] Ibid., 12:496B.

[6] *Lettera 56*; *Œuvres complètes*, ed. P. Glorieux (Tournai, 1960–), 2:266.

fitting to her in every way possible. There are other gifts that were not granted to her, even though they may perhaps have been fitting.[7]

Mary's Role in the Work of Salvation

Contemplating the mystery of the Blessed Virgin's participation in the Passion of her Son, Jean Gerson sees its root and foundation in the mystery of the Incarnation, since Christ suffers in his flesh, which is also his Mother's flesh. And so, in a sermon delivered on Good Friday, he places the following words on the lips of the Sorrowful Virgin:

> My God, my God, why have you abandoned the precious flesh that was taken from me, in perfect holiness and purity, conceived and born by the working of the Holy Spirit? I suffer in his flesh because his flesh and my flesh form one single reality, and his pain comes down upon me as well. Just as, in the past, sin passed from the woman to the man, so now I repair Eve's deceit. I wish it to happen thus, because it pleases God to happen thus.[8]

In the Eve–Mary parallel, as found in Irenaeus, the Blessed Virgin's role in salvation history was to ruin the ruinous role played by Eve in the Fall. This brings back the image of woman as a symbol of the expiation of the sin, into which she had caused the man to fall. As Eve induced Adam to sin, so now the second Adam calls the second Eve to cooperate in repairing humanity's evil. Mary agrees to do her part in obedience to the divine will, and she would do even more if the Lord wished it:

> Hearken, devoted people, to Mary's loving offer. Consider that she would want to pay our debt for us, as any good mother would want to do for her children, if the Son's offering were not enough. But that redemption sufficed for the salvation of a hundred thousand worlds.[9]

Mary's participation in Christ's Passion was not absolutely necessary. St. Ambrose had already stated this explicitly in these terms.[10] However,

---

[7] See *Opera Omnia*, ed. du Pin, 1:452B–453A.

[8] Jean Gerson, *La Passion*, ed. Georges Frénaud (Paris: Wittmann, 1947), p. 101.

[9] Ibid.

[10] See *In Lucam* 10, 132; SC 52, 200; *De institutione virginis* 6 (PL 16, 319); *Epist. 631*, 100 (PL 16, 1218).

it can be recognized as relatively necessary, along the lines of St. Paul's thought in Colossians 1:24.

Mary's mission on our behalf continues to unfold during the course of the centuries-long history of redeemed humanity. Our author contemplates this mission in the light of his own Christian experience. His prayer and personal devotion lead him to see her as more than just a creature who has a privileged relationship with the heavenly world, whose glory and eternal happiness she shares, as Queen of heaven and mistress of the angels. He also recognizes that the Mother of the Lord has a special bond with us as well. She is our Mediatrix in God's presence:

> We make you the Mediatrix of our prayer, O Blessed Virgin, most pleasing to God.[11]

Mary fulfills her office as Mediatrix by intervening on our behalf as a concerned advocate, especially when she makes our prayers and invocations her own:

> Come then, O our advocate, open that glorious mouth to pray for us, as we, in this day of solemnity and joy, open our mouths to greet you! [12]

The Virgin's role as Mediatrix has a solid foundation in her divine motherhood, from which came the Body of the incarnate Word, which became the Bread of Life for men. Thus, Gerson does not fail to bring out the profound link uniting the eucharistic mystery to the Incarnation, calling the Virgin "Mother of the Eucharist", because she is the Mother of grace. More than anyone else, after her Son, she was aware of this great sacrament:

> You are the Mother of the Eucharist because you are the Mother of good grace. More than anyone else, after your Son, you were aware of this Mystery, hidden for ages.[13]

Because of the intimate bond connecting the Virgin and the sacrament of the Eucharist, in virtue of the mystery of the Incarnation, Gerson turns to Mary to ask for the gift of divine grace:

---

[11] *De humilitate; Opera Omnia*, ed. du Pin, 3:1123B.

[12] *In festo omnium Sanctorum; Opera Omnia*, ed. du Pin, 3:1505B.

[13] See *De susceptione humanitatis Christi*; ed. Glorieux, 9:413.

We turn to you, then, O glorious Virgin, to beg this grace, since you are the one in whom was created and formed this Bread of Life, the Bread of angels.[14]

Mary's Greatness

Standing before the Mother of the Lord, that masterpiece of grace, Jean Gerson lets all his enthusiasm and admiration burst forth in his commentary on the *Magnificat*. For him, the most striking aspect of this wonderful canticle is that Mary preferred to exult more in her lowliness than in the greatness to which God raised her:

> Our great Lady, who is greatly to be praised, observed this [rule of humility], because she made the fame of her own blessedness redound totally to God's glory, when she said, "For he who is mighty has done great things for me" (Lk 1:49). Then not to me, but to you alone be the glory.
>
> In this, O Blessed Virgin, you were like an angel of God, so that a blessing would not induce you to lift yourself up, nor would a curse induce you to cast yourself down. The harder you ran away from glory, the more closely it followed you, as a shadow follows a body. You wanted, not to appear good, but to be good.[15]

With this attitude of extraordinary wisdom, she made up for the prideful conduct of the rebellious angels.[16] But for Gerson, commenting on the *Magnificat* does not mean limiting himself to a mere exercise in hermeneutics. Rather, it means achieving a deep understanding of the exceptional creature, Mary most blessed, rejoicing in her motherly tenderness and protection, being filled with her love, in order to grow in the Christian life.

---

[14] *De Eucharistia*; *Opera Omnia*, ed. du Pin, 3:1284A.

[15] *Collectorium super Magnificat*; ed. Glorieux, 8:222.

[16] See *Collectorium super Magnificat*, 3; *Opera Omnia*, ed. du Pin, 4:259A–264B.

READINGS

MARY'S TEMPTATIONS AND OTHER TRIALS

Since Satan dared tempt her Son, who was God, does it not follow that he must have tempted his Mother? This befell her that she might win the palm of victory and a golden crown, that she might be crowned, who fought [Satan] properly. For, unlike Eve, she did not succumb to the tempter.

Moreover, she wept with those who wept and rejoiced with those who rejoiced, but in either case with supreme moderation, so that she was tortured more by the defect of the wounds and limitations that affect the spirit than by the physical pestilence or sword that harm the body. In this she followed the example of her Son, who suffered more from our wicked ingratitude than from the torment of his own death.

Therefore, do not doubt that Mary, after her Son's Ascension, cried out her most delightful song [the *Magnificat*], which she had begun so delightfully, with holy fear and goodly zeal, with heartfelt compassion, with hope and great desire, as charity urged her on: "Daughters of Jerusalem, tell my Beloved that I am faint with love" (Song 5:8).

—Jean Gerson, *Collectorium super Magnificat*; ed. Glorieux, 8:233

INVOCATION OF THE BLESSED VIRGIN

O Mary, Star of the Sea, loving Queen of heaven! O Virgin, bend down to us, tossed by the storms of this world.

Rejoice and be glad that you merited to bear God. Beautiful Rose, and more comely than the rose, you are a unique rose. For you are the only rose who is also called lily and violet, sweet and full of honey.

Pleasant to your dear ones, a burden to none. You are joined to our heart; you speak to our mind. Make us spurn frivolous things!

Rejoice, verdant paradise, in whom our face comes alive, from whom arises the flower of beauty, from whom flows the fountain of love and everything that is best.

Rejoice, sweet nightingale, whose voice is full of love. Your sweet songs are the pleasant praise of the saints and the joy of the angels.

Rejoice, crowned with roses, adorned with every flower! O beautiful one, pray for us to your sweet Son before his throne, that he might give us himself as our reward.

O sweet Virgin and Mother, whom God the Father chose! Hail, full of grace! Pray to Christ your Son, that he might crown this choir in glory everlasting. Amen.

—Jean Gerson, *Poetic Works* 164; ed. Glorieux, 4:141

5

BERNARDINE OF SIENA
(d. 1444)

In the first half of the fifteenth century, the preaching of St. Bernardine of Siena stirred up a wave of enthusiasm and fervor in the crowds of faithful who hurried to hear him. As a result, Marian piety and doctrine became particularly widespread. This phenomenon could not be explained only by the oratorical abilities of the popular Franciscan preacher. Above all, his listeners were captivated by the example of his holy life and his burning and unlimited love for the Mother of the Lord. The exceptional impact of his words on the faithful was especially reflected in his preaching in the vernacular. He was able to establish an incredible rapport with his listeners, to such an extent that he became an astonishing interpreter of their feelings and reactions. He tried to give an answer to their problems and to the demands of their Christian life.

A Son of St. Francis, in Love with Mary

Bernardine was born at Massa Marittima, near Siena, in 1380, to the noble Sienese family of the Albizeschi. Left an orphan at an early age, he was raised by aunts and a cousin, who inculcated in him a tender and intense devotion to the Blessed Virgin. In Siena, outside the Porta Camollia, there was a fresco depicting Mary assumed into heaven. As a youth, Bernardine often went to pray before this image, and one day he confided to his cousin Tobia, "I am in love with the Most Blessed Virgin, Mother of God. I have always loved her, I have a burning desire to see her; I love her with all my heart, and so I have chosen her as my most chaste betrothed. I would like to keep my gaze fixed on her constantly, and that is why I decided to visit her every day." [1]

---

[1] P. Thureau-Dangin, *Un Prédicateur populaire dans l'Italie de la Renaissance: Saint Bernardin de Sienne* (Paris, 1896), pp. 9ff.

After studying rhetoric, philosophy, and law, in 1402 he took the habit of the Friars Minor and entered the novitiate at Colombaio, a convent of the strict observance. After his religious profession and ordination to the priesthood in 1404, his superiors assigned him to preaching. Bernardine dedicated himself to this ministry, beginning in the countryside and villages, but very quickly he came to understand that the Lord was calling him to a more extensive apostolate, and then he decided to go through all the cities and regions of Italy, focusing his preaching on more defined themes: the reform of habits, conversion to God, worship of the Eucharist, devotion to the Holy Name of Jesus, and devotion to the Blessed Virgin.

Although troubled by illness and other tiresome distractions, he remained faithful to his mission of preaching the word of God to the end of his life. He died in 1444 in Aquila, where today his mortal remains rest in a church dedicated to him. Six years after his death, Pope Nicholas V proclaimed him a saint.

His Marian devotion appears primarily oriented toward achieving practical objectives: to call the faithful back to the Christian life and to instill in their hearts a love for the Mother of God. However, it did not lack a significant theological foundation, anchored in his fidelity to Scripture and to Church tradition. His developed his Marian doctrine especially in his *Tractatus de Beata Virgine*, which contains eleven Latin sermons,[2] and in eight sermons in the vernacular.[3] All these writings are about the mysteries and events of Mary's life.[4]

---

[2] *Sancti Bernardini Senensis opera omnia*, vol. 6 (Quaracchi, Florence, 1959), pp. 65–180, with ref. to 4:537–61 and 2:153–62, 371–97. Hereafter cited as *Opera omnia*.

[3] Four of these can be found in *Le prediche volgari di San Berdardino da Siena, dette nella piazza del Campo l'anno 1427*, ed. L. Banchi, 3 vols. (Siena, 1880–1888), 1:7–34; 2:239–69, 388–429, 430–60. One is found in *San Bernardino da Siena. Le prediche volgari inedite, Firenze 1424–1425*, ed. D. Pacetti (Siena, 1935), pp. 317–47. Three are collected in *San Bernardino da Siena. Le prediche volgari*, ed. D. Cannarozzi, 5 vols. (Pistoia, 1934–1946), 1:272–86; 2:407–21, 422–32. A recent edition of the *Prediche volgari sul Campo di Siena 1427* was edited by C. Delcorno (Milan: Rusconi, 1989).

[4] Studies of the Marian doctrine of St. Bernardine of Siena include: G. Folgarait, *La Vergine bella in San Bernardino da Siena* (Milan: Ancora, 1939); idem, "La mariologia di San Bernardino da Siena", in *San Bernardino da Siena: Saggi e ricerche* (Milan, 1945), pp. 301–40; E. Blondeel ab Izegem, "De doctrina mariologica Sancti Bernardini Senensis", CollFranc 10 (1940): 383–94; L. Di Fonzo, "La mariologia di San Bernardino da Siena", MiscFranc 47 (1947): 3–102; F. Affelt, "The Marian Doctrine of Bernardine of

Two Franciscan authors especially inspired Bernardine's Marian thought: Pietro Olivi (d. 1298) and Ubertino of Casale (d. 1330). Bernardine copied entire chapters from their works.[5]

Doctrinal Exaggerations?

It cannot be ignored that some of Bernardine's statements about the Virgin can sound exaggerated, or downright strange and unacceptable, unless they are understood within the context of his mariological doctrine and unless one takes into account the circumstances in which they were pronounced. Bernardine was a popular preacher, attentive and sensitive to the mentality and religiosity of his listeners. He would try anything to get his message across to them in a way they could understand, to convince them to live out an authentic and intense devotion to the Mother of the Lord. It is understandable, then, that intemperate thoughts and expressions are particularly abundant in his sermons in the vernacular. In his Latin sermons, however, Bernardine usually appears more controlled and tends to use more rigorous theological language, reinforced by frequent references to the tradition of the Fathers and theologians of the Church.

In any case, when attempting to achieve an accurate understanding of the Sienese preacher's Marian thought, it would be wrong to limit ourselves to a search for statements that sound exaggerated or odd.[6] Instead, we need to seek out his true intentions, focusing on the many marvelous pages in which he exalts the greatness and holiness of the Mother of the Lord. For a lover of the Blessed Virgin like St. Bernardine, the words of the great convert and cardinal John Henry Newman are more relevant than ever: "What mother, what husband or wife, what youth or maiden in love, but says a thousand foolish things, in the way of

---

Siena", FrancEducConf 35 (1954): 196–222; L. Cignelli, "San Bernardino teologo e apostolo di Maria", in *San Bernardino da Siena nel VI centenario della nascita* (Jerusalem, 1980), pp. 45–104.

[5] We have already discussed Ubertino of Casale. Olivi was also a leading figure in the movement of the Franciscan spirituals.

[6] Hilda Graef considers Bernardine of Siena precisely a representative of the kind of so-called "Mariolatry" she thinks provoked the Protestant reaction in the next century. Cf. *Mary: A History of Doctrine and Devotion* (New York: Sheed and Ward, 1964), pp. 315–18.

endearment, which the speaker would be sorry for strangers to hear; yet they are not on that account unwelcome to the parties to whom they are addressed." [7]

Mary, a Matchless Mother

Devotion and filial love impel Bernardine to praise Mary in enthusiastic and superlative terms. After her Son, he considers Mary to be the noblest and loftiest human of all, the Queen of heaven and earth, the crowning achievement of all creation. He exalts her perfection so far above that of other created beings that, compared to them, she is a category unto herself. To an unparalleled degree, she brings together in herself all the gifts that God has distributed and continues to distribute to all his creatures. Commenting on the angelic salutation, he explains at length how the Virgin excels every other human being because of the excellence of her nature, the abundance of grace she received, and the glory to which she was predestined: [8]

> She has been made mistress in her Assumption, when "she was exalted above the choirs of angels in the heavenly kingdom" [9] and became "Queen of heaven and mistress of the angels".[10] But she had already been wonderfully illuminated the instant her soul was infused into her body; and she was illuminated even more wonderfully when she conceived the Son of God; and she was illuminated in the most wonderful way possible in her Assumption and glorification.[11]

The Virgin Mary's greatness and perfection are so excellent that they are beyond our understanding:

> Just as the divine perfections are beyond the grasp of any understanding, in the same way the perfections of the grace the Virgin received when she

---

[7] John Henry Cardinal Newman, "A Letter to the Rev. E. B. Pusey, D.D., on Occasion of His *Eirenicon*," in *Certain Difficulties Felt by Anglicans in Catholic Teaching Considered*, vol. 2 (London: Longmans, Green, and Co., 1900–1901), p. 80.

[8] See *De salutatione angelica*, sermon 52, a. 1; *Opera omnia*, 2:155–58, 162, 372, 379, 388; 6:68.

[9] Antiphon for the feast of the Assumption; see Renato-Joanne Hesbert, *Corpus antiphonalium officii* (Rome: Herder, 1968), 3:214, n. 2762.

[10] Hymn *Ave regina caelorum*; see, e.g., U. Chevalier, *Repertorium hymnologicum*, vol. 1 (Louvain, 1892), p. 122.

[11] *De salutatione angelica*, sermon 52, a. 1, c. 1; *Opera omnia*, 3:156.

conceived the Son of God can be understood only by the divine understanding, by Christ and by Mary herself.[12]

God wanted the Virgin to be so great and perfect because he had
predestined her to become the Mother of the incarnate Word. Thus, the
mystery of her divine motherhood is the reason for her greatness, so that
her predestination is connected with the predestination of Christ.[13] Her
fullness of grace and her role in the mystery of the incarnate Word, as
well as her compassion on Calvary and her Assumption into heaven,
make Mary the human being nearest to Christ and most like him.[14]

Mary's Holiness

Bernardine of Siena avoided participating in the controversy over the
dogma of the Immaculate Conception. In his time, the theologians of
his order opposed those of the Dominican order. We should also recognize that his statements do not help us clarify his thought on the matter
definitively.

He speaks of the Virgin's holiness with unbounded admiration. From
her birth, he holds, the Lord gave her all the fullness of grace that a
human being could possibly have, because she had been chosen to be the
Mother of God. He thinks that her own conception was absolutely
immaculate and affirms that there was no sin whatever in her life.[15] At
the moment of the Incarnation, a special intervention of God took place
in her, which confirmed her in the practice of good, freed her from the
fomes[16] of concupiscence, and took away the possibility of sinning.[17]
Nevertheless, we do not know for certain whether our preacher meant
to include exemption from original sin among the extraordinary gifts
that God gave his Mother.

---

[12] *De gratia et gloria beatae Virginis*, sermon 61, a. 1, c. 12; *Opera omnia*, 2:381.

[13] This opinion of Bernardine is very close to that of Augustine. Cf. Augustine, *In
Joannem*, tr. 8, 9; PL 35, 1455; *De peccatorum meritis et remissione*, 2, 24, 38; PL 44, 175;
Sermo 69, 3, 4; PL 38, 442; *Sermo 186*, 1; PL 38, 999.

[14] See *Opera omnia*, 2:387; 4:71ff.

[15] See *De admirandis gratiis beatae Virginis*, sermon 51, a. 2, c. 3; *Opera omnia*, 4:548.

[16] *Fomes*, i.e., the inclination to sin—Trans.

[17] See *De admirandis gratiis beatae Virginis*, a. 3, c. 2; *Opera omnia*, 4:553.

Mary's Assumption into Heaven

Bernardine's teaching on Mary's bodily Assumption into heaven is so clear and exhaustive that he has been acclaimed "Doctor of the Assumption". While, in his Latin works, he presents this truth in a theological way, his sermons in the vernacular describe the event in a lively, imaginative style, with intense emotional involvement. A beautiful example of this is found in the first of the sermons he preached in Siena's Piazza del Campo in 1427. Obviously influenced by the pseudo-Augustine, Bernardine wrote:

> The most holy flesh of the Mother, from which the flesh of the Son had been taken, did not have to suffer decay or be reduced to ashes or fall into dust.[18]

In another sermon in the vernacular, Bernardine, as if inspired by Dante's ascent from one heaven to the next in the *Divine Comedy*, follows in the Virgin's train, which, passing through various heavens, finally reaches the empyrean:

> Higher yet it goes; it climbs and reaches the empyrean heaven, with such festivity and gladness, with such glory, with such singing, with such dancing, that just to think of it is a joy. Oh, consider how they make merry there! In the Song of Songs, some tiny portion of its sweetness is recounted, in the second chapter (see Song 2:3ff.).[19]

Pius XII, in his apostolic constitution *Munificentissimus Deus*, by which he defined that Mary's Assumption into heaven was a truth of the faith, praises Bernardine's teaching on this point.[20]

Universal Queen and Mediatrix

Mary's universal queenship is evident after her glorious Assumption into heaven, but Bernardine also emphasizes its foundation, which, according to him, is Mary's role as Mother of God:

---

[18] *In Assumptione gloriosae Virginis Mariae*, sermon 9, a. 3, c. 1; *Opera omnia*, 6:173.

[19] *Prediche volgari sul Campo di Siena 1427*, sermon 1; ed. Delcorno, 1:104.

[20] *Acta Apostolica Sedis*, 42 (1950): 765–66.

The conception of the Son of God conferred upon the Blessed Virgin the right to administrate and govern everything that was granted to the Son.[21]

Mary's queenship is expressed, above all, in the working of mercy and the distribution of grace, since she is the Mother of Christ, the very source of mercy and grace. The connection between the mediation of grace and the divine motherhood recalls the strong influence of St. Bernard on Bernardine of Siena's Marian doctrine. We give one statement from among a great many on the subject:

> From the moment when she conceived God in her womb, she had—if I may be allowed the expression—a certain jurisdiction and authority over all the temporal processions of the Holy Spirit, so that no creature receives any grace of virtue except through the distribution of that grace by the Virgin Mary.[22]

Moreover, as Mediatrix, the Blessed Virgin is called to administer, as it were, the riches of the Holy Spirit as well, because the Paraclete is one of the gifts that Jesus gave to the Church. Our author writes:

> Because she is the Mother of the Son of God, who is the one who gives the Holy Spirit, it follows that all the gifts, virtues, and graces of the Holy Spirit are granted through her hands to whomever she wishes, when she wishes, and in the measure she wishes.[23]

Obviously, Bernardine is not unaware that Jesus is the only Mediator by his nature; nevertheless, this fundamental truth does not prevent him from seeing that Mary sits next to her Son, as intercessor and Mediatrix on behalf of us all. He explicitly recognizes this role, even when speaking to the more simple faithful, less well-prepared theologically, who came to hear him preach in the vernacular:

> O Queen of heaven, Mother of God, Milady of the world, Advocate of this our city, Fountain of mercy, in whom every virtue is found and from whom all graces flow, direct my speaking so that what I say may be for the praise and glory and honor of your sweet Son, our Creator and Redeemer.[24]

---

[21] De gratia et gloria beatae Virginis, sermon 61, a. 1, c. 7; Opera omnia, 2:377.

[22] De salutatione angelica, sermon 52, a. 1, c. 2; Opera omnia, 2:157.

[23] De gratia et gloria beatae Virginis, sermon 61, a. 1, c. 8; Opera omnia, 2:379.

[24] Prediche volgari sul Campo di Siena 1427, sermon 1; ed. Delcorno, 1:86.

We have already called attention to Bernardine's intemperate expressions, which may be explained as the Franciscan saint's verbal ventings of his passionate love and enthusiastic devotion for the Blessed Virgin. This notwithstanding, it bears repeating that Bernardine of Siena surely deserves to be numbered among the great masters of Marian doctrine at the close of the Middle Ages. His preaching strongly influenced the development of popular piety in subsequent centuries.

READINGS

MARY, TABERNACLE OF GOD

"In sole posuit tabernaculum suum" (Ps 18:6). He has placed his tabernacle in the sun. Hence, this morning of the Incarnation of the Son of God. What is his tabernacle? The Virgin Mary. What was put inside that tabernacle? The Son of God. Who put him there? The Holy Spirit: "Qui conceptus est de Spiritu Sancto"; who was conceived by the Holy Spirit. In this sacred utterance, divine grace shows you three things to contemplate: first, a radiant place: *in sole*; second, a loving action: *posuit*; third, the beautiful fruit: *tabernaculum suum*.

Where was the tree of life planted? In the earthly paradise. Who planted it? The Holy Spirit. What was born of it? The beautiful tabernacle. Take the first part: the radiant place. But he says: *in sole*. Whence you have in chapter twelve of the Apocalypse: "Signum magnum apparuit in coelo: mulier amicta sole, et luna sub pedibus eius, et in capite eius corona stellarum duodecim" (Rev 12:1). A great sign appeared in heaven: a woman clothed with the sun, and the moon under her feet, and on her head a crown of twelve stars. And so we contemplate her under three aspects: first, considering her as well adorned, clothed with the sun; second, as well honored, the moon under her feet; third, as well crowned, with twelve stars.

Take the first aspect under which we consider her: how she is well adorned. But it says: clothed with the sun. The sun has three natures: vigor, radiance, and warmth, and these natures it bears always. What do they signify? Her three singular excellences. *Ab aeterno*, it was ordained that she should be a unique woman: first, in her vigorous virtue; second, in her radiant knowledge; third, in her warm charity.

Take the first: her vigorous virtue. The vigor with which the Virgin

Mary's soul was clothed signifies a great virtue, which she put on when she was conceived in her mother's womb and her soul was infused. And immediately she had these three virtues. The first condition of the soul, vigor, was infused into her soul: at once, she had all the virtues. Whence says David the prophet: "Astitit regina a dextris tuis, in vestitu deaurato, circumdata varietate" (Ps 44:10). The queen stands at your right side, clothed in clothes of gold, surrounded with wonders; that is, with all the virtues. And so her soul was given all the virtues she ever needed, although she increased them when she conceived the Son of God. And so it says that she is clothed in gold and with the sun.

—Bernardine of Siena, *Le prediche volgari inedite* (Florence, 1424–1425; Siena, 1425), ed. D. Pacetti (Siena, 1935), pp. 317–19

MILADY OBEDIENCE [25]

The first of the other four companions of the Virgin Mary was Milady Obedience. She heard the angel's word, which seemed to her in accord with what she herself wanted, namely, that her virginity should be preserved always, and said to Mary: Remain content, for God has sent this angel to you. Answer him promptly, and tell him that you are content and prepared for the will of God. Then Mary said to the angel, "How can this be?" The angel said, "The Holy Spirit will come upon you, and the power of the Most High will overshadow you. . . . And behold, your kinswoman Elizabeth in her old age has also conceived a son; and this is the sixth month with her who was called barren. For with God nothing will be impossible" (Lk 1:35–37).

When she heard these words, Mary at once freely said, "Behold!" (Lk 1:38). Do you see this "behold"? It contains such sweetness as well as an abundance of every virtue. And there is a very great willingness in that word. And the swiftest readiness. And it contains the most abundant cheerfulness.

First, the greatest willingness was in readiness. And so, O maiden, when your father or your mother commands you, or your grandmother, or even your aunt, do what is commanded you. Do it willingly, as David says, "Voluntarie sacrificabo tibi" (Ps 53:8); willingly will I sacrifice to you and do what you will command me. Do it cheerfully and do not act

---

[25] Bernardine imagines that Mary, in the home at Nazareth, was assisted and served by twelve allegorical damsels, to each of which he gives the name of a different virtue.

as many do, who pout when they are commanded to do something. Don't act that way; be obedient.

This *ecce* also signifies readiness, teaching, O maid, that when your father or your mother commands you to do something, you should move to do it even before they speak, if possible. Know this: "Quia qui cito dat, bis dat"; who gives quickly gives twice. And someone who is not so quick gives only once. Hence, St. Bernard says on this subject, When your prelate commands you, make ready your body, hands, eyes, feet, mouth, every sense; make it prompt to obey his orders. *Ecce, ecce,* Behold, here I am, what do you command?

There is a third thing in this *ecce*; namely, cheerfulness. Oh, to have seen the Virgin Mary when she did anything! With what great cheerfulness she did it—how marvelous! For, whatever she did, she was always prepared to do it in God's sight, and so she did it with great pleasure.

—Bernardine of Siena, *Prediche vulgari sul Campo di Siena 1427*, sermon 30; ed. Dalcorno, 2:881–82

MILADY DILIGENCE

The third companion damsel of the Virgin Mary was Milady Diligence. She kept the whole house in order. And whatever she did, she did it with such love and order that even when eating, she ate in an orderly way, up to the time for bed. She did everything at the time ordained for it.

Learn, O maiden, to do with order and love whatever you have to do. If your task is to spin or cook or sweep or to govern the household goods, or anything else, do it with diligence. Learn from Mary. This is how she acted when the angel said to her: "Behold, you will conceive in your womb and bear a son, and you shall call his name Jesus. He will be great, and will be called Son of the Most High; and the Lord God will give to him the throne of his father David, and he will reign over the house of Jacob for ever; and of his kingdom there will be no end" (Lk 1:31–33). She said to the angel, "How can this be?" (Lk 1:34). Oh, how could this fact come to pass? I want to know, before I answer you. This diligence is a wonderful thing. Whence you find in Ecclesiasticus, "The diligent woman will be praised." The woman who demonstrates diligence in everything she does will be praised.

—Bernardine of Siena, *Prediche volgari sul Campo di Siena 1427*, sermon 30; ed. Dalcorno, 2:877–78

6

ANTONINUS OF FLORENCE
(d. 1459)

Antoninus was gifted with a singular sensitivity and openness to the people and problems of his time. He is remembered as a tenacious promoter of Church reform in Florence, of which he was the zealous pastor, and as a determined promoter of charitable and social works. In his Marian doctrine, he laid special emphasis on Mary's cooperation in the mystery of salvation, and he dedicated himself to spreading devotion to the Mother of the Lord.

Antoninus was born in Florence in 1389 to a good middle-class family named Pierozzi. His father was a notary by profession. In 1405, Antoninus entered the novitiate of the Dominican fathers at Cortona and made his religious profession there. After having been a prior in various convents, he was named archbishop of Florence in 1446. He had a special prophetic intuition about the necessity of reforming the Church before serious problems occurred, such as those that actually happened less than a century later in the Protestant Reformation. He had to content himself, however, with working within the limits of his own diocese, where his reform happened especially on a practical level, as he urged his faithful to works of charity and social solidarity, especially on behalf of the most needy. This goal of building up the Christian life was greatly helped by the witness of his own life, in which Antoninus continued to think and live as a mendicant friar, even after his elevation to the episcopacy, living in exemplary poverty according to the spirit of his order.

For understanding his Marian doctrine, his forty-six sermons on the Mother of God and his commentary on the first chapter of Luke's Gospel are essential. Also, he discusses Marian themes, with a properly theological method, in his voluminous *Summa Theologica*,[1] published for

---

[1] We will cite the edition published at Verona in 1740, which was reprinted in a facsimile edition at Graz in 1959. (Hereafter cited as Verona.)

the first time in 1477, at the dawn of the age of printing. The influence of the *Mariale super missus est* of the pseudo-Albert is easily perceptible in Antoninus' Marian writings. To appreciate his Marian doctrine, it is necessary to remember that his interests are focused primarily on practical disciplines such as moral and pastoral theology. Consequently, his Mariology is marked with a decidedly practical stamp, at the service of the Christian life and devotion to the Mother of the Lord. In his exposition of Marian themes he follows a rather arbitrary order.[2]

Mary's Holiness

The theme of the Blessed Virgin's preservation from original sin was much debated in Antoninus' time. He remained faithful to the tradition of his order and, consequently, opposed this truth, preferring the old solution according to which Mary had been sanctified in her mother's womb very soon after the infusion of her soul:

> She was sanctified in her mother's womb when she was totally cleansed from original sin. In this sanctification, a richer grace was infused in her than in the case of others who were sanctified in the womb, such as John the Baptist and Jeremiah.
>
> And it may also be piously believed that she was sanctified earlier than anyone else; but not before the infusion of her soul, because the flesh is not subject to sin or grace, but the soul is. But once the soul was infused, on that same day and hour, even if not at the same moment, she was cleansed from the original sin she had contracted, immediately after it entered her body.[3]

He believed that Mary had not only been purified from original sin but that she had also been filled with grace, which came to her because of the presence of the Incarnate Word within her:

---

[2] For the Marian doctrine of Antoninus of Florence, see E. Brand, *Die Mitwirkung der seligen Jungfrau zur Erlösung nach dem hl. Antonin von Florenz* (Rome, 1945); G. Defrenza, "Maria madre della Chiesa nel pensiero di S. Antonino, arcivescovo di Firenze", *Rivista di Ascetica e Mistica* 11 (1966): 172–80; L. Ciappi, "S. Antonino O.P., teologo e testimone del culto mariano nella Firenze del '400", in CongrRom 5:259–66; D. Montagna, "Un volgarizzamento toscano della formula integrale dell'Ave Maria alla metà del Quattrocento", Mar 37 (1975): 53–54.

[3] *Summa Theologica*, pars 4, tit. 15, c. 3; Verona, col. 923.

Among mere creatures, only the Virgin Mary was *full of grace*, because she could not have a greater grace. For one could not conceive of a greater grace than being united to divinity itself, and this grace she did receive. That is, no greater grace could be conceived than to be the Mother of God, unless she should become God himself.[4]

This fullness of grace was the font of every kind of blessing, gift, privilege, and virtue in the Virgin, making her a creature uniquely perfect, both in body and, of course, in soul. This personal condition placed her at the summit of creation, for in her God brought together all the gifts and blessings accorded to other creatures. Moreover, she found herself placed higher even than angelic creatures. It is in the mystery of her Assumption into heaven that the superiority and glory of the Mother of the Lord shine forth fully. Antoninus states that of all creatures, only Mary, the Mother of Christ, is situated between the glorified creatures and Christ, the one creature united to divinity by his nature.[5]

In response to the amazing fact that God chose her, Mary consecrated her whole life to him. The clearest expression of this consecration is the vow of virginity she made, even before the angel of the Lord gave her the news that the Lord had chosen her. This vow was an unusual proposition in the time and cultural context in which she lived; nevertheless, she was always ready to lay aside her own plans, should God ask her to.[6]

Mary's Cooperation in Redemption

The bishop of Florence bases his thought on the principle of Mary's association with Christ, which makes her a helper and instrument similar to him. He recognizes the Blessed Virgin as a true collaborator with the Redeemer in the work of human salvation, so that she placed her whole self at his disposal: her very being, her conduct, her diligence, and, above all, her suffering as the Mother of a Son whose existence was marked by a tragic destiny. In him, the Redeemer, she became the Mother of all the living:

---

[4] Ibid., c. 15; Verona, col. 1009.
[5] Ibid., c. 45; Verona, col. 1268.
[6] Ibid., c. 6; Verona, col. 946.

And she is the Mother of all men to the greatest possible degree, with regard both to bearing [children] and to taking care of them, because she bore the one man through whom she recreated or regenerated all men. And in her Son she obtained for us everything necessary for the present life and for the life to come.[7]

Antoninus goes so far as to attribute a kind of priestly status to the Blessed Virgin; he actually calls her "priestess of justice" (*sacerdotissa iustitiae*) because, as she stood beneath the Cross, she did not spare her only Son. Rather, with a high sense of duty, she offered him according to the eternal Father's will for the salvation of the human race:

She was also the priestess of justice, because she "did not spare [her] own Son" (Rom 8:32), but "stood by the cross of Jesus" (Jn 19:25) not, as Blessed Ambrose says, so that she might look upon her Son's death, not so that she might contemplate her Son's suffering, but so that she might await the salvation of the human race, for she herself was ready to offer her Son to God for the salvation of the world.[8]

Mary's Spiritual Motherhood

The role Mary plays on our behalf within the Church is simply the consequence of her cooperation with Jesus in the salvation of the world, so that she has become the Mother of our spiritual rebirth. Antoninus actually uses the expression *mater spiritualis*:

O Church, I want her who is my Mother to become your Mother also. She is my natural Mother; she is your spiritual Mother. Behold: the Mother of the Savior is the Mother of the sinner in the Church.[9]

To support the reality of Mary's spiritual motherhood, the bishop of Florence cites the words of Christ to his Mother and John on Mt. Calvary (Jn 19:25–27):

As a man is called "father" because of generation, care, age, honor, and affection, so in all these ways the Blessed Virgin is our Mother. First, just as Christ, by his word of truth, by suffering the pains of the Cross, gave us birth to the spiritual existence of grace, which is more perfect than

---

[7] Ibid., c. 20; Verona, cols. 1059–60.

[8] Ibid., c. 3; eVerona, cols. 926–27.

[9] Ibid., c. 2; Verona, col. 917.

natural existence, so too the Blessed Virgin Mary conceived and gave us birth in the greatest pain, suffering together with her Son, suffering the greatest pains for our sake.[10]

Antoninus goes on to explain at length the other reasons why the Virgin Mary is our spiritual Mother: the concern and tenderness with which she truly takes care of us, her age, which transcends all times (in that God predestined her from all eternity), the dignity and honor that is hers as Mother of God and Queen of heaven and earth, and the great affection she bears toward her people, whose good she constantly considers.[11]

He lists the various ways in which the Virgin carries out her spiritual motherhood on our behalf in the Church: she assists those who have been entrusted with the governance of the Christian community; she obtains reconciliation with God for those who undertake the path of conversion to the Christian life; she assists and inspires by her example those who are progressing in the way of holiness; and she gives hope to the perfected, assuring them of achieving eternal beatitude.[12]

Antoninus employs a great many metaphors and images to illustrate his Marian doctrine; however, he always seeks to interpret them within the limits imposed by Scripture, which imparts a theological and biblical character to his presentation.

Mediatrix

The Blessed Virgin's maternal role is not limited to our spiritual birth on Calvary; rather, it continues in the services and care she renders us through her maternal mediation. For Antoninus, the term "Mediatrix" means that Mary stands in the middle (*media*) between God and human beings:

> She has been made the middle term, or Mediatrix, between God and men, for which reason the Church sings: "Mediatrix of men, washer-away of offenses, forgiveness of sins", because she obtains these things. And so sinners, who have become rivals and enemies of God by their offenses, should have recourse . . . to this Mediatrix, in order to be recon-

---

[10] Ibid.

[11] Ibid., Verona, cols. 917–18.

[12] Ibid., Verona, col. 919.

ciled to God. For just as the lawsuit between God and men is settled by her mediation, in the same way, the cases between men and the devil are ended by her.[13]

Our author attributes extraordinary power to Mary: through her Son, she absolves us of all our faults and the punishments that follow from them. But she carries out this role with a special preference for sinners, so that she may be called both their great Mediatrix and their Advocate.[14]

READINGS

MARY AT CANA

"The mother of Jesus was there" (Jn 2:1), that is, at the wedding feast. It was the wedding celebration (as is commonly said) of John the Evangelist, who was a nephew of the glorious Virgin on his mother's side.[15] For the mother of John and of James the Greater, who was called Mary Salome, the wife of Zebedee, by whom she bore John and James, was a sister of the glorious Virgin. And so, as a relative, she was invited to her nephew's wedding as was her Son together with his disciples.

Even though she was the Mother of the Lord and Queen of heaven, being humble, she did not disdain to be present at the wedding of a poor little fisherman who was so poor that the wine for his wedding celebration was running short. But she made sure that this need was taken care of by her blessed Son, for, being truly merciful, she had sympathy for the embarrassment of the needy couple.

Moreover, her presence and that of her Son did not reprove the state of spouses who celebrate their wedding in fear of the Lord, as is read of the holy man Tobit and his wife (see Tob 8:4), but approved of it, even while preferring the virginal or widowed state to that of a married couple, as having greater merit. For [John] did not consummate the

---

[13] Ibid., c. 5; Verona, col. 937.

[14] Ibid.

[15] The source of this tradition is the *Monarchian Prologue* to the fourth Gospel, composed probably at the end of the fourth century or the beginning of the fifth. Cf. H. Lietzmann, *Das muratorische Fragment und die monarchianischen Prologe ze den Evangelien*, Kleine Texte 1 (Bonn, 1933), p. 13.

marriage he had contracted, but when he saw the miracle of the water changed into wine, he left his wife, laid down the world and took up the discipleship of Christ and remained a virgin forever.

This wedding also symbolizes the spiritual wedding celebrated between Christ and the Church in general, or between God and any individual soul in particular, and in all these cases "the Mother of Jesus was there", the Blessed Virgin Mary.

—Antoninus of Florence, *Summa Theologica pars* 4, tit. 15, c. 38;
Verona, cols. 1194–95

MARY'S PILGRIMAGE TO THE HOLY PLACES

[Mary] visited the places where her Son had done any miraculous deed, and there she contemplated the sacred mysteries. Sometimes in Nazareth she went to the place where the angel had made his announcement to her and she had conceived the Son of God, and there she contemplated God's boundless charity. Sometimes in Bethlehem she meditated on God's humility, for there he had his humble birth. Sometimes she went to the Temple in Jerusalem, where she had been presented on the fortieth day and where [her Son] later preached, recalling his most sweet and wondrous teaching, reflecting on his wisdom. Sometimes she visited the river Jordan, where when Christ was baptized he had made all the waters holy for washing away the sins of those receiving baptism and where John had heard the Father's voice: "This is my beloved Son", and the Holy Spirit was seen in the likeness of a dove. And considering how great and generous the Lord is, she was caught up in spiritual ecstasy, as might well be believed.

Passing by Mt. Calvary, where her Son was crucified amid such great insult for the salvation of men, she completely dissolved into tears because of the immense sweetness of God's love that was revealed there. And, going on from there and reaching the tomb, she rejoiced with all her heart that he had come forth from it risen and appeared on the third day. And going up the Mount of Olives, and recalling that her Son had ascended from there into heaven, she eagerly longed to be with Christ.

—Antoninus of Florence, *Summa Theologica pars* 4, tit. 15, c. 43;
Verona, col. 1228

7

DIONYSIUS THE CARTHUSIAN
(d. 1471)

Dionysius [Denys] van Leeuwen was a prolific author whose works became very widely read, greatly influencing religious learning in the West. Even though we cannot say that his thought is very original, he did leave us an enormous literary output, covering the most varied fields of theological learning: questions of exegesis, commentaries on the Bible and ancient writers, systematic treatises, spiritual and mystical works. He was called *Doctor Ecstaticus* because of his mystical experiences. He touched on Marian themes in nearly all of his works, as if he sensed a continual need somehow to express his particular love for the Blessed Virgin, which he had fostered since his youth.

Dionysius was born in 1403 or 1404 in Rijkel, in the region of Limburg (Belgium), to a family of modest means. Having manifested a precocious affinity for study, he was first sent to the school of Saint-Trond. At the age of thirteen, he transferred to the more famous school of Zwolle. In 1421, he enrolled at the University of Cologne, where he earned the degree *Magister Artium* in 1424. After overcoming a serious spiritual crisis, he embraced the religious life in 1425, in the Charterhouse of Roermond. There his Marian piety was further reinforced, for he loved to recite the Angelus and to repeat the words "As God lives, in whose sight I stand" (cf. I Kings 17:1), which he believed had been continually on the lips of the Blessed Virgin. In 1433, he was named procurator, but very quickly he was exempted from this responsibility so that he might be free to dedicate himself to writing.

He lived an intensely ascetical life, composed of penance and the practice of Christian virtues, and was also graced with mystical gifts, such as ecstasies and supernatural visions. His intense commitment to the Carthusian life did not prevent him from becoming a counselor to famous personages of his time. In 1466, he was given the post of rector of the new foundation of Bois-le-Duc; but some years later he had to return to Roermond because of the precarious condition of his health. He died on March 12, 1471.

Dionysius left an impressive literary legacy. His works take up forty-four folio volumes.[1] The following works are dedicated to Marian doctrine: the two treatises *De praeconio et dignitate Mariae* and *De dignitate et laudibus Virginis Mariae*, as well as Marian hymns and thirty-five sermons for the feasts of the Mother of God (Conception, Nativity, Purification, Annunciation, Visitation, and Assumption). As was said above, however, references to the Virgin are quite frequent in all of his works, especially in his commentaries on Marian texts in the Old and New Testaments.[2]

An Authoritative Witness to the Marian Tradition of the Church

Dionysius' teaching on the Blessed Virgin does not offer any exceptionally original points. Instead, it is valuable because it firmly and competently continues the reflection to which the great masters of the Middle Ages were already committed. This reflection, which preexisted the medieval masters, is coupled to the tradition of the Fathers of the Church. Dionysius prefers to appeal to the authority of Jerome, Augustine, Bernard, Bonaventure, pseudo-Albert, and others. Nevertheless, we must recognize that this strong attachment to tradition sometimes makes it difficult to consider and accept new perspectives, such as the theme of Mary's holiness, for example. In any case, he is accustomed to attribute many titles to Mary, understanding them in the light of her greatness and the importance of her mission. In virtue of her divine motherhood, he calls her Light-giver (*illuminatrix*), Companion, and Cooperatrix in the Redemption, "Savioress" (*salvatrix*), Advocate, Mediatrix, and Spouse of God.

---

[1] We cite the following edition: *Doctoris Ecstatici D. Dionysii Carthusiani Opera omnia*, vols. 1–42 (Monstrolii [Montreuil-sur-Mer/Tournai], 1896–1913); vols. 43–44 (Parkminster, 1935).

[2] See F. M. Bauducco, "L'Illuminatrice nelle opere de Dionigi il Certosino", Mar 10 (1948): pp. 191–210; idem, "Due mariologie di Dionigi il Certosino", Mar 13 (1951): 453–70; idem, "De Maria et Ecclesia apud Dionysium Carthusianum", in CongrLourd 3:375–88; idem, "Fonti della mediazione nella mariologia di Dionigi il Certosino", Mar 33 (1971): 457–501; B. Tonutti, *Mariologia Dionysii Carthusiani* (Rome, 1953); Y. Gourdel, "Le Culte de la très sainte Vierge dans l'Ordre des Chartreux", in Maria, 2:625–78.

The Question of the Immaculate Conception

On the question of the original holiness of the Mother of the Lord, Dionysius' thought shows a certain evolution. At first, he did not hold that she had to be excluded from the common inheritance of sin, which all the members of the human race incur at the moment of their conception. He strictly interpreted the law formulated by the Apostle, "[In Adam] all men sinned" (Rom 5:12), and would admit only that Mary had been sanctified before her birth, in her mother's womb:

> Christ chose and created for himself a Mother, whom he preserved all pure from every stain of sin, and he sanctified her in her mother's womb.[3]

Later, after the Council of Basel had declared the Immaculate Conception a truth of the faith, and notwithstanding that the decree on the Immaculate Conception was later considered invalid because of the historical vicissitudes that Council had to negotiate, Dionysius considered the conciliar definition to be valid. Making Duns Scotus' teaching his own, he upheld the truth that the Virgin had been exempted from original sin.[4] This new position included the idea that, in the Immaculate Conception, the Virgin had also been confirmed in grace and therefore could not fall into sin, even a venial one. Dionysius declares this explicitly:

> [God] protected the glorious Virgin, not only from every mortal sin, but from every venial sin as well.[5]

After having postulated the various degrees in which the Lord shows how he protects his creatures, he concludes that this grace, reserved to Mary alone, constitutes the highest degree of divine protection against evil and sin.

Mary's Gratitude for the Gift of Her Divine Motherhood

The birth of the Son of God from a woman would be unimaginable had God not prefigured the event in the Old Testament. Dionysius compares the Mother of God to Sarah, with whom she may repeat:

---

[3] *In Psalmum 45; Opera omnia*, 6:15A.

[4] *In librum 3 Sententiarum*, d. 3, q. 1; *Opera omnia*, 23:98A–D.

[5] *Enarratio in cap. 15 Genesis*, a. 1; *Opera omnia*, 1:224A.

"God has made laughter for me" (Gen 21:6), that is, he has given me a reason for the highest exultation by making me the inviolate Mother of his Only-begotten. "Every one who hears will laugh over me" (ibid.), that is, let all the faithful congratulate the Most Blessed Virgin for this [favor]. The fact that this Virgin nursed a son was so far beyond the law of nature that it seemed almost unbelievable.[6]

Mary's divine motherhood gives her a position of greatness and dignity higher than any the Almighty has ever granted to a mere creature. The Virgin's response to God for this incomparable gift finds its greatest expression in her *Magnificat*, in which she recognizes her lowliness and the Lord's immense goodness and generosity to her:

> You, Elizabeth, praise, extol, and magnify me, but I, knowing that I possess nothing on my own, give the credit for all these things to God. Him do I praise; myself I depreciate.... Him do I magnify; that is, I confess, witness, and designate him as great, most high, and immense; I honor him who must be magnified with all my powers; I desire him to be worshipped with all zeal. I consider myself to be of little account.[7]

Mary's Cooperation in Redemption; Mediatrix of Grace

Our author does not hesitate to present the Mother of God as Mediatrix between her divine Son and human beings; what is more, in his ardor he goes so far as to call her "Redemptrix and Savioress of the world".[8] He begins with the principle that, just as Adam had a woman as his partner in sin, so the new Adam, in accord with the free decision of God, had to have a partner in the work of salvation.[9] And it is because of this free decision that Mary beseeches God for all the graces that we obtain:

> After God, Mary is the origin, Mother, and generous giver of all the gifts that are granted us; for to her has the kingdom of mercy been handed

---

[6] *Enarratio in cap. 21 Genesis*, a. 62; *Opera omnia*, 1:284D–285A.

[7] *Enarratio in cap. 1 Lucae*, a. 4; *Opera omnia*, 11:393CD.

[8] See *De praeconio et dignitate Mariae*, lib. 2, a. 8 and 9; *Opera omnia*, 35:516CD. Statements of this kind are dangerous if isolated from their context, where it is always understood that Christ is the true Redeemer of the world. The term "redemptrix" is meant only to emphasize the special role that Mary played, alongside her Son and subordinate to him.

[9] See ibid., lib. 2, a. 9 (*Opera omnia*, 35:516B); lib. 3, a. 25 (*Opera omnia*, 35:563B).

over, and through her hands God gives and has decided to give whatever grace he bestows on us.[10]

The power of her intercession comes from the fact that she was present beneath the Cross on Calvary. This circumstance makes the Redeemer particularly inclined to be generous to us and to assure us of his assistance in the order of our eternal salvation.[11]

Mary and the Church

Dionysius emphasizes the close connection between the Virgin and the Church in his commentary on the Song of Songs, which he considers a certain prophecy of the Church herself, the universal Bride of the incarnate Word. In the Church, the faithful soul also participates in his mystery as a particular bride of Christ. Mary can be well described as the unique Bride of her Son. On this point, Dionysius' thought is quite clear:

> Christ has three brides, namely: a universal bride, who is the Church of all the elect, whom he began to wed at the beginning of the world by faith and charity; a particular bride, who is the holy soul, whom he weds daily by converting individuals to himself by grace; a singular bride, who is the most blessed Virgin, whom he wed in the womb of his Mother. But these last two brides are contained in the first, as the part is contained in the whole.[12]

Even though the Virgin, being the Mother of God's Son, is in a particular and unique personal situation compared to other believers, she still participates in the universal spousal mystery of the Church just as they do. In this perspective, Dionysius can rightly consider her a member and spiritual daughter of the Church.[13] Nevertheless, she is also the Mother of the Church, because her Son, as he hung on the Cross, designated her as Mother of all Christians.[14] The title "Mother of the

---

[10] *Enarratio in cap. 4 Cantici Canticorum*, a. 14; *Opera omnia*, 7:384A.

[11] *De praeconio et dignitate Mariae*, lib. 3, a. 25; *Opera omnia*, 35:563B-D.

[12] *Enarratio in cap. 3 Joannis*, a. 10; *Opera omnia*, 12:340B. Some centuries earlier, Isaac of Stella (d. ca. 1169) had expressed himself in the same terms. Cf. his *Sermo 51 in Assumptione Beatae Mariae*; PL 194, 1863AB; SC 339, 204.

[13] See *Enarratio in cap. 6 Cantici Canticorum*, a. 20; *Opera omnia*, 7:415B.

[14] See *Enarratio in cap. 19 Joannis*, a. 46; *Opera omnia*, 12:595D.

Church", which Dionysius explicitly attributes to Mary, is to be understood in this sense.[15]

She is a Mother who also exercises the role of advocate on behalf of
her children, the members of the Church. Indeed, human beings obtain
salvation thanks to her maternal intervention. This is shown by her
intervention with her Son at Cana:

> The most kind, affectionate, and sweet Virgin felt compassion because of
> the shame of the bride and bridegroom as well as for their penury or for
> their guests' lack [of wine]. And if she felt with them the sorrow of their
> physical poverty and came to their aid, even without being asked, how
> much more will she have compassion on our spiritual neediness and offer
> assistance if she be called upon with faith? Yes, she offers assistance
> generously, even before she is asked.[16]

Our author maintains that Mary's intercessory role was willed by
Christ himself:

> Indeed, you willed that she should be a cooperatrix in the work of the
> salvation of all of us; you established her as the advocate of the Church
> and decreed that many should be saved through her.[17]

READINGS

THE VIRGIN'S EXTRAORDINARY FAITH

In truth, who could think, conceive, or tell how manifest, sure, and solid
was the faith of the most splendid Virgin? For she super-certainly knew
that she was a virgin, that she had conceived by the Holy Spirit, that she
had given birth without any lessening of her chastity, that is, the seal of
her virginity being preserved. She knew that she was the Mother of
Christ, the only begotten Son of the eternal Father; she knew that she
had conceived and borne God and man in a single person; and because
she was full of the grace of the discernment of spirits, she knew that she
had conversed with the archangel Gabriel. She heard the words of the

---

[15] See *Enarratio in cap. 6 Cantici Canticorum*, a. 20; *Opera omnia*, 7:415B.

[16] *Enarratio in cap. 2 Joannis*, a. 7; *Opera omnia*, 12:313D.

[17] *De praeconio et dignitate Mariae*, lib. 3, a. 25; *Opera omnia*, 35:563B.

shepherds and Simeon and Anna; she saw the three Magi and the star; she saw Christ's miracles; she was most highly aware of all of his mysteries; and it must be believed that Christ appeared to her first after his Resurrection. Therefore, enlightened by all these things and others besides, how greatly strengthened and informed must her faith have been! This is why, even at the hour of the Passion, she alone remained fully unshaken and perfected in explicit faith.

THE VIRGIN'S PERFECT HOPE

Moreover, who could say anything worthy of the perfection, excellence, and certitude of her faith? Oh, how super-certain and perfect was this most excellent Virgin's faith! For she knew that she was the Mother of the God of gods, that she had borne, embraced, nursed, and brought up the salvation and glory of all the elect! She knew that she stood out among the predestined and that she had a throne in the heavenly kingdom, higher than the choirs and ranks of all the angels. For this reason she confidently sang, "My soul magnifies the Lord, . . . for he has regarded the low estate of his handmaiden. For behold, henceforth all generations will call me blessed; for he who is mighty has done great things for me" (Lk 1:46, 48–49).

She knew most certainly that she was to be most supremely and eternally honored by her only Son, God and man . . . and that her prayers would never be rejected by him. She knew that she was the most chosen of women, indeed, of all creatures. Nor did she doubt that she was the one whose person, dignity, and glory the patriarchs and prophets had foretold from the beginning. Therefore her hope was inexpressibly perfect.

THE VIRGIN'S OUTSTANDING AND ARDENT CHARITY

We can say nothing fitting about her charity, about how outstanding and ardent it was. For how could she not love God super-fervently, seeing herself so incomparably chosen by God, who went before her with his grace so graciously, seeing herself made his Mother, experiencing his goodness and generosity in her life so unceasingly and lavishly given, whom she loved not only as her God and Creator, but also as her Son, for whom she burned with love without limit, as she daily looked upon him, hugged him, fed him, and brought him to man's estate?

In the same way she most ardently loved God the Father, from whom, she knew, her only begotten Son had been sent, seeing herself made a co-parent with the eternal Father. And she loved the Holy Spirit most fervently, knowing that she had conceived by his power and overshadowing and that he had filled her with so many graces and charisms.

MARY AND THE GIFTS OF THE HOLY SPIRIT

The seven gifts of the Holy Spirit are granted to strengthen the virtues. They especially reinforce the three theological virtues, bringing them to perfection. For this reason, the more perfect one is in practicing the theological virtues, the more perfect he will be in the aforementioned seven gifts. So we have to believe that the most august Virgin Mary excelled in the practice of the theological virtues and that this excellence corresponded to her excellence in the enjoyment of the gifts [of the Holy Spirit].

Thus, she was most distinguished in the gift of wisdom. This gift has three levels, as is the case with charity. Wisdom, considered in its third or highest level, is in fact to be identified with mystical theology, which is theoretical, unitive, affective, and ardent wisdom. The Virgin Mary's perfection in this kind of wisdom was beyond measure, greater than that of all other wayfarers [on this earth]. The same may be said with regard to all the other gifts and lesser virtues.

—Dionysius the Carthusian, *Sermo 6*, vol. 31, 63B–64B

8

ALANUS DE RUPE

(d. 1475)

This Dominican friar, who died in the odor of sanctity, dedicated his most exceptional talents as an untiring preacher to spreading the Holy Rosary.[1] He preferred to call this pious practice the "Marian Psalter". He entrusted its recitation especially to the so-called "Confraternities of the Rosary", which he established as pious associations of prayer and which became enormously popular.

Teacher and Preacher

Alanus was born around 1428 in the region of Brittany and entered the order of St. Dominic when he was still young, around 1450. His first experience of the religious life took place in the convent of Dinan, from which he was sent to the convent of Saint-Jacques in Paris to continue his studies. Later he was called back to Dinan to teach; then, in 1460, we find him once again in Paris, commenting on the *Sententiae* of Peter Lombard. This stay in Paris was brief. In the autumn of 1461, he was sent to the convent of Lille and lived there until 1464, working as a *lector* (lecturer) and preacher. In October of the same year, he transferred to the autonomous congregation of the Dominicans in Holland and continued his activity as a lecturer, first at Douai (1464–1465), then at Ghent (1468–1470), and finally in the Dominican *studium* of Rostock (1470–1474), part of the University of Mecklenburg. He founded the first Rosary Confraternity in 1470, at Douai. In 1473, at Rostock, he received the title of Master of Theology and, as such, took part in the chapter of the Dutch congregation, held at Lille in 1475. At that time, he

---

[1] See, e.g., A. Wilmart, "Comment Alain de la Roche préchait le Rosaire ou Psautier de la Vierge", *La Vie et les arts liturgiques* 11 (1924–1925): 108–15.

lived in the convent of Zwolle, where, in the same year, he took ill and met his death.

His Marian Devotion

Alanus' importance for Marian devotion and spirituality is primarily tied to his distinguished contribution to establishing the Rosary as a Christian practice. It was he who introduced the recitation of 150 Hail Marys subdivided into decades, instead of the fifty usually said before. The idea of meditating on the mysteries of the life of Christ and of the Virgin is usually attributed to the monk Dominic Helion of Prussia (d. 1460), a Carthusian of the monastery of Trier. Dominic, in order to encourage the practice of meditation, introduced short phrases into the middle of the *Ave Maria*, after the word "Jesus", referring to the mystery being meditated upon.

Alanus' biographers tell us that he was driven to spread devotion to the Rosary by his own burning devotion to the Mother of the Lord and that this devotion never failed, even when he underwent a grave spiritual crisis between 1457 and 1464. Even then, he never stopped his daily recitation of the "Marian Psalter", or Rosary.

In 1464, the Virgin appeared to Alanus, put a ring on his finger as a sign of spiritual betrothal, and asked him to spread the Rosary and his Confraternity. For this reason, he came to be called "new bridegroom" of the Blessed Virgin Mary.

His Writings

In essence, the works of Alanus de Rupe are a collection of his preaching on the pious practice of the Rosary. The earliest witness to his preaching is offered by a work of his contemporary Michel François, who, in 1479, published his *Quodlibet de veritate Fraternitatis Rosarii*, a lecture he had given in Cologne in 1476. In an appendix, he added a work of Alanus': *De Psalterio beatae Mariae Virginis: exempla valde motiva ad amorem illius.*

Among the other important works of Alanus is the one entitled *De immensa et ineffabili dignitate et utilitate psalterii praecelsae ac intemeratae semper virginis Mariae* (published posthumously in 1498 at Stockholm).

His writings, widely published in adulterated form after his death, contributed to the propagation of various legends, including the legend that attributes the origin of the Rosary to St. Dominic. The changes made to his writings make the preparation of a critical edition of his works a demanding task. The psalter was published in 1610 in Fribourg, edited by the Dominican A. Coppenstein, who explains that the contents of the treatise are by Alanus, while the form is that of the editor. The work consists of five parts:

— a response to questions about the Rosary posed by the bishop of Tournai;
— stories, revelations, and visions concerning the Rosary;
— sermons of St. Dominic revealed to Alanus;
— sermons and treatises by Alanus himself;
— examples and miracles that illustrate the excellence and effectiveness of devotion to the Rosary.[2]

The Holy Rosary

In his treatise *Compendium psalterii beatissimae Trinitatis*,[3] Alanus offers a clear and complete summary of his teaching on the recitation of the Rosary. The title of the treatise is explained by the fact that in reciting the Rosary we are able to praise the Blessed Trinity through Christ, through the Virgin Mary, and in communion with all the saints.

Alanus divides his presentation into fifteen short chapters. In the prologue, he recalls that this pious practice consists in 150 Hail Marys, subdivided into groups of ten, each of which is preceded by the recitation of the Our Father. Against those who considered the recourse to numbers banal and artificial, Alanus appeals to the Fathers of the Church, expressly mentioning the eminent names of Augustine, Ambrose, and Jerome, who thought that numbers were the criterion according to which divine wisdom had arranged the universe, "lest dullness and confusion and impudence reign in divine things".

---

[2] Some bibliographical pointers: A. Duval, "La Dévotion mariale dans l'Ordre des Frères Prêcheurs", in *Maria*, 2:768–76; T. Koehler, *Maria nella storia della devozione cristiana, dal sec. XIII al sec. XVIII* (Verbania Pallanza: Centro Mariano Chaminade, n.d.), pp. 85–87; M. O'Carroll, *Theotokos: A Theological Encyclopedia of the Blessed Virgin Mary* (Wilmington, Del., 1982), pp. 9–10; *Marienlexikon*, vol. 1 (St. Ottilien: Eos Verlag 1987), p. 74.

[3] We cite the Italian translation by S. Orlandi, O.P., *Libro del Rosario della gloriosa Vergine Maria* (Rome: C.I.D.R., 1965).

The 150 Hail Marys are understood by way of analogy with David's Psalter, in which we read, "Praise God in the psaltery" (Ps 150:3). Adding the fifteen Our Fathers, you have a total of 165, which corresponds, according to a revelation received by St. Bernard, to the 165 wounds inflicted on Jesus in his Passion.

Alanus then calls for preaching the Rosary to the general public, because this practice has the advantage of being short (compared to the Psalter, obviously) and within the grasp of all, even the simple.

With an obvious sense of exaggeration, he claims to trace the Rosary back to apostolic times, whence it was passed down to his day by Christian tradition. Alanus attributes the enormous success of the Rosary to St. Dominic. He says that Mary revealed to Dominic that the first fifty Hail Marys are to honor the mysteries related to the Incarnation of the Son of God, the next fifty are for venerating the mysteries of his Passion and death, and the last fifty are recited in honor of his Resurrection and glorification. These three parts of the Rosary may be recited together or separately, at morning, midday, and evening, or any time at all, according to each person's devotion. As is the case with the Psalms of David, the Rosary invites us to enter into the four senses of each mystery: literal, allegorical, moral, and anagogical. In entrusting this practice to the faithful, Alanus fervently exhorts them:

> All of you who are lovers of Christ and of the glorious Virgin Mary, receive this psalter, which, according to St. Anselm, contains two queens among prayers, namely, the Our Father and the Hail Mary. These two prayers are two most common and worthy gospels, which are to be preached to every creature.[4]

The Confraternity of the Rosary

Speaking of the Confraternity of the Rosary, Alanus repeats that it was founded at the request of the Virgin, who suggested it to St. Dominic. In order to avoid simony, the faithful were to be admitted to membership at no cost whatever. Further, its members put all their merits and all the fruits of their spiritual life in common and committed themselves to the daily recitation of the Rosary, but not under pain of sin. Their names

---

[4] Ibid., pp. 184–85.

were inscribed in a special register so that they all might know each other and encourage a shared spirit of peace, charity, goodwill, mercy, and communion. Finally, they were invited to the practice of frequent sacramental confession and to participate in a special eucharistic celebration on the feast of St. Dominic.

Young people were also allowed to enter these confraternities. They could substitute for the recitation of the Rosary other prayers more appropriate to their age level.

Everyone was encouraged to carry a Rosary at all times as a sign of belonging to Christ.

Alanus' theory presents the Rosary as a universal prayer, suitable for all kinds of people: prelates, theologians, preachers, and devout persons in general. Its excellence and usefulness are confirmed by the miracles obtained by those who prayed it. Alanus describes fifteen types of miracles, especially those of a spiritual character, which correspond to the fifteen mysteries. His treatise concludes with this invitation:

> Let all praise our glorious Jesus Christ in this psalter so that, in the end, with the holy angels, they may praise without ceasing the Bridegroom and the Bride in endless joy.[5]

The great merit of Alanus de Rupe was to give the recitation of the Rosary a stable structure that could be used by even the most simple Christian. In meditating on the mysteries, he united the events of Mary's life to those of the Lord's life. Notwithstanding a certain exaggeration in the value he placed on legendary traditions about the origin of this devotion, the preaching of this zealous Dominican and his untiring work in founding the confraternities of the Rosary had a positive result, namely, spreading this pious practice, which was destined to play such an influential role in the Marian piety of later centuries, right up to our own day.

---

[5] Ibid., p. 203.

READINGS [6]

PRIVATE REVELATIONS OF MARY REGARDING CHRIST'S PASSION

The Virgin Mary revealed many things about the Lord's Passion that are not found in the Gospel, all of which should be piously believed. For, according to the testimony of John, not all the things Christ did were written down by the evangelists. But some persons, skeptical and devoid of devotion, incapable of tasting the things of God, to say nothing of the things that cannot be proven from Holy Scripture, scorn these other things and make fun of them, publicly stating that they are false or sophisms. By doing this, they often trouble the minds of the devout.

—Alanus de Rupe, *Alanus de Rupe sponsus novellus beatissimae*
Virginis Mariae (Mariefred, Stockholm, 1498), fol. 211r, B

THE ROSARY IS PRESENTED AS AN ANCIENT PRACTICE

Master Alanus de Rupe, of happy memory, the distinguished professor of sacred theology of our order, reported that he had read in a treatise by Master John del Monte how blessed Dominic championed this confraternity [of the Rosary] and how he had converted many people through it, how he performed many miracles, on which I will not dwell for the sake of brevity. I add what was said of him earlier, that is, in many ancient books . . . many beautiful stories and accounts of miracles related to the Rosary are read. From these facts one deduces that preaching the Rosary and convincing others to pray it, or becoming a member of the fraternity that bears its name, does not constitute something new but is merely the renewal of an ancient devotion, temporarily abolished in some places.

—Alanus de Rupe, *Alanus de Rupe sponsus novellus beatissimae*
Virginis Mariae (Mariefred, Stockholm, 1458) fol. 18r

---

[6] One needs to remember that the writings of Alanus de Rupe have been reworked by editors.

9

BERNARDINE DE BUSTIS
(d. ca. 1515)

This humble Franciscan friar bequeathed to later generations an impressive and weighty work: his *Mariale*. It offers a magisterial summary of the Marian doctrine and mentality of his time, even though the author's plan for the overall structure of the book is sometimes disrupted by certain of its copious contents.

Bernardine was born in Milan around the year 1450. He completed his first studies in that city, then went on to Pavia, earning a doctorate in law at the local university. Around 1475 he heeded the call to religious life and entered the order of Friars Minor. He died in the odor of sanctity sometime between 1513 and 1515. His life as a disciple of St. Francis was continually inspired by a tender devotion to the Mother of the Lord. This exemplary Marian charism also pervaded his intense activity as an apostle and preacher of God's word. He kept the feasts of the Lord's Mother with special fervor, composing for them sermons full of sound doctrine and the deepest veneration and love for the Virgin. Because of his reputation as an outstanding orator, he had a strong influence on the preachers of his time as well as those of the following century.

His writings address all the questions connected with Christian asceticism and sacred eloquence (preaching). His best-known work, which became an enormous success, is the above-mentioned *Mariale de excellentiis Reginae coeli*, which appeared in numerous editions in various European countries. It contains sixty-three sermons in which our preacher reviews the entire life of the Virgin and the divine mysteries in which she played a part. We have already mentioned that many exaggerations, trifles, and banalities are mixed in with more valuable material.[1] This may

---

[1] René Laurentin expresses a rather severe judgment on this work and concludes that the position of the Virgin must have been pretty solid to have avoided being

be considered telling evidence of the decadence that infected the historical period in question. Some decades later, in the Renaissance and in the
years of the Protestant Reformation, this same decadent tendency would
give rise to lively controversies.

The *Mariale* of Bernardine de Bustis was first published in Milan in
1494. We have been able to consult this *incunabulum* in a copy that the
Marian Library of the University of Dayton (Ohio) has kindly put at our
disposal.[2]

The Immaculate Conception

Faithful to John Duns Scotus, whose theory of the Virgin's preservation
from original sin had by then become part of the tradition of the
Franciscan theological school, Bernardine strongly favors this doctrine.
He does so with such zeal that he even cites, as supporters, theologians
who actually upheld the opposite thesis. Among others, such is the case
with St. Thomas Aquinas, whom the Franciscan counts among the
defenders of the dogma. Bernardine alleges that St. Thomas appeared to
a certain Santino, a bishop of Padua much devoted to Mary, who,
reading part 3 of the *Summa*,[3] was amazed that Aquinas denied the
Immaculate Conception. In this alleged apparition, St. Thomas clarified
what he had intended to uphold, namely, that even the Mother of the
Lord, in her conception, would have had to contract original sin according to the law of nature had her Son not made an exception, intervening
to preserve her from it.[4] It cannot be denied that this interpretation of
the Angelic Doctor seems to have been pulled out of thin air. Bernardine
dedicated the first nine sermons of the *Mariale* to Mary's Immaculate
Conception, followed by an Office composed for the same feast, which
obtained public approval from Pope Sixtus IV.[5]

---

compromised by such pietistic devotion. Cf. *Court traité sur la sainte Vierge* (Paris, 1968),
pp. 80–81.

[2] For the Marian thought of Bernardine, see F. Cucchi, *La mediazione universale della
SS. Vergine negli scritti di Bernardino de Bustis* (Milan, 1942); Comune di Busto Arsizio,
Bernardino de Bustis e il Mariale (Busto Arsizio, 1982). [The translator has worked from a
rare edition of the *Mariale* kindly made available to him by the library of the Pontifical
College Josephinum, Columbus, Ohio.]

[3] Thomas considers the theme in the six articles of Pars 3, q. 27.

[4] See *Mariale*, 1.7.1.

[5] Ibid., fol. 44v–52v.

Mary's Divine Motherhood

Bernardine shows a marked tendency to attribute to the Blessed Virgin every grace and heavenly gift that a creature so highly favored by God could possibly receive. So it is no wonder that he recognizes in her a certain right to the privilege of the divine motherhood, and he specifies in what sense this right ought to be understood. Before the mystery of the Incarnation of the Word of God was accomplished in her womb, this was a right of pure fittingness (*de congruo*). The Virgin was personally aware of this, as is seen from what she confided to her confessor, the Apostle John:

> For she recognized that she had received such a great grace, which she could never merit by right [*de condigno*], nor could any other creature merit it in that way. She merited it by way of fittingness [*de congruo*].[6]

After she gave her consent to the angel, however, this right of fittingness was transformed into a right of justice (*meritum digni*), because of her voluntary fidelity to God's plan of salvation.[7] This unique personal status puts Mary on a higher level, with regard to merit, than all the elect.[8]

The Mother of God and Redemption

Because of her privileged condition, Mary was able to collaborate with the Redeemer in his work of salvation to a greater extent than any other believer. Bernardine describes her as "collaborator in our redemption" (*adjutrix sive auxiliatrix nostrae redemptionis*), because it is through her aid that all persons achieve the grace of justification and salvation. Our author writes:

> Inasmuch as she binds and unites, she is Mediatrix of salvation [*mediatrix salutis*], of justification, of reconciliation, of intercession and of communication.[9]

---

[6] Ibid., 2.6.4.

[7] The problem of Mary's merit had already arisen in preceding centuries. Such prominent writers as Albert the Great and Thomas Aquinas held that the Virgin had merited to be Mother of God in some way (*quodammodo*).

[8] *Mariale*, 7.4.2.

[9] Ibid., 3.1.3.

Because the Lord entrusted her with the task of dispensing all the graces that human beings needed in the order of their salvation, Bernardine does not hesitate to apply to the Virgin titles that express this salvific role more or less directly. In the lengthy invocation to Mary that concludes his *Mariale*, Bernardine addresses Mary in very bold terms, some of which border on rashness:

> O spring of supernal grace! O armory of all treasures of wisdom and knowledge! O food and refreshment of the human mind! O our life! O artery of our salvation! O Redeemeress [*redemptrix*] of the universe! O changer [*mutatrix*] of the natural course of things! O recoverer of the lost world! O renewer of human nature! O Mediatrix between God and man! . . . O foundation of our faith!. . . O most faithful advocate in the presence of our Judge!. . . O dispenser of God's gifts!. . . O treasure of the Most High![10]

Some of these statements could not be submitted to careful analysis without facing the suspicion of heresy, since their meaning, if taken strictly, applies to Christ, not to Mary. But, in this case, they can be salvaged by the intention that inspired them, namely, to find a language capable of expressing the most ardent possible veneration and love for the Mother of God, going beyond the limits imposed by strictly theological language.

Mary's Glory in Heaven

Bernardine defended the doctrine that Mary was assumed into heaven, body and soul, after her earthly death. For him, death was an important event in Mary's life. While her preservation from original sin through the merits of her Son undoubtedly eliminated the fault of sin itself, nevertheless it left untouched the punishment of sin, which includes subjection to the natural law of death. Without this submission to death, our author doubts that Mary and Jesus could have truly been numbered among Adam's descendants.[11]

In heaven, the Virgin is enthroned as universal Queen and empress; her power extends to heaven, to hell, to purgatory, and throughout the

---

[10] Ibid., 12.2.1.
[11] Ibid., 1.2.2.

whole earth.[12] But she continues to be the Mother of Mercy and, as such, is dedicated to her role as Mediatrix and distributor of grace.

READINGS

MARY RECEIVED BAPTISM

The sacraments are a kind of avowal or profession of faith. But faith was present in the Virgin more than in any other person. Therefore, she had and received the sacraments.

Therefore, the Virgin herself observed the requirements of the Law, such as the requirement of purification, and so on, and so she observed the requirements of the Gospel law as well. The Lord himself said to John, "Thus it is fitting for us to fulfill all righteousness" (Mt 3:15), namely, in perfect humility, and he was speaking of receiving the sacrament of baptism. And so, for the same reason, the Blessed Virgin had to be baptized and receive the other sacraments. . . .

Whoever possesses every grace also possesses everything that confers grace. But the most blessed Virgin possesses every grace, and therefore she had everything that confers grace. Therefore, she had baptism, which confers grace.

Again, the precept of baptism, once it was promulgated, binds everyone to receive baptism. Therefore, the Blessed Virgin was also bound to receive baptism.

Again, the Lord was baptized, even though he did not need it. Therefore, the Blessed Virgin had to be baptized, too.

Again, in the Gospel of John the Savior says, "Truly, truly, I say to you, unless one is born of water and the Spirit, he cannot enter the kingdom of God" (Jn 3:5). But the Blessed Virgin entered the kingdom of God. Therefore, she was baptized.

Further, if she had not been baptized, it would have scandalized those who did not know that she had been sanctified. But Mary never scandalized anyone. Therefore, she received baptism.

---

[12] See ibid., 3.2.3.

MARY RECEIVED THE SACRAMENT OF PENANCE

Mary did not sin, but that was no obstacle [to her receiving the sacrament of penance]. It is characteristic of the spiritually good to acknowledge fault where there is no fault. Therefore, she recognized that she was bound to contract original sin and that she had been redeemed by her Son. For this reason, she would have been subjected to original sin had she not been preserved by prevenient divine grace. And she received this from the sacrament of penance in excelling measure.

For, by contrition, she had the preservation of innocence.[13] Instead of confessing her sins, she gave thanks. Instead of offering satisfaction, she received a superabundance [of grace]. Now confession has three parts: the accusation of sins, the recognition of the incongruity or greatness of the benefits [God has conferred], and the confession of the merits poured into the soul.

This, precisely, was the case with the Virgin's confession. For she recognized that she had received such a great grace, which she could never merit by right (*de condigno*), nor could any other creature merit it in that way. She merited it by way of fittingness (*de congruo*). She confessed this and other like things to Blessed John the Evangelist, her confessor.

MARY RECEIVED THE EUCHARIST

Albert shows that Mary received the sacrament of the Eucharist. In John's Gospel, [the Lord says], "Unless you eat the flesh of the Son of man and drink of his blood, you have no life in you" (Jn 6:53). Therefore, all the faithful are bound to receive the Eucharist during the time determined by the Church. Therefore, the Blessed Virgin also received the Eucharist. Further, in the same place the Savior says, "For my flesh is food indeed, and my blood is drink indeed. Whoever eats my flesh and drinks my blood has eternal life" (Jn 6:55–56). And again, "He who eats this bread will live for ever" (Jn 6:58). Therefore, there is no doubt that the Blessed Virgin devoutly ate this bread.

Again, this is the sacrament of love. Therefore, Mary had to receive it, since she was the highest in the order of love. Therefore, Albert says that

---

[13] It is possible that the text is corrupt here and should read "instead of [*pro*] contrition" and not "by [*per*] contrition".—TRANS.

the Blessed Virgin received from this sacrament a remembrance of the Lord's Passion, an exercise of practical devotion that made up for the desolation of her Son's physical absence.

—Bernardine de Bustis, *Mariale*, fol. 120v

Select Bibliography *

Balić, C., ed. *Bibliotheca Mariana Medii Aevi*. 8 vols. Rome, 1931–1954.

Barré, H. *Prières anciennes de l'Occident à la Mère du Sauveur*. Paris, 1963.

Baumer, Remigius, and L. Scheffczyk, eds. *Marienlexikon*. St. Ottilien: EOS Verlag, 1988–1994.

Besutti, G. *Bibliografia Mariana*. 8 vols. Rome: Marianum, 1948–1993.

Carol, J. B., ed. *Mariology*. 3 vols. Milwaukee, 1955–1961.

Courth, F. *Mariologie*. Texte zur Theologie, Dogmatik, vol. 6. Graz: Styria, 1991.

DeFiores, Stefano, and S. Meo, eds. *Nuovo dizionario di mariologia*. Milan: Edizioni Paoline, 1985.

Delius, W. *Geschichte der Marienverehrung*. Munich and Basel, 1963.

Gambero, L., ed. *Testi Mariani del Secondo Millenio. Autori Medievali*. Vols. 3 and 4. Rome, 1996.

Graef, H. *Mary: A History of Doctrine and Devotion*. New York: Sheed and Ward, 1964.

Koehler, Theodore. *Storia della Mariologia*. Verbania Pallanza: Centro Mariana Chaminade, 1971–1976.

Laurentin, R. *Court traité sur la Vierge Marie*. Paris, 1968.

Leclerq, J. "Grandeur et misère de la dévotion mariale au Moyen Âge". In *La Liturgie et les paradoxes chrétiens*. Lex Orandi, 36. Paris, 1963.

O'Carroll, Michael. *Theotokos: A Theological Encyclopedia of the Blessed Virgin Mary*. Wilmington, Del.: Michael Glazier, 1982.

Roschini, G. *Maria Santissima nella storia della salvezza*. 4 vols. Isola del Liri, 1969.

Söll, Georg. *Storia dei dogmi mariani*. Rome, 1981.

Gharib, G., E. Toniolo, L. Gambero, and G. DiNola, eds. *Testi mariani del primo millenio*. Vol. 3, *Padri e altri autori latini*. Rome: Città Nuova, 1990.

Toniolo, E. *Bibliografia Mariana*. Vol. 9 (continuation of Besutti). Rome, 1998.

---

* As we have already given specific bibliographical references for each medieval author, we limit ourselves here to works of general interest.

Index

Aaron's rod, 67–68, 83
adoptionism, 61
Aelred of Rievaulx, 162–69
Akáthistos hymn, 25–26
Alain de Lille, 185–91
Alan of Auxerre, 132
Alanus de Rupe, 315–20
Albert the Great, 222–33, 326–28
Alcuin, 60–65
almond analogy, 176
Amadeus of Lausanne, 155–61
Ambrose, 91, 241
Ambrose Autpert, 43–52
Aminadab, 191
Anna, 214
Annunication (teachings about): seventh
    through eleventh centuries, 28, 39, 96–
    97; twelfth century, 127, 145, 163, 188;
    thirteenth century, 226–27, 240;
    fourteenth and fifteenth centuries, 266
Anselm, 39–40, 107, 109–16
Anthony of Padua, 197–205
Antoninus of Florence, 300–306
aqueduct analogy, 135
Arnold of Bonneval, 148–54
art/icons, 25, 52, 195, 290
Ascension of Christ, 120, 123, 278
Assumption (teachings about): seventh
    through eleventh centuries, 42, 46–47,
    50, 53, 56–58, 71, 77–78, 80, 87, 101;
    twelfth century, 107, 120, 138–39, 151,
    159, 164–65, 173–74, 175–76, 179–80,
    189; thirteenth century, 228, 238, 242;
    fourteenth and fifteenth centuries, 293,
    295, 302, 324–25
Augustine, 240–41
Ave maris stella hymn, 69

baptism: of Jesus, 306; of Mary, 325; of
    men, 172–73, 175

Barré, H., 65
Basel, Council of, 309
Basil the Great, 85
basket analogy, 156–57
beauty: of Jesus, 279–80; of Mary, 163–64,
    179, 182–83, 202–3, 218, 220–21
Bede, 36–42
bee allegory, 203–5
Benedictine order, devotion to Mary, 19
Bernard of Clairvaux, 117, 131–41, 208
Bernardine de Bustis, 321–27
Bernardine of Siena, 290–99
Bethlehem, 176n12, 265–66, 306
Bonaventure, 206–15
Bride–Church parallel: seventh through
    eleventh centuries, 39–40, 71, 97;
    twelfth century, 125–26, 128–29, 163,
    169, 179, 186–88; thirteenth century,
    209, 226–27, 230; fourteenth and
    fifteenth centuries, 311–12. *See also*
    Church–Mary parallel
Bridget of Sweden, 275–80
burning bush, 67
Byzantine Church, 17, 25, 26

Calvary (teachings about): seventh through
    eleventh centuries, 40, 45–46, 62, 87,
    92; twelfth century, 126–27, 130, 140–
    41, 149–50, 153–54, 158–59, 168–69,
    188; thirteenth century, 209, 212, 213–
    15; fourteenth and fifteenth centuries,
    268, 269–71, 273–74, 278, 303–4
Cana wedding, 40, 61–62, 232, 305–6, 312
Carolingian Renaissance, 51–52
cathedrals, 105, 195
Chalcedon, Council of, 61
charity, 190, 203, 313–14
Charlemagne, 51, 52, 60
Chartres, 81
chesnut analogy, 118–19

Church–Mary parallel: seventh through
    eleventh centuries, 39–40, 48–49, 70–
    71, 99; twelfth century, 125–26, 128–29,
    171, 172–73, 175, 180–81, 188–89;
    thirteenth century, 212–13, 230;
    fourteenth and fifteenth century, 311–
    12. See also Bride–Church parallel
circumcision of Jesus, 267–68
Cleophas, 214
Cluniac tradition, 88–94
conception of Mary: seventh through
    eleventh centuries, 82, 83–84; twelfth
    century, 110–11, 117, 118–19, 137–38.
    See also Immaculate Conception;
    original sin (teachings about)
Confraternity of the Rosary, 318–19
Conrad of Saxony, 216–21
Constance, Council of, 282
counsel gift, 159
Crucifixion. See Calvary (teachings about)

Dante, 131, 132, 255
devil. See Satan (teachings about)
devotion to Mary: seventh through
    eleventh centuries, 31–33, 34–35, 40,
    62–63, 65, 75, 78–79, 90, 99–100, 101;
    twelfth century, 111–15, 132, 137, 143–
    47, 167–68; thirteenth century, 208,
    213, 219, 231; fourteenth and fifteenth
    centuries, 290, 316
diligence of Mary, 299
Dionysius the Carthusian, 307–14
divine motherhood: seventh through
    eleventh centuries, 29, 37, 55, 61, 64,
    69–70, 72–73, 96–97; twelfth century,
    114, 133–34, 158; thirteenth century,
    199–200, 226–27, 231, 236–37, 241–42,
    245–47; fourteenth and fifteenth
    centuries, 266, 293–94, 309–10, 323
Dominic Helion, 316, 318–19, 320
Duns Scotus, John, 107, 119, 243–52

Eadmer of Canterbury, 117–23
Elizabeth, 42, 72, 92, 298
Ephesus, Council of, 61
Esther, 174, 220
Eucharist, 74, 98–99, 209, 286, 326–27
Eve–Mary parallel: seventh through
    eleventh centuries, 38–39, 49, 97–98;

    twelfth century, 158, 183; thirteenth
    century, 210, 211, 212; fourteenth and
    fifteenth century, 285, 288. See also
    Satan (teachings about)

faith of Mary, 85, 144–45, 187–88, 231–32,
    312–13
fear gift, 157
feast days: seventh through eleventh
    centuries, 20, 25, 44, 46–47, 97; twelfth
    century, 110, 117, 137–38; thirteenth
    century century, 248
fortitude gift, 158–59
Fulbert of Chartres, 81–87

Gandolf, 112
grace (teachings about): seventh through
    eleventh centuries, 37; twelfth century,
    144–45, 164; thirteenth century, 199–
    200, 211, 238, 239; fourteenth and
    fifteenth century, 260, 286–87, 293–
    94, 296, 301–2, 309, 310–11, 325,
    326
greatness of Mary: seventh through
    eleventh centuries, 37, 47, 49–50, 54,
    71–72, 78–79, 101; twelfth century,
    117–18, 160–61, 163–64, 169;
    fourteenth and fifteenth centuries, 287,
    288–89, 293–94
Grosseteste, Robert, 248

Helvidius, 28
Herbert, St., 128
Holy Spirit (teachings about): seventh
    through eleventh centuries, 32–33, 37,
    39–40, 49, 54, 56, 61–62, 64, 96–97;
    twelfth century, 115, 120, 125, 126, 129,
    145–46, 157–59, 172–73, 186;
    thirteenth century, 210, 225–26, 236,
    246; fourteenth and fifteenth centuries,
    260–61, 280, 296, 297, 314
hope, 313
humility of Mary: seventh through
    eleventh centuries, 41–42, 47, 48, 54–
    55, 71–72, 79, 82, 86, 92; twelfth
    century, 134, 190–91; thirteenth
    century, 203, 204–5, 220, 221;
    fourteenth and fifteenth centuries, 259–
    60, 287, 310

hymns: seventh through eleventh centuries, 20, 25–26, 40, 68, 69, 98, 101; twelfth century, 106, 143, 146–47

icons/art, 25, 52, 195, 290
Ildephonsus of Toledo, 27–33
Immaculate Conception: twelfth century, 125; thirteenth century, 225, 248–52; fourteenth and fifteenth centuries, 258–59, 276–77, 283–84, 284–85, 294, 297–98, 309, 322. See also conception of Mary; original sin (teachings about)
Incarnation (teachings about): seventh through eleventh centuries, 32–33, 34, 41, 61–62, 64–65, 69–70, 71, 72–73, 97, 99; twelfth century, 126, 127–28, 133–35, 152–53, 163–64, 178–79, 190–91; thirteenth century, 209–10, 211, 225–26, 229, 236–37, 245–47; fourteenth and fifteenth centuries, 259–63, 285–87, 294, 297–98, 301–2
intercession (teachings about): Newman's, 21–22; seventh through eleventh centuries, 57, 58–59, 63, 65, 71, 85–86, 87, 100; twelfth century, 112–14, 115–16, 121–23, 135–37, 151–52, 159–60, 161, 165–66, 181, 184, 187–88; thirteenth century, 201–2, 204, 210–12, 219–20, 221, 229–30; fourteenth and fifteenth centuries, 279, 282, 286–87, 295–96, 304–5, 310–11, 312, 325
Isaac of Stella, 170–76

James the Apostle, 214
Jean Gerson, 281–89
Jeremiah, 118, 217
Jerome, 69
Jews, 28, 46, 48
Joachim, 214
John Rylands Library, 26n2
John the Apostle (teachings about): seventh through eleventh centuries, 46, 87, 92, 101; twelfth century, 118, 127, 141; thirteenth century, 214–15, 217; fourteenth and fifteenth century, 270–71, 305–6
John Chrysostom, 214, 232
Joseph, 38, 144, 227, 272, 280; marriage to Mary, 38, 163, 227, 240–41, 280

Jotslad, 91, 93
Jovinian, 28, 30
Jude, 214

Koehler, Theodore, 105, 136

Lady (Marian title), 68–69, 167
Light-Bringer (Marian title), 68–69
lily symbol, 54
love of Jesus and Mary: seventh century, 55–56; twelfth century, 113, 150, 168–69, 174; thirteenth century, 214, 259; fourteenth and fifteenth centuries, 259, 267–70, 272–73, 278, 313–14. See also Bride–Church parallel

Marian doctrine, overviews, 18–21, 25–26, 51–52, 105–8, 195–96, 255–56. See also specific topics, e.g., Assumption (teachings about); intercession (teachings about)
Mary Magdalene, 214
Mary of Cleophas, 214
Mary Salome, 305
mediation. See intercession (teachings about)
medieval era, overviews, 17–18, 105–8
mercy (teachings about): seventh through eleventh centuries, 58–59, 88–89, 93; twelfth century, 136, 190–91; thirteenth century, 204, 212–13, 219, 229–30; fourteenth and fifteenth century, 296, 310–11
Messianic prophecies, 67–68, 82–83
Middle Ages, overviews, 17–18, 105–8
monastic life, Mary as model for, 90–94
Moses, 21, 67, 83
Mother of Mercy (Marian title), 88–89, 93, 136

names of Mary: seventh through eleventh centuries, 68–69, 84–85; twelfth century, 139–40, 161, 167, 168; thirteenth century, 242; fourteenth and fifteenth centuries, 283–84, 308. See also individual Marian titles, e.g., Mother of Mercy, Queen, Star of the Sea
Newman, John Henry, 21–22, 292–93
Nicaea, Second Council of, 18, 25, 52

obedience of Mary, 41, 298–99
Odilo of Cluny, 89–93
Odo of Cluny, 88–89, 93–94
Olivi, Pietro, 292
original sin (teachings about): seventh
    through eleventh centuries, 37; twelfth
    century, 107, 110–11, 118–19, 125,
    136–38, 178–79; thirteenth century,
    217–18, 225, 237–38, 248–52;
    fourteenth and fifteenth centuries, 258–
    59, 276–77, 284–85, 294, 301, 309, 322,
    326. See also Immaculate Conception

Paschasius Radbertus, 74–80, 107
Paul the Deacon, 53–59, 85
penance sacrament, 326
Pentecost, 145
Peter Damian, 95–101
Peter of Prussia, 222n2
Peter the Venerable, 142–47
Philip of Harveng, 177–84
piety gift, 158, 164, 212–13
pilgrimages, 105–6, 275–76, 306
Planctus Mariae hymn, 106
poverty of Mary, 91–94
prayers to Mary: seventh through eleventh
    centuries, 20, 21, 26, 28, 32–33, 38, 40,
    58–59, 62–63, 65, 71, 89, 93; twelfth
    century, 110, 111–14, 121–22, 137;
    thirteenth century, 202, 219–20;
    fourteenth and fifteenth centuries, 286–
    87, 316–20
prophecies, 67–68, 82–83, 164. See also
    Messianic prophecies
prudence, 190–91
Purification of Mary, 44

Queen (Marian title): twelfth century, 119–
    21, 127–28, 160–61, 167; thirteenth
    century, 209, 218–19; fourteenth and
    fifteenth centuries, 279, 286, 293, 295–
    96, 298, 304, 324–25

Rabanus Maurus, 66–73, 74
Ratramnus, 70, 74, 75–76, 77
Raymund Lull, 257–63
redemption. See salvation (teachings about)
Resurrection (teachings about), 271, 273–
    74

Rosary, 316–20
Rupert of Deutz, 124

Salome, 214
salvation (teachings about): seventh through
    eleventh centuries, 29–31, 37, 38–39,
    49–50, 70, 84–85, 86–87, 97–98, 100–
    101; twelfth century, 107, 114, 115–16,
    120–21, 134–35, 149–52; thirteenth
    century, 201–2, 210–12, 228–30, 235–
    40, 249–50; fourteenth and fifteenth
    centuries, 266–67, 277–78, 285–87,
    302–3, 310–11, 323–24
Salve Regina hymn, 106, 219
sanctification of Mary. See original sin
    (teachings about)
sanctuaries, 106
Sangallese 95, 69
Sarah, 309–10
Satan (teachings about): seventh through
    eleventh centuries, 38, 39, 54–55, 67,
    82, 83, 85, 86–87, 94; thirteenth
    century, 210; fourteenth and fifteenth
    centuries, 288
Scholastic age, overview, 195–96
serpent, 39, 55, 67, 82, 86–87, 158. See also
    Eve–Mary parallel
Simeon, 40, 44–45, 140–41
Simon, 214
Song of Songs, 182, 186–87
spiritual motherhood: seventh through
    eleventh centuries, 45; twelfth century,
    122–23, 126–27, 166, 173, 175, 180–81,
    189; thirteenth century, 212–13, 230,
    266–67; fourteenth and fifteenth
    centuries, 270–71, 273–74, 302–4,
    311–12
Stabat Mater hymn, 106
Star of the Sea (Marian title), 68–69, 84–
    85, 139–40, 161, 242, 283–84, 284
Sub tuum praesidium confugimus, 26
suffering of Mary. See Calvary (teachings
    about)
Sword of Simeon, 40, 44–45, 140–41

Temple image of Mary, 30, 49, 53–54, 92,
    112, 119, 200, 208–9, 266
Temple in Jerusalem, 48–49, 91, 144, 200,
    268, 269, 306

temptations of Mary. *See* Eve–Mary
    parallel; Satan (teachings about)
Theophilus, 85, 229
Theotókos title, 56, 61, 64, 195
Thomas Aquinas, 234–42, 322
Tobit, 305
Transitus Mariae, 77

Ubertino of Casale, 264–74, 292

virginity of Mary (teachings about):
    seventh through eleventh centuries,
    29–33, 37–38, 39–40, 54, 61, 64–65, 67–
68, 70, 75–77, 82–83, 86–87, 91–
94, 98, 101; twelfth century, 115, 134,
139, 153, 171–72, 175, 180, 183;
thirteenth century, 200–201, 203–4, 220,
226–27, 241–42, 247–48; fourteenth and
fifteenth centuries, 260–61, 302
visions of Mary, 31–32, 89, 93, 128, 276–
77, 316

William of Saint-Armour, 206
William of Ware, 248
wisdom gift, 144–45, 159, 164, 314
wool analogy, 61, 64

Scripture Index

GENESIS

3:15	55, 67, 82, 86, 201
21:6	310
28:16	232
29:17	163

EXODUS

3:2	67
20:12	214

LEVITICUS

12:8	93

NUMBERS

17:6–24	83
17:23	67

1 KINGS

2:20	221
17:1	307

2 CHRONICLES

9:1	218

TOBIT

8:4	305

ESTHER

2:15	220
2:17	220
4:11	174
5:1	174
15	174

PSALMS

9:15	163
18:6	227, 297
19:5	41, 169
23:2	80
38:12	214
39:2	190
44:10	298
45:2	163
45:9	219
47:10	49
48:9	49
53:8	298
87:4–5	154
92:1	161
92:4	161
97:2	31
98	31
122:3	49
131:4–5	232
131:8	242
150:3	318

PROVERBS

8:22–23	128
9:1	96, 100
25:4	217
31:10	211
31:29	164, 174, 205

SONG OF SONGS

1:2	129
1:12	169
2:1	204
2:3	295
2:4	187
2:16	232
3:3	272
3:4	168
3:6	56
4:7	164
4:12	49
5:8	288
5:12	80
6:10	218
6:11	176
6:12	190
8:5	141, 157, 176, 232

WISDOM

8:1 86

SIRACH

3:18 . . . . 42, 72
6:31 141
11:3 . . . . 203, 204
24:11 173

ISAIAH

7:14 . . . . 68, 83
11:1 . . . . 68, 204
11:2 . . . . 157, 164
35:2 242
43:3 69
52:10 30
66:10 56

EZEKIEL

16:12 141
44:2–3 30

MATTHEW

1:18 230
1:20 240
1:21 237–238
2:13 144
3:15 325
12:42 218
12:48 149
27:52–53 228

LUKE 313

1:26–27 241
1:27 139
1:28 . . 37, 141, 164, 169, 183, 238
1:29 190
1:30–31 129
1:31–33 299
1:34 . . . . 247, 299
1:35–37 298
1:35 . . . . 33, 129, 203, 248
1:37 153
1:38 . . . . . 41, 92, 129, 190, 298
1:42 . . . . 72, 73, 169
1:44 72
1:45 231
1:46 313
1:48–49 313

1:48 204
1:49 287
2:14 65
2:19 203
2:34–35 140
2:35 . . . . 214, 268
2:48 . . . . 168, 272
2:51 . . . . 35, 233
3:6 30
10:41–42 230
10:42 203
11:28 176
11:31 218
22:28 215

JOHN

1:1 . . . . 50, 153
1:3 120
1:14 . . . . 37, 64, 144, 238
1:16 164
1:29 93
2:1–2 63
2:1 305
2:2–5 219
2:3 . . . . 232, 233
3:5 325
3:16 . . . . 41, 268
6:38 236
6:53 326
6:55–56 326
6:58 326
16:21–22 130
16:21 126
19:25–27 . . . 62, 126, 256, 274, 303
19:25 . . . . 130, 303
19:26–27 . . . . 127, 270
19:26 . . . . 141, 270
19:27 . . . . 122, 180

ACTS

1:14 282

ROMANS

1:31 141
5:12 309
8:32 303

I CORINTHIANS

1:24 232

3:17 49

7:34 242

2 CORINTHIANS

1:7 271

12:2 47

PHILIPPIANS

2:7 190

2:10 80

COLOSSIANS

1:24 286

I TIMOTHY

4:10 238

5:8 214

HEBREWS

4:12 141

4:16 211

I JOHN

2:1–2 86

REVELATION

12:1 297